GROW RICH SLOWLY

GROW RICH SLOWLY

THE
Merrill Lynch Guide to RETIREMENT PLANNING

Don Underwood and
Paul B. Brown

VIKING

VIKING
Published by the Penguin Group
Penguin Books USA Inc., 375 Hudson Street,
New York, New York 10014, U.S.A.
Penguin Books Ltd, 27 Wrights Lane,
London W8 5TZ, England
Penguin Books Australia Ltd, Ringwood,
Victoria, Australia
Penguin Books Canada Ltd, 10 Alcorn Avenue,
Toronto, Ontario, Canada M4V 3B2
Penguin Books (N.Z.) Ltd, 182–190 Wairau Road,
Auckland 10, New Zealand

Penguin Books Ltd, Registered Offices:
Harmondsworth, Middlesex, England

First published in 1993 by Viking Penguin,
a division of Penguin Books USA Inc.

1 3 5 7 9 10 8 6 4 2

PUBLISHER'S NOTE
This publication is designed to provide accurate and authoritative information in
regard to the subject matter covered. It is sold with the understanding that the
publisher is not engaged in rendering financial, legal, or other professional service.
If financial advice or other expert assistance is required, the service of a competent
professional person should be sought.

LIBRARY OF CONGRESS CATALOGING IN PUBLICATION DATA
Underwood, Don.
Grow rich slowly : the Merrill Lynch guide to retirement planning /
Don Underwood, Paul B. Brown.
p. cm.
Includes index.
ISBN 0-670-84674-0
1. Retirement income—United States—Planning. 2. Aged—Finance,
Personal. I. Brown, Paul B. II. Merrill Lynch & Co. (1973–   )
III. Title.
HG181.U523   1993
332.024'01—dc20   92-56717

Printed in the United States of America
Set in Garamond Light
Designed by Kathryn Parise

For Pat, Martha, and Steven Underwood,
who, through different perspectives, are much
concerned with the trials and
tribulations of retirement
—D. U.

For Scott R. Brown,
who is still at least *30 years away*
from retirement
—P. B. B.

FOREWORD

Merrill Lynch is "Bullish on America."

In that spirit, we're on a crusade to deliver a clear and simple message to all Americans: The most crucial economic challenge we face is to rediscover the old habits of saving and investing that made us the most affluent nation and the leading economic power on earth.

It's crucial if some 75 million Americans who'll turn 65 in the first decades of the new century are to have a reasonable prospect of enjoying the freedom that comes with a financially secure retirement. If that were the only reason, it would be reason enough.

But it's also crucial for a second, equally important reason. Money saved and invested does not sit idly in a cookie jar. It funds investment in new plants and equipment, in research, development, and training. In short, it fuels the entrepreneurial drive that will keep America on top in an increasingly competitive global economy.

We need a three-way partnership between government, the private sector, and individuals to close America's savings gap. This book addresses the third part of that trio—you, the individual.

What follows is a superb primer on personal finance, written in a simple, straightforward style that's easy to digest, and enjoyable to read. We're proud that a great many Merrill Lynch experts have dedicated their careers to helping people plan their financial futures. Here their wisdom and experience is collected and distilled; we don't think you'll find better or more comprehensive advice anywhere.

In planning for retirement, you'll find that the paths are many but the destination is the same: the freedom to pursue your dreams in a nation that is constantly reinventing and reinvigorating itself, and which remains a shining example for the rest of the world.

William A. Schreyer
Chairman of the Board

Daniel P. Tully
President and Chief Executive Officer

Merrill Lynch & Co., Inc.

PREFACE

Listening and Learning

by John L. Steffens
Executive Vice-President, Private Client Group
Merrill Lynch & Co., Inc.

This book is the result of not just listening to, but also learning from, a lot of concerned Americans.

Let me tell you some of the things I've been hearing in recent years. Not too long ago we talked with a panel of Americans—some retired, some facing retirement—and they said:

"I think there exists, in today's society, too much of the feeling 'live for today.' "

"I think a lot of people think they are planning when they're just sort of aspiring to something."

"I know some people, relatives, who have planned, but not well. They're going to get along, but not as well as they might have had they been able to properly manage their money . . . or manage their lives."

As you keep listening, you try to find solutions to the problems facing Americans.

At a Senate Finance Committee hearing in Washington, after I testified as an "expert" on savings proposals, I listened to the rest of the committee's witnesses. And I have to confess that, although my points were well received, what really electrified the senators—what really made them sit up and take notice—were words of simple eloquence from these Americans:

A woman from Boston: "Our needs are simple. We want to grow up, get a job, marry, and somehow buy a home."

A man from Raleigh, North Carolina: "The government has got to do something to change us from a nation of spenders to savers."

A man from Columbus, Ohio: "I have three kids—and a fourth on the way—and I've got to have some way to get them to college."

There's another way of listening and understanding and learning: you listen to your friends, to your family.

A friend told me that his father lived to be 94. That's a long life, but for the last 24 years of his life, the father suffered from Alzheimer's disease. The toll, emotional as well as financial, on the son was horrendous. My friend was able to take care of his father to the end, but what bothers me is that not everyone will be as well prepared financially to care for his or her loved ones.

Seeking Independence

If that seems bleak, here's a brighter picture. This came of my son and I talking to—and listening and learning from—each other.

He had finished college, landed his first full-time job at age 21, and I said I'd make a deal with him. I would kick in the money—some $2,000 as a starter—for his first year's IRA, if he'd take it from there. When the second year rolled around, although his entry-level salary was pretty modest, he somehow dug up his own $2,000. I know that finding the $2,000 was a strain.

Why did he, at age 22, save rather than spend? The answer is that he saw what the first $2,000 IRA contribution would be worth some 40 years later when he might be thinking about retirement. He translated those future dollars into something very tangible: independence.

That's what all of us—my son, who is a post–baby boomer, the 76 million baby boomers themselves, and my middle-aged friend—have to find: financial solutions that lead to independence.

From my role as national chairman of the Alliance for Aging Research, I also see—in addition to these personal reflections—a range of statistical proof of this aging phenomenon.

- Life expectancy at birth has increased from 47 in 1900 to 78 years in 1989. As baby boomers reach age 65, their life expectancy should reach the mid to late 80s.

- By 2030 there will be more older persons than younger persons in this country. Persons under 18 will account for 18% of our population; those over 65 will total 22%.

- The health care costs of Americans over age 65 currently account for 37% of our total health care bill.

- The decline in our national savings rate—from more than 9% in the 1970s to under 4% now—comes at precisely the wrong time. The savings gap is widening.

- Families headed by individuals aged 45 to 54 have median financial assets—not including equity in their home—of only $2,300.

I also look at the future from another perspective—from some 30 years of listening to our clients tell us of their concerns about the future. Our approach to retirement planning has been shaped from what I've learned. At present, more than 1.8 million clients have invested more than $66 billion in self-directed retirement accounts as part of their total scheme of retirement planning. They have come to understand the power of time and compounding. They have taken control of their future as they share their concerns with their financial consultants and receive advice and counsel in turn. They are actively involved in the many different facets of retirement planning.

Unfortunately, this is not the case for most Americans. For some years now we've conducted an annual survey across the country of trends in retirement planning. These surveys invariably tell us that a large percentage of middle-aged Americans have some seriously inaccurate notions about how they'll live after they retire.

Through one recent study we found that people believe that on their retirement, Social Security and pensions will provide for more than 65% of their income. Yet, only 46% of Americans have pensions, and many of these pensions are relatively small.

Social Security, in reality, may likely account for only 23% of what most Americans need in retirement, with pensions adding some 20%. That means that for retirees 65 years and older who are living on $20,000 or more per year, some 57% of their income *must come* from earnings on investments or savings.

The fact is that as Americans leave the work force, if they cannot rely on additional savings, investments, and earnings, they will find it incredibly difficult to maintain their standard of living.

This savings shortfall that so many Americans face is a growing crisis for the entire nation. It will not be resolved easily.

Our Lengthening Life Span

As we go into the twenty-first century, every American—and I mean everyone: the young and the old—should be concerned about how the Aging of America will drastically change this country. This lengthening of the life span and the advance of the baby boom generation—now coming at the same time, with each doubling or tripling the impact on the other—will force major changes on us. We—our country as a whole and each of us as individuals—have to figure out how to weather this tempest, how to respond to this rapidly changing environment, and how to take control of our destiny.

So in a very positive way, that's what this book is all about: the need in the future to find independence, and to be financially strong. The best reason to build reserves—to try to grow rich s-l-o-w-l-y—is to create independence through wealth.

The young need independence, the old need it. I know that far too many Americans today are more afraid of outliving their resources than they are of old age itself. As they do age, Americans want to be assured of a decent quality of life. I believe that as Americans achieve financial freedom, psychological and social well-being will follow.

The authors of this book are a generation apart in age. This age spread brings a wise perspective to their advice. They know, and they're pretty blunt in telling you, that you can't depend any longer on your rich uncles—your Uncle Sam or your uncle employer—to take care of you.

Your government can't solve all your problems.

Your employer can't be the sole underwriter of your future.

But you, in partnership with your government and your employer, can help yourself. You *can* fill the gap between Social Security and private pensions and what you will need in your retirement years.

Changing Habits

The heart of this book is that to find financial independence you may need to change some financial habits. This country over the last several decades has become a spending society. We must once again become a saving society. We need to get back to basics.

I wish I could say to all Americans, "Ladies and gentlemen, we may have to start over again. Through disciplined savings— and the two miracles of time and compounding—you *can* take control."

That's what this book is all about.

I am an optimist. My most personal hope is that this guide, and its many suggestions on how to accumulate assets, and how to build retirement nest eggs, will lead to an enhanced quality of life for your retirement years.

In any financial path there will always be roadblocks. You don't have to go it alone. You need partners. Ask your attorney, your accountant, your financial consultant to be your advisers. My prescription for financial success: You need a plan. You need time. You need a trusted adviser to counsel you on your follow-through. You need to be consistent. You need to stick to your plan.

Earlier in your life—it might have been in grade school, or high school, or possibly even as late as college—some teacher got your intellectual juices flowing by promising you that from time to time, if you were lucky, you would read something that would turn a light on.

I believe this book will be one of those times.

CONTENTS

Contents

II
Saving Systematically and Tax-Advantaged

III
Saving Smarter

Contents

IV
Harvesting Your Savings

GROW RICH
SLOWLY

An Overview

You're not getting any younger.

Even if you eat right, exercise daily, and have worked out a pact that involves a portrait hidden in the attic, the fact remains that you are older now than you have ever been.

At some point, be it in a year—or twenty—you're going to start *seriously* thinking about what your life is going to be like when you retire.

This book will help.

"Maybe, but it's going to be about as much fun as an IRS audit, right?" we hear you cry.

To be honest, we understand your reaction. Thinking about retirement is hard enough without having to slog through retirement books, which tend to be deadly dull. They're usually filled with arcane cost-of-living formulas that never seem to apply to anyone, and the material always reads as if it were lifted straight from the (yawn) Social Security Administration or a textbook for actuaries.

A Look at Real People

Why would anyone want to read a book like that?

We have no idea.

That isn't the kind of book we've written. We think we've created a retirement book that will do four things:

1. **Focus on the concerns of real people.** As you'll see, we have chosen five couples and two individuals who represent the differing needs of just about everyone thinking about retirement. The idea here is simple. We didn't want to present our information in a vacuum. Even the most eloquent explanation of a retirement strategy is worthless if you can't figure out if it's right for you. So when we talk about funding an IRA, planning for college, purchasing an annuity, increasing your 401(k) plan, or setting up trust funds for your children, we'll show how those decisions will affect the people we've chosen as our models.

At least one of these people (or couples), we're sure, will have many of the same retirement questions and concerns that you do.

The idea of using real people has seldom been tried before in a retirement book, and that's hard to believe. When it comes to retirement planning, one size does not fit all. Some people begin preparing early, others late. While an older couple may start getting ready for retirement with lots of money in the bank, others may not. Their needs are different, and so is the information we provide.

2. **Pay a lot of attention to the needs of baby boomers**—the oldest of whom has already turned 47. This was an important reason why we wrote the book. People aged 29 to 47—all 76 million of them—are different from the generations who have come before. You can blame it on Dr. Spock, the affluence of their

parents, or even Elvis and the Beatles, but the fact is that they—and the "they" includes one of the authors—are different.

If you are a baby boomer your attention span is shorter, your loyalty to organizations is less (try to find a "company man" [or woman] under the age of 40), and if you're honest you'll admit you expect immediate gratification.

While it's true that baby boomers should be able to relate to a discussion of the retirement planning needs of a 55-year-old, since a nervous portion of them are close to turning 50, the fact is that very few can.

It's not completely their fault. Their retirement concerns *are* different from the ones their parents have, and need to be treated that way.

Upwardly Mobile? Yes.
Pension? No.

Take the matter of upward mobility, which often involves switching companies to obtain a better job. That's great for your career, as baby boomers know, but awful when it comes to planning for your retirement. While people now in their 50s or 60s are grappling with concerns about shrinking employer pension plans, their children face different problems.

They may end up, at retirement time, with an impressive résumé. They may have always made more money with each job change. In just about every measurable way but one, they've moved up the career ladder. Their one problem—and it's a big one—is that in their successful upward trek they have never been in one job long enough to have *significant* vesting (or participation) in a corporate pension plan. In short, they may have *no* appreciable employer pension money coming their way upon retirement.

And then there are other unique problems that many baby boomers face, merely because they are baby boomers. Having put off the decision to marry and have children until they were in their late 20s or into their 30s, a vast number of them will be putting kids through college while simultaneously trying to figure out how they're going to take care of their aging parents. When you are facing financial burdens like that, it's hard to think about retirement. Yet baby boomers have to, and we will try to help. (And it wouldn't hurt, if you are the parent of one of these people, to suggest they start thinking about these things.)

3. **This guide won't ignore the "mature" person**—the one who's facing retirement five years from now (or maybe has just retired). We'll give you a plan on how to put your financial house in order, and we'll even tell you of ways to spend (or transfer to others) your hard-earned savings.

4. **Finally, in most chapters we'll give you investment ideas.** It's not enough to save; it's equally essential that you invest wisely. We'll tell you how to assess your tolerance for investment risk, and then how to allocate your assets accordingly.

Having (Some) Money Sure Helps

One thing this book won't do: it won't waste many words on life-style issues. We won't be drawing you into debates on the merits of retirement living in Clear Creek, Florida, versus Deep Water, Idaho, or the advantages (or disadvantages) of retirement villages versus life-care complexes.

This is a *financial* book. Money clearly isn't everything in retirement. But having some sure helps. So we're doing the financial end of retirement. Period. We'll leave the other stuff to books like *Better Fishing After 80.*

But *Better Fishing After 80* raises an interesting question: Are there really shortcuts to providing for a well-funded retirement? After all, if a fishing book can promise to turn you into a better angler within 15 minutes, and diet books can "guarantee" that you will lose 10 pounds in 10 days, why can't a retirement book ensure that you will live happily ever after, with "absolutely no effort on your part"?

It could. It also would be lying with every page.

If you want to lose weight, you have to eat less and exercise more. If you want to be a better fisherman, you somehow have to develop patience. If you want to have money when you retire, you have to start putting it away now. You'll have to do something old-fashioned: save. You'll have to learn how to think and invest long-term.

Sorry, but them's the facts. There's a reason this book is called *Grow Rich Slowly.*

The news is not totally depressing, however. There is a world of things you can do to make planning for your retirement easier. As you'll see, we have filled the book with checklists and fill-in-the-blank forms, wherever possible, to reduce some of the stress that comes with planning for your retirement.

Similarly, there are certain financial strategies you can follow that will also reduce stress. They'll help your money grow faster.

For example, most people are *too conservative* when it comes to picking investments for their future. We're not necessarily going to advocate putting all your retirement money in soybean futures, but the fact is if you pick "safe" investments yielding 4% for the next

20 years, and inflation averages 6% over that time, you will steadily lose ground.

We will be spending a lot of time talking about money-saving, or money-stretching, ways—such as prepaying your mortgage—that can keep you ahead of inflation. You don't have to work the investment side day and night to keep ahead of the game, but you do have to be alert.

Small moves add up.

As you can already see, our focus won't be on the importance of retirement planning. Our assumption is that if you've picked up this book, you know the subject is important. Instead, we'll be stressing the *uncertainty* that surrounds preparing for your retirement.

The Gold Watch—Ahead of Time

You may be planning for a gold watch, and a graceful exit at age 65, but your company may suddenly have other ideas. The offer (you can't refuse) of early retirement (as a result of restructuring—now euphemistically called "right-sizing") may come without warning. Then there's the growing trend among corporations to shift more of the burden of retirement planning onto the backs of their employees. Entitlements are out; self-help is in. We'll explain how a combination of a 401(k) plan and your trusty IRA can add up to an enormous nest egg. But the burden is on you—not on your employer.

This won't be news to you: company pension plans are shrinking. But even if you're lucky, and your pension isn't being cut, you have to remember that pensions, unlike Social Security, are rarely indexed for inflation. The problem with that is obvious. While your expenses keep rising, your income remains fixed. That's no way to enter retirement.

All this uncertainty can be expressed in a good news/bad news joke:

The good news is: We're living longer.
The bad news is: We're living longer.

It's easy to see the problem. Not only are people living longer, they're retiring earlier. As a result, *many people will spend as much time retired as they did working.*

When that happens it's easy to outlive your money. And more and more that's likely to happen. Consider:

- By the year 2000, now less than seven years away, average life expectancy will be 78.8 years.

- There are 63,000 Americans aged 100 or older today. By the year 2030, their number will total 360,000.

- Today's fastest-growing population segment is people 85 or older.

Even a quick glance at those numbers underscores that if you want to be happy in retirement, you'd better be taking action now. If you don't, you run the risk of having to rely on the kindness of strangers, or the government. The kindness of neither, we're afraid, is guaranteed.

No one is willing to say, with any degree of conviction, that Social Security will survive forever in its present form. Social Security is built on the premise that the young will pay for the retirement of the old. But the baby boomers are having only 1.8 kids on average. That means they aren't replacing themselves, and so the country's median age keeps climbing. What happens when there are fewer young and more old? Will it be possible to maintain benefits at their current level, a level we hasten to point out that doesn't support a way of living guaranteed to get you on "Lifestyles of the Rich and Famous"?

Once upon a time planning for retirement was simple.

You got married in your 20s, had your kids, bought the house, paid for college, and woke up one day when you were in your 50s and happily realized the largest bills were behind you. Writing tuition checks was an unpleasant memory and the kids were out of the house—a house, by the way, that was probably yours free and clear. It was then, and probably only then, that you started seriously thinking about retirement. But that was fine. You had 10 or 15 years—years in which you were making more money than you ever had in your life—to prepare for retirement and build your nest egg.

The old days may not have been necessarily better, but they sure were a lot simpler. Today, the number of people we know who fit into that old model seems to be decreasing by the day. For example, there are a growing number of people—either because they decided to have children late, or because they now head a second family—who are seeing their outgoing college tuition check and incoming Social Security benefits cross in the mail.

Given this new reality, and all the uncertainty that now surrounds retirement planning, a new kind of retirement book was called for.

We don't intend to just warn you about the financial thickets out there; we'll show you how to get through them.

We've even tried to make it fun to read.

The Future Doesn't Add Up

This book grew out of two independent ideas that have turned out not to be so independent after all.

First, one of the authors, a card-carrying member of the baby boom generation, woke up one morning and realized that while he had started to put money away for his children's college education, he hadn't done one darn thing about planning for his retirement. Worse, he had no idea how much money he'd need, or where he should put it, if he was able somehow—after paying the mortgage, buying clothes that the kids seemed to outgrow daily, and supporting the local supermarket—to figure out how to start saving.

Second, the other author, whose hair is alarmingly (to him, anyway) going from gray to white, and who soon expects to be awarded senior citizen discounts from his friendly neighborhood 16-screen movie palace, concluded that baby boomers aren't alone in their unease at retirement planning. This author has been preaching the gospel of retirement planning, of one sort or another, for almost two decades, but the world is vast. Obviously, not everyone has heard the message. Merrill Lynch's own retirement planning surveys, which for several years have surveyed Americans annually to see how prepared they are for retirement, show that: *Far too many Americans, no matter what their ages, are not financially prepared for retirement.*

9

There's Financial Fantasy Out There

Oh, we all say we're ready for the day when we stop working. Approximately eight in ten pre-retirees surveyed said they feel financially prepared to face retirement, but if you look a little deeper into the survey results, you find that simply isn't true. In the last survey, some 28% of the people questioned said they are now putting less money toward their retirement than they had in the past. And nearly one in five saved nothing at all. There's a lot of financial fantasy out there.

If these people were starting from a huge retirement savings base, this would be understandable. But they're not. As we said earlier in the preface, many 50-year-olds, for example, have an average of just $2,300 put away for retirement. That's not even enough to buy a decent used car these days, let alone finance the retirement people say they want, one in which they are free to do—and pay for—everything they have ever dreamed of.

This gap between expectations and financial reality remains consistent in virtually every retirement survey Merrill Lynch has undertaken.

For example:

• Pre-retirees express growing concern about government and employer support during retirement, yet they remain unrealistically optimistic about their ability to maintain their standard of living during retirement. Some three-quarters of them fully expect their standard of living to remain the same once they stop work, even though they have done virtually nothing to replace the income they'll lose once they stop receiving a regular paycheck.

- People in their 30s, 40s, 50s, and 60s increasingly say they consider the funding of retirement to be primarily an individual responsibility, but they are saving no more for retirement today than they did last year, or five years ago.

- After Social Security, most people cite employer's pensions as their primary source of expected income, yet only 46% of employees even have a pension plan. Moreover, among people over 65 with an annual income over $20,000, Social Security currently represents 23% of their retirement income. (Pensions are just 20%.)

And things may actually be bleaker than they appear because future retirees are likely to have even smaller proportions of their living costs covered by government and corporate pension sources than current retirees do.

Just consider the corporate contribution for a moment. The majority of firms surveyed in the Merrill Lynch annual retirement planning study said that their companies will try to cut their benefit costs over the next five years. The number of companies saying they offer retiree health care benefits in 1991 fell to 40%, and you can expect it to go even lower.

Given all this, the lack of savings is startling, especially when considered in the context of a growing retiree population and increasing questions regarding the level of income replacement to be provided by Social Security and other traditional sources of retirement income.

Plainly put, at the present rate of savings, a large majority of people will not be able to afford to retire.

Americans simply do not understand the costs of retirement and old age. They have vague and unrealistic expectations for Social

Security and employer pensions, and they are neglecting to put aside significant funds of their own to pay for retirement. The future doesn't add up when you look at most people's perceptions about retirement, and then compare those perceptions with reality.

Everyone knows that America is aging rapidly—due to longer life expectancies and the maturing of the baby boom generation— yet few people know how dramatic this aging actually is. On average, women who reach their 65th birthday this year can expect to celebrate their 87th. Remember, that's the average. Men who are turning 65 can expect to live at least until they're 82. In 1990, over 30 million people were over age 65; by 2030 that number is projected to more than double.

As has been well documented in your daily paper and on the nightly news, the cost of retirement is rising far faster than our ability to meet that cost, yet very few people are preparing to deal with that ever-growing gap.

Consider: Nine out of ten pre-retirees in the Merrill Lynch survey say the issue of long-term health care is important to them, but they aren't doing anything about it. Pre-retirees accurately estimate the average cost of a nursing home to be approximately $32,000 a year, yet this cost exceeds the average size of their *total* savings and investments ($19,500) to such an extent that the typical pre-retiree currently could afford to pay for only seven months of nursing home care, *and it would require them to spend virtually all of their total assets to do so.*

The conclusion from this, and all the other things we have talked about, is painfully clear. Without immediate attention to the problem of retirement planning, we face the prospect of personal tragedy on a national scale.

That is true for four reasons:

1. Large numbers of retirees will outlive their savings by an increasing number of years. To be blunt, what this means is that not very long from now, America's future elderly could become a sprawling class of the underprivileged.

2. A likely conclusion that follows from the first point is that more older Americans will increasingly need to depend on their children, placing a huge financial and emotional burden on the next generation.

3. There will be increased pressure on our social systems to deal with the problems caused by having an impoverished class of older Americans.

4. The last point logically follows the first three. Taxes to help care for the aged will take more out of the average paycheck. That seems inevitable.

Warning—This Is Not a Typo!

Just consider the future of Social Security. One United States senator, peering into the twenty-first century, has even gloomily predicted that the time soon will come when payroll taxes (that is, your basic FICA, or Social Security tax) will take 35% of your income. No—that's not a typo. We repeat his prediction: *an annual Social Security tax of 35%*. (If you work for someone, your share would be half; if you're self-employed, you would get hit with all of the 35%.)

How could we face such an enervating tax? Well, it will take two chapters for us to explain Social Security's good points (the benefits you'll surely receive), but also the bad points (the shortfall this country's future generations will have to make up).

In short, there has been a steadily increasing demand for Social Security benefits without a corresponding increase in those contributing to the system. The ratio of workers to Social Security beneficiaries has declined from 42:1 in 1937 to just over 3:1 today.

Americans seem to be aware of some of the problems facing them as they grow ever closer to retirement, but it is clear that most don't understand the scope or intensity of those problems. Certainly, they have not yet been able to absorb the information in a way that encourages them to act.

A Hopeful Sign

There is one small, hopeful sign. Gradually, attitudes are changing. Increasingly, pre-retirees say that preparing for their retirement is *their* responsibility, not their government's or their employer's. This change in attitude might signal a shift in future savings.

But that's a big "if" and one that is far off in the future.

While attitudes may be changing, current preparation for retirement remains woefully inadequate for an America with a greatly increasing retired population and the associated costs that this aging population brings. The problem is unlike any the United States has faced before. It is not cyclical, and it will not recede or correct itself with time. It will only grow.

If this overview has fulfilled its purpose as a prelude to serious retirement planning on your part, forge ahead. Keep reading—keep listening. You'll find that the rest of the book tells you what you can do.

The constant theme is that you can't depend on the kindness of strangers. The future *is* in your hands—and it's a future you can change.

We are an aging nation. We may live longer than we think we will. We know we have to save more—because we're going to live longer—but we're not always saving systematically. Many Americans want to take early retirement, but unless we change spending (savings) habits, a large number simply won't be able to afford the high costs of any sort of retirement.

The "4-S" Savings Formula

This is it—the beginning of retirement planning. And if you are the impatient sort, it's also the end, because we're going to boil down for you all you really need to know.

When it comes to retirement planning there aren't a lot of "tricks." This entire guide—from "Keeping Records and Making Budgets" to "Spending Down"—comes down to a very simple system. We call it the "4-S" approach. You:

1. **Save more.**
2. **Save systematically.**
3. **Save tax-advantaged.**
4. **Save smarter.**

Let's take them one at a time.

Save more. In the following chapters we will give you several ways to figure out exactly how much money you're going to need to achieve your financial goals, goals that may range from funding your children's (or grandchildren's) college education to ensuring you're going to have a pleasant retirement.

Are you saving enough now? Probably not. Odds are you'll need to put away a lot more today, if you want to have a relatively worry-free retirement tomorrow.

Save more. That's simple to say, hard to do. But we'll show you some long-term methods (and a couple of short-term ways as well) that will help you to save more money than you might think possible.

Save systematically. We know this is not going to win us many friends, but the plain fact is that you have to be disciplined when it comes to savings. The way most of us go about saving money ("Let's see, I'll pay all the bills, and then if there is anything left over and I can't get a good deal on a trip to Disneyland/new boat/new sweater, I guess I could save what's left.") just isn't going to cut it, if you want a comfortable retirement.

By disciplined savings we mean budgeted savings. And by budgeting, we don't mean creating a paper goal that has all the staying power of a New Year's Eve resolution—something to look at, but soon to be forgotten. We mean you stick to the budget, and put money away regularly—weekly, monthly, or quarterly. One of the easiest ways to do this is through payroll deductions. Or, you

---

Are You One Out of Twenty?

Only one in twenty people is currently prepared to pay for the kind of retirement they all envision.

If you are the one in twenty, congratulations! You may want to fast forward to the part of the book where we talk about how retirement planning also means retirement spending. It's fun to give your hard-earned money away to your local Porsche dealer, the travel agent who books around-the-world cruises, or to someone else.

Unfortunately, the rest of us are going to have to read the stuff in between.

---

can employ an automatic transfer of money—generally, $100 a month and up—directly from your bank account to your brokerage account. Once the money is there, it can automatically be invested, say, in a mutual fund of your choice.

What you don't see, you don't miss. What you don't have in your pocket, you can't spend. Start saving in January. Don't wait till the December countdown—after you've totaled up the year's numbers—to see if anything is left for the savings pot.

Save tax-advantaged. When you start to save systematically, put your money in accounts that have tax advantages. At best, your savings should be tax-deductible; at the least, you want the earnings and gains produced by your savings to be tax-deferred or even tax-free.

There are two major benefits to taking this approach to savings. First, if taxes are not taken out of your investment—or at the very least, the taxes are deferred—there is more money to invest.

Second, if you are saving tax-deferred, it means that you're putting off paying taxes until some future date. Ideally, that date will be once you are retired and in a lower tax bracket. The best retirement plans—401(k)s, employee stock plans, Keoghs, SEPs (all of which we will talk about in detail)—will be tax-advantaged.

Accumulate enough and savings becomes wealth. One of the best ways to save—sometimes tax-deductible, but always tax-deferred—is through your trusty old IRA. It's still the linchpin of solid retirement planning. Because it is so important, we will be discussing it in detail in Chapter 11. In just about any retirement plan you're directing yourself, you'll have tremendous leverage through the power of compounding. We'll show you many examples of how that can work for you.

Save smarter. Don't get nervous. We're not asking you to become smarter overnight. In fact, we firmly believe that you know more about retirement planning than you might think. Our goal is to educate you a bit more, and see if we can get you to raise your investment sights a notch or two.

Instead of settling for an annual return of 4% on your retirement investments, let's see what happens if you seek 6%, and what happens if that 6% becomes a doable 8% or even a more difficult 10% over the long term? Combine higher returns with tax-advantaged savings and the power of compounding and the results can make you look very smart indeed.

Saving smarter also means hiring the investment smarts of others, as needed. "My rise to the top has been easy," says a friend of ours who runs a multibillion-dollar company. "I always hire people smarter than me." You do the same. If you need help preparing for retirement, go to people who are smarter than you. (Smarter, we hasten to add, in ways of investment!) We'll show you how to find them.

As you go through this guide, you'll see that the authors' musical tastes run from Beethoven to the Beatles. But almost all music, from two-hundred-year-old symphonies to rock operas, has a reprise of one sort of another.

This book has a reprise too:
  1. *Save more.*
  2. *Save systematically.*
  3. *Save tax-advantaged.*
  4. *Save smarter.*

Those four steps are the real way to grow rich slowly.

PART I

Saving More

CHAPTER 1

Real People, Real Concerns: Do You Have a Savings Gap?

Retirement planning—projecting your future needs against present and future assets—is not an abstract exercise.

You're saving for real reasons: to live out your retirement years in good financial shape; to put your children, or grandchildren, through school; to leave a sizable estate.

Real people who do retirement planning have real concerns, and we're now going to probe some of those worries.

You'll read about a newly married couple, who in their early 20s have a remarkably firm idea of the road they'll be taking, and you'll meet a 75-year-old who is facing a problem we'd all like to have—how to give away his hard-earned money.

But you'll also meet a young professional who's still figuring out her retirement path, and you'll read about some baby boomers with high income who need to alter their courses to hit their marks.

With our examples—five couples and two singles in all—we span several generations (52 years, to be exact, from age 23 to 75) and we sweep the country—from California to Vermont, Utah to Missouri, Texas to Georgia.

Although every single financial fact is true, and our solutions in the following chapter have indeed been offered to these people, we've changed their names and some identifying information in order to protect their privacy.

A master retirement plan is not, as Shakespeare might have put it, "the be-all and the end-all"—it's a living draft that's never finished. It's something that will grow, and change.

Read on. We suspect in these different scenarios you'll find cases similar to yours. In fact, if you alter a few facts, and a couple of dreams, these people could well be you.

Read on.

"When we retire . . . we want to live comfortably, the way we do now, maybe better."

Steven and Patti Harrison are young (23 and 24), relatively well off (together they make $50,000 a year), and are starting to save for retirement. However, they plan to have a couple of kids, there is this house they want to build, and they know putting money away for retirement is going to become a lot harder in the future. How much money should they be saving? How much can they?

For Steven and Patti Harrison of Orange, Texas, on the Louisiana border, retirement is a long way off, but they are already planning for it.

Steve, 23, is a superintendent for a company that installs industrial insulation. Patti, 24, is an elementary school teacher. Together they are earning about $50,000 a year (Steve earns $30,000, and Patti makes $20,000), and so far they have been pretty good about making sure that at least part of each paycheck is put away for their retirement.

Steve has no pension plan at work, and he doesn't believe he'll ever be covered by one. His main retirement investment is in an IRA, to which he has contributed $2,000 in each of the past three years. That money is invested in zero coupon treasury bonds that will be worth $57,000 when they mature in 2019. That's when Steve will be 50 (a good age to begin seriously thinking about retirement, he thinks. Steve plans to retire when he is in his mid to late 50s.). Until then he plans to keep contributing the $2,000 maximum annually to his IRA, although his contribution is currently not tax-deductible.

Patti's retirement investment is in the form of the state's teachers' pension plan, which requires a mandatory contribution of 6.4% of her salary. She has been in the plan one year, and has about $1,200 in it. The plan is structured so that she will receive monthly retirement benefits of between $1,200 to $1,500 at age 55, or after 25 years of service, whichever comes first.

"We want to live comfortably, the way we do now, maybe better," says Patti about the day when she and Steve stop working. Steve dreams about having a second home—probably a mobile home—located in the lake region of East Texas. There he'd like to hunt, boat, and fish, and if they have planned right, there will be enough money to satisfy Patti's passion for travel and ski trips. Says Steve: "There's no way I can hurt myself by investing in our retirement."

Toward that end, Steve and Patti have been saving all they can. They also have $8,500 in cash, and a Treasury note that will be worth $11,000 when it matures in 1999. Steve also has $6,000 in a credit union account at his company, and another $1,100 in a bank CD.

Having about $25,000 in cash, in addition to some money put away for retirement, puts the Harrisons financially ahead of people twice their age.But, they are planning on having two children—the first one soon—and they are also going to build a house.

They are currently renting a home from Patti's uncle, but about a year ago they bought 3½ acres of land, taking out an $8,000 note. They have since paid it down to $5,000. Steve is clearing the land himself, and plans to do as much of the home building as he can, but he concedes that the house is still going to cost $50,000. Steve says he is in no hurry to finish it, and they would prefer 10-year financing, rather than tie themselves up with a 30-year mortgage.

Patti and Steve know that the house and kids probably will force them to tap some of the money they've already put away, in addition to making it harder to save in the future. But no matter what, they agree, "We won't touch the IRAs."

By any measure, the Harrisons have a remarkable amount of savings for young people who haven't inherited any money, but given the uncertainty of the future, they think saving a lot is the only prudent course to take.

"I don't know if Social Security is going to be there when I retire," says Steve. "We want to be able to take care of ourselves."

"Just about everything we'll do in retirement will cost us money."

John Peters, 51, and Lori Peters, 46, of Ogden, Utah, represent a problem many of us are going to face: How can you save enough money to retire well, when, at the exact mo-

ment you plan to quit work, you will have a child going to college?

"All the retirement books say you need seventy percent to eighty percent of your current income to retire comfortably," says John, a middle-level manager at the Internal Revenue Service, "but I don't buy it. My own logic tells me that the cost of living will be exactly the same as it is now—or even higher—once I stop working. I don't see where I can cut expenses much, once I retire, but I sure can see where expenses could increase.

"We have a low-key life-style; in the summer I ride my bike the almost five miles to and from work, and I brown-bag lunches every day. But just about everything we'll do in retirement—even going to a concert or the movies—will cost us money."

The money will be constantly going out, but will enough—generated from retirement investments, and John's pension—be coming in?

Fortunately, the Peterses are starting from a fairly strong base.

Together John and Lori, a secretary, make $78,000 a year, and recognizing that retirement is not that far off, they are now pouring $1,500 a month—or 23% of their *gross* pay—into various retirement plans. In addition, they are increasing their mortgage payments by $100 a month, to $570, in the hopes of having the $30,000 that remains on their mortgage paid off by the year 2000, six years early.

You can see that this planning has started to pay off. The couple has $243,000 saved, aided in large part by a $120,000 inheritance Lori received in 1989. Most of that money, which is invested in conservative mutual funds, is earmarked for retirement. "But will it be enough," John constantly wonders, to support them forever once they stop working?

And indeed will there even be $243,000 there?

The Peterses have saved $28,000 to put their only child—Karen, now age 14—through college. They figure Karen's college fund, which is made up of zero coupon bonds, U.S. savings bonds, and mutual funds, will be worth $40,000 when she starts school. But while that might be enough to cover most of the state college tuition, what happens if Karen wants to live away from home, or go to a private university?

Another potential drain is the Peterses' sideline business, which they are hoping will supplement their retirement income. They raise and breed quarter horses, and have for the last 10 years. In their best year, the Peterses have made $5,000 from their breeding business; in the worst, they lost $11,000. Every time they need money to finance the business, they borrow from their savings and "write an IOU to ourselves." Currently there is a $14,000 IOU outstanding.

John, who could retire from the government with a full pension of $36,000 a year at age 55, has already decided he will work another five years beyond that, even though it will not increase his retirement benefits. "That raised a lot of eyebrows at the office, but the principal reason I am going to keep working is to pay for Karen's education."

John's decision, of course, will give him another five years to contribute to his own retirement accounts. "But even then," the couple wonders, "will we have enough?"

"It's hard picturing retirement, when you're barely thirty."

Martha Skylar, 30, single, rising Atlanta ad executive. Bright future, but the future could be a ways away. Current income:

$50,000. Has started to fund her 401(k), which her company matches $1 for every $2 she puts in. She has $13,000 in the 401(k), but may use the money as a partial down payment should she buy a house. The rest of her nest egg is $32,000 that her parents gave her.

The good news? Martha, at some point in her career, could find herself making a very nice living as a creative director in the advertising business. She is widely recognized as being a "comer," and she's planning to soon tackle New York's "Big Apple," where the competition may rise a notch or two. When you see, on page 53, Martha's financial "snapshot," her state income tax projections will be based on New York's rates.

The bad news? Advertising is a notoriously fickle field—wholesale firings after a client switches to a new agency are common—and for all the awards she has won, and all the glowing annual performance reviews she has received, Martha's raises have been slow, although steady, so far.

"It's hard picturing retirement, when you're barely thirty," says Martha, who nonetheless has a pretty good—if perhaps unrealistic—idea of what she would like it to be like. "I'll stop working at sixty-five. But business tends to burn people out, and besides, there just isn't a whole lot of room at the top. After I quit, maybe I'll travel and sculpt. I've taken some courses, but I just never have the time to do it now. I picture retirement as the time when I can step back a little bit." She thinks she'll inherit some money, "but of course I can't count on it."

While she's clear about what she would like retirement to be like, Martha is not as certain about how she'll pay for it. She finds saving money "next to impossible."

"My grandmother recently gave me a hundred dollars. I guess she still thinks I'm a kid, and I used it to open the first savings account I've ever had." She doesn't have an IRA.

Martha readily concedes that she wouldn't have much put away for her retirement if the company hadn't instituted a 401(k) plan three years ago.

"They take the money out of my paycheck, so I never see it. If I don't see it, I don't miss it. If they gave me the money, I wouldn't save it, I'd just go out and buy something, or have a little fun."

The company contributes $1 to her 401(k) for every $2 she puts in, "so I'm getting a 50% return on my money right off the bat." However, the ad agency only matches up to the first 6%—$3,000—of Martha's salary, and that's all she is putting in.

Martha says: "I've thought about contributing more." She has also thought about contributing less.

In the course of talking about her financial future, Martha wistfully mentions twice how she would have more take-home pay if she stopped funding her 401(k). And even if she keeps putting money in, she currently plans to use her 401(k) money as a down payment when it comes time to buy a house. "I guess I think of it more as an emergency fund, rather than something that will pay for my retirement."

The money that she has put away in the 401(k) is invested in a balanced mutual fund—a mixture of stocks and fixed income investments. About $30,000 of the gift from her parents is in the stock market.

Why stocks?

"I remember my Dad pointing out a chart that showed long-term stocks outperformed every other investment. I figure this money is certainly intended for the long term. Besides, if I lost it all tomorrow, it wouldn't be that big a deal. I could go save it all again. I'm still young.

"How much money will I need to retire the way I want? I have no idea. I hope to get married. And I hope to have a family. If that happens, that will change everything. But I do want to work—even after kids. As to the future, I have watched my grandparents trying to get by on Social Security and their small savings, and I know I don't want to go that route, but I have no idea other than that."

"Right now, we aren't budgeters. . . . Putting the kids through school will require a huge sum, and we're going under the assumption that we aren't saving enough."

Dick and Mary Frank of Montpelier, Vermont, have it easier than most couples in their mid-30s. Together they make about $270,000 a year. They would like to retire early and in comfort. But with two young children to put through college, and perhaps another child somewhere in their future, they are not sure how much money they are going to need, or how it should be allocated.

Dick, 35, an attorney, and Mary, 34, owner of a company that supplies coffee to nearby businesses, have already put away $200,000 toward retirement. They feel that the money, which is invested mainly in growth mutual funds, through Mary's Keogh plan and Dick's 401(k) plan, gives them a good start toward retiring early, but they don't know how much more they are going to need.

That uncertainty is compounded by the fact that they have two boys, aged 5 and 3, who they'll have to put through school. Each child has a college fund invested in fixed income securities. They have put aside $32,000 for their older boy, $22,000 for the younger. "We know putting the kids through school will require a huge sum, and we're going under the assumption that we aren't saving enough for their education," says Dick. As a partner in his law firm, Dick takes as his paycheck a weekly draw against the firm's earnings. Once a year he takes an exceptionally large draw and puts about $3,000 in each of the boys' college funds. "I don't do it on a calculated basis, just when the mood strikes us and the money is there."

And so far, the money has always been there. Dick and Mary have a comfortable life now, and they expect it to continue. Dick projects that their combined $270,000 annual income should increase by between 8% and 15% in the years ahead, and that is good because the family goes on skiing, canoeing, hiking, and fishing trips regularly. And that's in addition to the trips to Bermuda and Florida and long weekends to Boston and the Maine coast. This is the kind of life the Franks want to continue after they retire. Partly in anticipation, they are planning to buy a ski condo within the next 10 years.

When the kids go to college—which means about 15 years from now, provided that they don't have another child—the Franks plan to sell their recently acquired $350,000 home and build a smaller one outside Montpelier. Dick figures by then the information age will have advanced to the point where he can do much of his law work at home. But even if commuting becomes easier, he—and Mary—are adamant about retiring early. Says Dick: "I have seen so many people put off retirement and then they never live to enjoy it."

Mary plans to sell her business about the same time that Dick starts telecommuting. Her business grosses about $1 million a year, but it's tough, says Dick, to put a price tag on what it's worth. "There are no proprietary assets; it's mostly good will." Still, they are hoping to get between $700,000 and $900,000 for it when the time comes to sell.

Dick and Mary realize that saving for college and their retirement is going to require more discipline than they currently have. "Right now," they admit, "we aren't budgeters. If we want to do something, we just do it."

"Five years ago, we had a retirement plan. We've got to resume it as soon as possible."

Linda and Harry Fox have suddenly swerved into the fast lane—and they're having problems keeping up. Two years ago, Linda, 54, the principal breadwinner, left her job back East to become marketing chief at one of Hollywood's hot new record companies. Her income has zoomed to $260,000 a year, but expenses have soared even faster. As a result, preparing for retirement, and for their daughter's education, has been put on hold.

Both Linda and Harry say they don't expect their current high-pressured life to last forever. They talk of eventually moving from Los Angeles to Wyoming or Maine, and assuming a slower pace. But that is eventually. Now they are struggling to get by on the $260,000 a year Linda makes. (Harry, 49, is a sculptor and his earnings are erratic.)

True, no one is going to hold a benefit for the couple who until recently were living with their 8-year-old daughter in a one-bedroom apartment in New York City. Their current income puts them safely within the top 1% of the nation's wage earners.

But expenses have a way of absorbing the money available. Between their $590,000 mortgage (on their $800,000 home), a personal trainer for Linda, psychotherapy for Harry and Linda, a live-in housekeeper, someone to take care of the grounds and the like, there just isn't much left at the end of the month. "Five years ago," Linda says, "we had a retirement plan. We've got to resume it as soon as possible."

But currently, all thoughts of retirement planning have been put on hold.

With liquid assets totaling $500,000—$300,000 of which is in an IRA funded with rollovers from Linda's last two jobs—the Foxes do have a very solid foundation of retirement savings. But they don't know if that money, which is split fairly evenly between stocks and bonds, will be enough.

Besides, they both say, retirement is not the immediate concern. Linda talks about quitting work "eventually," and as an artist, Harry expects to be creating his steel sculptures until the end. (After all, Harry says, Picasso kept working into his 90s.)

In the short term, they want to make sure that they have enough money set aside to put their daughter through the school of her choice. They currently have $32,000 saved. They figure they'll need five times that when she starts college 10 years from now.

There are two big variables that could affect their financial future: Linda's job, and Harry's reputation.

It is all well and good being a senior executive at a hot music shop. But Hollywood is a place where a record producer who is hot today is known for producing dogs tomorrow. What will happen to Linda's income then?

On the plus side, Harry still dreams of the big break that will make his inventory of sculptures worth $1 million or more, although he concedes it probably won't happen. "If you take a napkin and tear off a tiny corner," he says "that's the percentage of people who make any money being artists."

That's a lesson Harry has learned firsthand. In the previous four years, his annual income has averaged less than $50,000. Last year it was only $20,000, not even enough to cover the cost of his studio. Between the steel, acetylene, and such, it costs Harry $35,000 annually just to begin work.

"We'll have to rely on Social Security quite a bit, something I would rather not do."

Carl and Connie Schmidt of St. Louis have the typical problems of many young couples: a tight budget, two young kids, and limited resources to put toward college and retirement. The problem is the Schmidts aren't so young anymore—he's 40 and she's 39. They know they'd better do some serious financial planning—soon.

It's hard to figure out where the money goes. Carl makes $57,500 as a project manager installing software at a manufacturing company. Connie works part-time for the state, investigating child abuse cases. She earns $11,000 a year.

But with the cost of raising two children—Ingrid, 8, and John, 6—and an $85,000 mortgage on the $116,000 home they bought three years ago, money is consistently tight. For example, the Schmidts have not yet been able to put anything away for their kids' college education.

The couple's retirement picture isn't much brighter. Carl, who has been at his present job less than a year, rolled over his $18,000 pension from his previous job and put it into an IRA. It is currently invested in a certificate of deposit.

Carl's present employer has a pension plan that will pay him $31,112 a year starting at age 65, if he stays that long.

"We hadn't thought about retirement until a couple of years ago, when both our fathers retired almost simultaneously," says Carl. "We don't have a concrete plan. We've talked about both of us quitting work at age sixty-five and then moving to some warm place on the ocean, but beyond that we don't have anything definite planned."

How are they going to pay for their retirement?

They are not sure about that either. "We'll have to rely on Social Security quite a bit, something I would rather not do," says Connie. "It's not that great a position to be in."

Connie talks about moving to a more pleasant job where she could work full-time, now that the children are older. The job would probably offer a better retirement package than the one she now has, but so far, Connie hasn't prepared her résumé.

As Carl concedes, there is a lack of focus in the Schmidts' financial planning: "I think we need to identify our goals."

"I'm too old to take chances."

Milton Quincy, 75, is set for life. Milton, a self-employed packager of home video and television programs who lives in Pasadena, is a year or two away from retirement, but his decision to stop working won't affect his life-style at all. (With a net worth of about $6 million, his investments generate about $350,000 of income a year.) The widower's main

**concern is protecting his assets from taxes, so that his heirs
and charities can receive as much as possible.**

Milton Quincy has always had an "ear" for talent. As an agent he
discovered some of the biggest singing stars of his generation.

But while that talent was innate—"I was born with music in my
blood," Milton says simply when asked to explain his success—his
retirement planning expertise was definitely learned.

Milton, who went on to found his own record company, which
was subsequently acquired by a media conglomerate, began thinking about his retirement in earnest some two decades ago, when
his record company was sold.

Eventually, he rolled his pension into a form of an IRA—a
Simplified Employee Pension (SEP) plan (see Chapter 12)—and in
1992 he contributed $30,000, the maximum allowed by law, to it
from his current business. Today that SEP is worth just about $1
million. Since he turned 70½, Milton, as required by law, has been
withdrawing about $135,000 a year from the plan. (Note: The
government's rules are quite precise on what *must be taken out* of
retirement plans. We explain this more completely in our final
chapter, "Spending Down.")

He has been plowing the proceeds back into equities and tax-
free bonds. "I'm too old to take chances," he says.

It's a philosophy that has served him well. By starting financial
planning years ago and investing in his business, Milton has
managed, after a lifetime of working, to become a millionaire many
times over.

His financial life is set. His home, valued at about $800,000, is
completely paid for. "I don't think I live frugally," he says. He
claims he doesn't lift a finger around the house, except "to call

someone to do something for me. I don't even change light bulbs."

He travels a great deal—both for business and for pleasure—and he entertains a lot. "I still love music, just about any kind, so I go to everything—from pop to classics to Broadway." His biggest concern, and we all should have such problems, is making sure that his estate planning is adequate.

His primary goal is to leave everything that he possibly can to his heirs, a son and four grandchildren, and his favorite charities. Individual trusts were set up for all five heirs about 20 years ago, and they contain $200,000 each.

That's good, Milton concedes, but he'd like to know what else he can do to keep estate taxes to a minimum.

In our next chapter, you'll see some possible solutions to the financial planning challenges facing these people.

Retirement planning isn't an abstract exercise. You save money for real reasons. For every financial worry—if you have time on your side and can alter your spending (saving) habits—there is a solution.

CHAPTER 2

Real People: Where You Are Now, Where You Want to Be

In the preceding chapter we outlined the basic problems our real-life examples are facing as they go about their retirement and financial planning. Now, we'll give some suggestions that might solve their dilemmas.

The key to financial planning is balancing present assets against future needs.

To do this, you are projecting, and that means you're taking calculated guesses. You're guessing what inflation will be; you're guessing how much your earnings may go up each year between now and the time you retire, and you are guessing how much your investments will earn. These are educated guesses, but they *are* guesses or assumptions.

Obviously, the longer the span between now and when you retire, or now and when you need the money for college, the wider the variations may be. If your child is newborn, and you're trying to project college costs some 17 or 18 years away, you are making a calculated guess now about whether your one-day-old baby will go to a private or a public school and what those schools will cost. It is quite possible that your projections will be off—quite possibly by a lot.

If you're 40, and you're projecting ahead to retirement, you'll probably pick a retirement date between your 60th and your 70th birthdays. If you actually retire earlier or later, then obviously your projections will be off, perhaps substantially.

But assume you must; project you must.

A do-nothing stance ("Gee, I just can't guess about that now. I'll wait a few more years, then I'll try.") means you're flirting with financial disaster. If there's a shortfall in savings, the earlier you detect it, the easier it will be to erase it by adjusting budgets (spending) and thus savings (investing).

No, you won't have all the information you need to make projections. But there is nothing wrong with you taking your best shot today at where you're going, and then as circumstances change, or you gain more information, making new assumptions a year from now, or five years from now. Retirement planning is an unfinished symphony.

Goals Change

You're setting goals. You're asking:

- How can I save enough to live comfortably in retirement?

- How can I put aside enough to pay for the college education of my children or grandchildren?

- How can I plan to take care of my parents, or my children, or best of all, myself and/or my spouse?

How do you do all this planning?

You could do it yourself. There are software programs available that will run on your personal computer. Or you could ask your financial consultant to do it for you. If you go that route, you have two choices.

Choice number one is to do the analysis piecemeal. Among the various free services available there are some that will project:

Retirement costs. These programs will show you how much you need to save or invest each year to be able to afford the retirement life-style you want. Based on your current income, and whether you or your spouse is covered by an employer pension plan, these programs may also tell you whether your IRA contribution is fully deductible or partially deductible, and might also project how much your IRA will grow in coming years.

College costs. This one shows how much you need to put aside to pay for your children's college education.

Rollover comparisons. These programs take your tax status and your age into consideration, and explain the various tax consequences you should take into account as you think about rolling over your pension assets. These programs compare the advantages and disadvantages of taking the money now (and paying taxes) versus rolling it over tax-deferred.

Your other choice, when it comes to getting this advice, is using an integrated service that will do all of the above, plus provide an in-depth analysis of your estate planning as well.

This option brings into play all of a financial consultant's resources and generally will cost you somewhere between $100 and $500.

The ultimate planning method, which employs attorneys and other experts who will review in detail your assets and your needs, can cost $5,000 and up. In this guide we used a service that cost

$175 per report to help us analyze the needs for our real live case studies. These reports are generally projected in terms of today's dollars, but obviously the amounts needed in future years may have to be adjusted to reflect inflation.

We'll start with the Harrisons, our young couple in Texas who are just starting out, and we'll end with our 75-year-old Californian who is living the good life; he also wants his children and grand-children to share his bounty.

"When we retire . . . we want to live comfortably, the way we do now, maybe better."—Patti Harrison

Only in their 20s, Steven and Patti Harrison are well on their way to a successful retirement. They are already saving

---

Assumptions

Financial planning—since it is looking ahead into the unknown—must be based on assumptions. In real life, a decade or even two from now, the assumptions today may turn out to be too high or too low. That is why you should constantly update your assumptions, and thus your projections.

But start with something. Here are the assumptions we used for the case histories:

	Annually
Inflation will average	4%
Taxable investment growth*	7%
Equities growth	10%
Tax-exempt growth	6%
Other investments' growth**	5%

*Includes money market funds, CDs, and corporate bonds.
**For example, real estate and collectibles.

---

significant sums for the day—still at least 30 years off—when they'll stop work. In fact, based on the money they have put away, they can already afford the modest retirement life-style they envision. While they still have to figure out how they'll put their children—should they have them—through college, they face the very pleasant problem of trying to see just how nice retirement can be.

The Harrisons are living proof that if you start early enough, you can afford to retire quite well, and in fact might be able to live

Snapshot

Current annual income (from all sources)	$51,100
Current federal tax liability	$8,980
Investment Assets	$37,270
Portfolio allocation:	15% cash, 0% equities, 85% fixed income
Net worth	$45,270

Net Worth Summary

Assets	Personal Assets	$8,000
	Investment Assets Portfolio	$30,570
	Other	$0
	Retirement	$6,700
Total Assets		$45,270
Liabilities		$5,000
Net worth		$40,270

better than you are now, once you stop working. In other words, you can indeed grow rich s-l-o-w-l-y.

The Harrisons tend to be conservative in just about everything they do, and it's no different when it comes to projecting how much money they'll need in retirement. They took a look at their current after-tax income of about $42,000 a year, subtracted some, and said they should be able to do just fine if, after taxes, they could have $30,000 (in constant dollars) coming in once they are retired.

Steven and Patti have already—at the ages of 23 and 24 respectively—almost saved enough money to pay for the kind of retirement they are projecting.

Indeed, if they were willing to spend their principal, they could afford to live on $34,500 a year in retirement—that's 15% more than they say they'll need—*and that's assuming they never save another dime.*

Odds are that they won't stop saving. The Harrisons can definitely be described as penny-pinchers and they have quite a bit of time before they plan to stop work. Patti won't retire for another 31 years; Steven for another 37. Even if they only put modest amounts away, it will be more than possible for them to live on double, or triple, their current income, once they stop work.

The only thing they have to worry about in their immediate future is figuring out how they are going to put their children through college. They must save as much as $10,000 a year *starting today* to make sure that their children can go to the college of their choice. That's an awful lot of money, especially when you consider that their kids haven't been born yet.

The Harrisons are talking about having two children—one in 1993 and another in 1995.

Still, if they want their future children to go to college, they better start saving now, and saving a lot. Based on current projections, it will take 6% of their present income to put both children through public colleges. They'll need to save 19% of their budget if the children go to private schools. These projections are based on the following facts and assumptions:

1. Tuition, room, and board at a state school in Texas is currently $5,000.

2. Nationwide, room, board, and tuition for private colleges is $15,000.

3. The annual increase in college costs will be 7%. (Educational costs continue to rise far faster than inflation.)

4. The after-tax return on their investments will be 7.5%.

(This assumption of a 7.5% return is based on the investments being a mixture of fixed income and equity, and that the taxes will be relatively low through the use of tax shelter devices. See Chapter 5—"Paying (Saving) for Your Children's College Education"—for full details on how long-term college funding strategies can be tax-advantaged.)

The following charts tell what they are up against:

To meet these costs, the Harrisons need to save $1,700 a year—every year for the next 18—if their first child goes to a state school, and $5,000 if she decides to go to a private one. The alternative would be investing $18,200 in a lump sum today. That would take care of a state school. An investment of $54,500 today would be needed to pay for tuition at a private university.

While the tuition bill for their second child will be more, they can actually get by with putting away a bit less each year, since they are starting two years earlier.

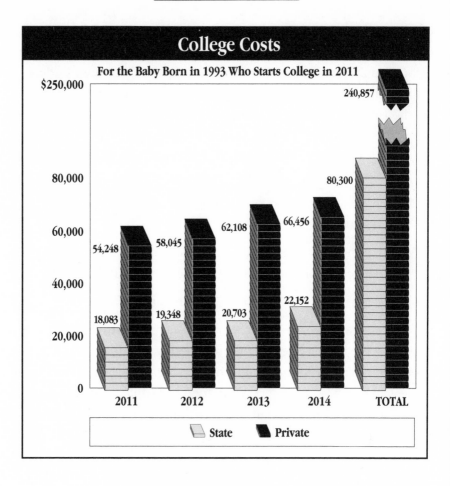

Savings of $1,600 a year would take care of four years at a state school; $4,700 would cover private school tuition. A lump sum investment of $18,000 today would pay for tuition at a state university for child number two; it would take $54,000 today to completely fund four years at a private school for him.

While preparing for future college costs should be taking up the bulk of the Harrisons' attention in the short term, they also need to spend a bit of time thinking about how their assets are allocated.

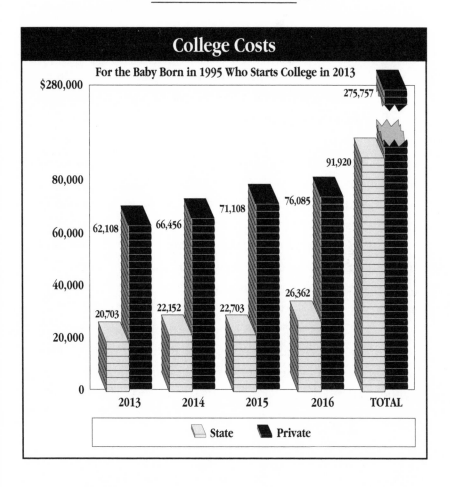

College Costs

For the Baby Born in 1995 Who Starts College in 2013

Year	State	Private
2013	20,703	62,108
2014	22,152	66,456
2015	22,703	71,108
2016	26,362	76,085
TOTAL	91,920	275,757

State   Private

(This is the only major flaw we can find in their considerable retirement planning to date.) The Harrisons are just too conservative with their investments for a couple so young.

They have $26,000—that's 85% of their investment assets—in fixed income securities. While those investments let them know with certainty what their money will be worth in coming years— for example, the $6,770 Steven has put away in a zero coupon municipal should be worth $192,299 when he retires 37 years from now (if he were to constantly reinvest in new tax-free securities as the old ones mature)—it does not allow them to participate in the growth that has traditionally come from investing in equities.

A more balanced portfolio would call for them to shift $12,275 from their fixed income investments, and another $1,450 from their cash equivalents (a money market account) and move that money into stocks—probably a growth and income mutual fund, given their conservative nature.

If they did, their investment portfolio would look like this: equities, 45%; fixed income, 45%; and cash, 10%.

With that small change, their retirement planning—which up until now has been excellent—will become even better.

When asked where they are now, Steven and Patti Harrison can answer, "In pretty good shape." That's putting it mildly.

We would offer only one other piece of advice. They should hedge their bets by taking out a term insurance policy of about $175,000 on each of their lives, so that college can be paid for even if either of them dies before the kids start school. They should also take out disability insurance. (For more on that, see Chapter 27, on insurance.)

Other than that, they are in great shape. Actually, we're understating.

Considering their age, and their financial discipline, they're in fantastic shape!

"Just about everything we'll do in retirement will cost us money."—John Peters

John Peters, 51, and Lori Peters, 46, of Ogden, Utah, represent a problem many of us are going to face: How can you save enough money to retire well, when, at the exact moment you plan to quit work, you will have a child going to college? The Peterses' solution appears sound. They are not going to try to do both simultaneously.

John is going to work a bit longer than he planned. He'll retire at age 60 instead of 55. Those extra five years will make all the difference in the world.

The Peterses are a wonderful example of what happens if you start your retirement planning soon enough, and can be a bit flexible. Like just about everyone, they found when they sat down

Snapshot	
Current annual income (from all sources)	$83,900
Current federal tax liability	$15,481
State income tax	$4,788
Investment Assets	$332,750
Portfolio allocation:	14% cash, 40% equities, 46% fixed income
Net worth	$514,390

Net Worth Summary		
Assets	Personal Assets	$222,000
	Investment Assets Portfolio	$193,650
	Other	$48,800
	Retirement	$90,300
Total Assets		$554,750
Liabilities		$40,360
Net worth		$514,390

to do serious retirement planning that they were going to need a bit more money than they had first thought.

However, all it is going to take is just a few adjustments to make sure that they can have the kind of retirement they want.

Let's start with the Peterses' biggest worry: the cost of sending Karen, their only child, to college. She's 14 now and they have put away $28,779 to pay for her education.

The Peterses have already put away more than they'll need, if Karen attends a state school. Should she go to a private school, there will be a shortfall, but, fortunately for them, not an insurmountable one.

If the Peterses were to stop work in four years, just as Karen began her freshman year, there could be a lot of financial stress. They'd be watching as $48,900 of their savings flowed out to pay for four years of college (the total shortfall in savings that they'd face if Karen attended a private school) with not a whole lot of money coming in.

However, they have eliminated that problem by deciding to keep working until Karen finishes school. In fact, even if Karen decides to go to a private school, it may be possible for her parents to pay for her education out of cash flow, thanks to their decision to put off retirement for a bit. The additional money they'll have to put away accounts for only 8% of their current income, and the Peterses are already used to saving large amounts of money.

Ever since they became serious about their retirement planning a few years ago, they began pouring $1,500 a month—or 23% of their *gross* pay—into various retirement plans.

They could take $567 of that $1,500 and set it aside for Karen's education. (That would take care of the private school tuition shortfall.) Even if they did that, they still would be saving about $1,000 a month for retirement.

They have that flexibility because they have decided to keep working. So, you can see how much easier their retirement life is going to be by deciding not to retire so young.

That decision to postpone retirement does something else as well. It ensures that the Peterses will have at least $55,000 a year in annual retirement, the minimum they say they'll need. (One advantage of working for the government is that his pension will increase each year because of automatic cost-of-living adjustments.) In fact, if they were willing to spend all the principal from their savings and investments during the 25 years they are expected to live once they stop work, they could live on $65,000 a year. If they didn't want to touch their principal, they could live on $61,500 a year.

And those numbers don't include the additional $60,000 they will be saving between now and retirement. (Assuming that money can generate 5% tax-free, that would give them another $3,000 a year.) Plus, if Karen goes to a state school, that will save them *another* $58,200, which will yield an additional $2,910 tax-free annually to supplement their retirement income.

If both things happen, the Peterses could live on $67,410 a year (in constant dollars) during their retirement, without ever touching their principal. They say that sounds quite pleasant indeed.

To get even more enjoyment out of retirement, they could make a few adjustments to their investments now. And they should also make sure that—given the big swings in their horse business—that it remains a sideline *business* and not a fixation.

For one thing, they may want to boost their investments in equities a bit from the current 40% of their portfolio to 45%. They could do that by decreasing the bond portion of their portfolio by 1%, and reducing their cash position from 14% to 10%.

In addition, there is absolutely no reason why they should carry a credit card debt of $9,860, especially when they have a total of $27,000 in cash sitting in their savings, checking, and money market accounts.

Finally, the Peterses may want to look at their taxable investments. They are now receiving $6,400 a year in taxable interest and dividends, and between state and federal taxes they are paying about a third of that money, $2,124 to be exact, to the government.

That argues for them to switch those investments to tax-free investments. The following table shows why they would be better off.

Taxable Equivalent Yield at 33.18% Tax Rate*					
Tax-exempt yield	4.50%	5.00%	5.50%	6.00%	6.50%
Taxable equivalent yield	6.73%	7.48%	8.23%	8.98%	9.73%

*Combined federal and state

But all these changes are minor. The Peterses have done a good job of retirement planning, and it shows.

"It's hard picturing retirement, when you're barely thirty."—Martha Skylar

If Martha Skylar had to prepare for retirement on her own, she'd be in trouble. As we have seen, she is just not a saver.

Recognizing that fact, she did something that cost her a bit of pride, but made preparing for her future a lot easier. She went to her parents and basically took a loan against her inheritance. Martha's parents have given her $32,000, roughly 10% of what she would receive if they died today. Her parents gave her the money with the stipulation that "it be invested wisely."

Without that present from her parents, we have serious doubts that Martha Skylar would ever be able to retire on the $60,000 a year she says she'll need. However, with that gift, she'll need to save just $1,347 a year in today's dollars, for the next 35 years, to produce an annual retirement income of $60,000.

Snapshot

Current annual income (from all sources)	$50,000
Current federal tax liability	$9,560
State income tax	$3,820
Investment Assets	$58,200
Portfolio allocation:	7% cash, 93% equities, 0% fixed income
Net worth	$58,200

Net Worth Summary

Assets	Personal Assets	$0
	Investment Assets Portfolio	$32,200
	Other	$0
	Retirement	$26,000
Total Assets		$58,200
Liabilities		$0
Net worth		$58,200

Martha's Retirement Lifestyle

Year	Retirement Income	+ Return on Investment	= Total Income (After-Tax)	− Anticipated Expenses	= Annual Surplus (Deficit)	Remaining Investment Balance
At Retirement						$204,805
2027	$22,974	$8,924	$31,898	$60,000	-28,102	184,911
2028	23,576	6,584	30,160	62,400	-32,240	161,535
2029	25,122	3,814	28,936	64,896	-35,960	135,149
2030	25,879	548	26,427	67,492	-41,065	101,686
2031	26,495	0	26,495	70,192	-43,697	62,908
2032	27,088	0	27,088	73,000	-45,912	18,983
2033	27,705	0	27,705	75,920	-48,215	0
2034	28,346	0	28,346	78,957	-50,611	0
2035	29,013	0	29,013	82,115	-53,102	0
2036	29,707	0	29,707	85,400	-55,693	0
2037	30,429	0	30,429	88,816	-58,387	0
2038	31,179	0	31,179	92,369	-61,190	0
2039	31,959	0	31,959	96,064	-64,105	0
2040	32,771	0	32,771	99,907	-67,136	0
2041	33,615	0	33,615	103,903	-70,288	0
2042	34,493	0	34,493	108,059	-73,566	0
2043	35,406	0	35,406	112,381	-76,975	0
2044	36,355	0	36,355	116,876	-80,521	0
2045	35,416	0	35,416	121,551	-86,135	0
2046	36,366	0	36,366	126,413	-90,047	0
2047	37,354	0	37,354	131,470	-94,116	0

True, a reasonable portion of that $60,000 will be coming from Social Security—some $11,925 a year—and from her defined benefit pension from work she'll get another $11,048 annually. However, the fact is, thanks to all the earnings that $32,000 gift will be producing for her between now and the time she retires in 35 years, Martha will only need to save a little bit more than $100 a month between now and retirement to accomplish her goal.

To show you exactly how important that gift was, let us restate it in slightly different terms. If Martha doesn't save another cent over the next 35 years, she could retire on $35,000 annually.

She would still be getting $22,973 a year in pension and Social Security, and that $32,000 gift from her parents would be producing $12,027 a year in interest by the time she retires.

Thanks, Mom and Dad.

To best achieve her ultimate goal, Martha may want to reallocate the $32,200 she has to invest. (That money is made up of the $32,000 gift from her parents, the $100 her grandmother sent her last year, and $100 she was able to save on her own.)

Right now she has $30,000 in equities, and $2,200 in cash, $2,000 of which is in her checking account. She may want to shift that money around so that she has 45% of it ($14,490) in stocks, 45% ($14,490) in bonds, and $3,220, or 10%, in cash.

A major reason for this shift would be so that she could reduce the amount of taxes she has to pay. Between federal and local taxes, nearly 34% (33.67% to be exact) of every dollar she earns goes to pay taxes. If she can find fixed income securities that are paying 6% tax-free interest, it would be the same as if she invested in something with a 9.05% taxable yield.

Now, we have built a couple of assumptions into Martha's retirement model. For one thing, we have assumed that nothing in her personal life is going to change over the next 35 years. In our projection we are assuming that she is never going to marry, never have children, and never buy a house.

If any one of those three events happens, all bets are off.

The other thing we are assuming, and it is a great big assumption, is that Martha will manage to save an additional $1,347 a year, for the next 35 years, to fund her retirement. If she doesn't, she will exhaust all her retirement savings five years after she stops work.

The table on page 54 tells the depressing story. We are assuming that Martha will retire in the year 2027, when she is 65, and that her investments will have grown to be worth $204,805 at that time.

Our hope would be that Martha would look at this table and realize the need to save more money. An IRA would be one way—or she could increase her 401(k) contributions. Failing that, we hope she can figure out how to live on $35,000 a year in retirement, because that is all that her current resources will allow.

"Right now, we aren't budgeters. . . . Putting the kids through school will require a huge sum, and we're going under the assumption that we aren't saving enough."—Dick Frank

Dick and Mary Frank of Montpelier, Vermont, know they are lucky. Their combined family income is $270,000 and their two boys are bright, funny, and healthy.

They wouldn't change a thing about their life now, and they don't want to change anything about it once they retire. To make sure they don't have to, they'll need $150,000 (after taxes) in retirement income coming in each year. Although they have been diligent savers so far, they still have a ways to go before they reach their goal.

Although the Franks *are* prosperous (they make more than 99% of their countrymen), they are looking for money-saving ideas, *and their search is totally justified.*

Snapshot	
Current annual income (from all sources)	$270,000
Current federal tax liability	$71,458
State income tax	$24,296
Investment Assets	$882,769
Portfolio allocation:	52% cash, 48% equities
Net worth	$1,175,769

Net Worth Summary		
Assets	Personal Assets	$443,000
	Investment Assets Portfolio	$31,264
	Other	$650,000
	Retirement	$201,505
Total Assets		$1,325,769
Liabilities		$150,000
Net worth		$1,175,769

While they have a net worth of more than $1 million, they still don't have enough saved to retire the way they want.

Dick and Mary project, realistically, they are going to need $150,000 a year tax-free once they retire to live the way they are living now. And despite all the money they have put away, they are not even close to having enough.

Should they stop saving today, they'd have two choices in thinking about retirement. They could either retire at age 55, as they had planned, and live on $115,500 a year, or they could postpone retirement until they reached age 63. By that time their assets would have grown enough to support the life-style they want.

There is a third option, of course. They can continue saving diligently. If they do, and they also reapportion their investment portfolio a bit, they may very well be able to retire on $150,000 at age 55.

How can they do it? They can start by looking at the way they have allocated their investment assets.

They are being too conservative. Instead of having 52% of that money in cash and fixed income investments, they may want to reduce it to 30%—5% cash and 25% fixed income—shifting more of their money into equities, which tend to do better over the long term.

And they'll also want to take the fixed income portion of their portfolio and invest it tax-free.

Between federal and state taxes, the Franks are paying 36.71% of their income in taxes. It's awfully hard to get ahead when you are losing more than a third of what you make.

The following table shows how much better off they would be if they switched as much money as possible into tax-free investments.

Taxable Equivalent Yield at a 36.71% Tax Rate					
Tax-exempt yield	4.50%	5.00%	5.50%	6.00%	6.50%
Taxable equivalent yield	7.11%	7.90%	8.69%	9.48%	10.27%

That's a significant difference in the rate of return.

We can show just how dramatically different it is by looking at the Franks' tax bracket another way.

Here is what kind of return their investments are earning, after taxes *and a 4% inflation rate are factored in.*

The Real World Rate of Return

Return (%)	Return After Taxes (%)	Inflation (%)	Return After Taxes and Inflation (%)
5	3.16	4	− 0.84
8	5.06	4	1.06
11	6.96	4	2.96

As you can see, tax-free investments for the Franks make a lot of sense.

And shifting the money around today will have another big advantage. The Franks will be able to take care of college costs for Jordan, 5, and Matthew, 3.

Because they were not certain how much money they would need for college, Dick and Mary periodically have been putting away $3,000 for each boy. At the moment, they have $32,000 earmarked for their older son, and $22,000 for the younger.

But the money is combined with the Franks' other savings. If they broke out that money separately, they'd find they have already set aside enough to pay for public school for each boy, and they are not far from having private school tuition covered as well.

They would need to invest an additional $23,800 today to make sure that Jordan will be able to go to the private college of his choice, and another $34,300 to cover private school tuition for Matthew. That's a lot of money, but the Franks already have it in their savings accounts. All they have to do is put the money aside for their children.

If they do, they'll find that all their financial worries—except one—will have been eliminated. The exception? Their retirement planning.

They are starting from a solid base. Assuming they don't save another dime, here are the resources that will be available to them come retirement.

Social Security Income

Annual After-Tax Income		Annual Increase
Mary's (Starts in 2020)	Dick's (Starts in 2018)	
$12,087	$11,318	4%

In addition to Social Security, the Franks will also have the following assets.

Other Retirement Assets

Assets	Current Value	Value at Retirement
Tax deferreds	$201,505	$1,672,530
Taxable fixed income/ investments	16,264	18,757
Equity	15,000	24,877
Other	650,000	585,946
Total	$882,769	$2,302,110

You will note that we are being extremely conservative in valuing Mary's business, which is currently mostly good will. In fact, we project a decline, because of the capital gains tax she will pay when it is sold. In reality, if the business continues to prosper, the value of the business may increase dramatically. But for the time being, it is best to consider this asset as the wild card of their retirement future. Still, going into retirement with over $1 million in liquid assets, and a guaranteed $21,702 coming in from Social Security each year, is a very nice position to be in. However, it will not cover all of the Franks' retirement needs.

In fact, if they tried to live on $150,000 a year, given the money they have put away up until now, their retirement assets would be exhausted in 15 years. That means that during the remaining 11 years they are expected to live in retirement they would have to depend exclusively on Social Security.

To maintain the life-style they want, the Franks will need to save another $26,904 a year—every year—from now until the time they retire. That's a large number, but it accounts for only 10% of their current annual income.

Simply by putting away 10% of their income each year, the Franks can be assured of the kind of retirement they want.

"Five years ago, we had a retirement plan. We've got to resume it as soon as possible."—Harry Fox

Linda and Harry Fox have recently arrived among the rich—last year their combined income was $260,200—and they'd like to stay there, even after they retire.

They are willing to retire on less—say, $150,000 a year—but figuring out how to secure that retirement income, in addition to putting their now-8-year-old daughter through college, will require discipline.

The Foxes face a difficult—but not impossible—task.

We've said from the beginning that preparing for your own retirement, while figuring out how you are going to pay for your children's college education, is probably one of the most difficult things you'll ever have to do, and Harry and Linda's situation proves it.

Snapshot	
Current annual income (from all sources)	$260,200
Current federal tax liability	$77,430
State income tax	$25,200
Investment Assets	$340,000
Portfolio allocation:	20% cash, 40% equities, 40% fixed income
Net worth	$690,000

Net Worth Summary		
Assets	Personal Assets	$960,000
	Investment Assets Portfolio	$0
	Other	$0
	Retirement	$340,000
Total Assets		$1,300,000
Liabilities		$610,000
Net worth		$690,000

Let's start with the relatively good news: the price of putting their eight-year-old through college.

If we project that current room, board, and tuition charges at a state school will grow at 7% a year, it will cost them a total of $36,000 to put Sarah through a state school. If she goes to a private school, the total tab will be about $107,000.

Why is that good news? Because the Foxes already have put $32,000 into Sarah's college fund. They figured they would need about $160,000 to pay for four years of school, so actually they estimated too high.

The Foxes could divide the $32,000 they already have into four parts and buy four $8,000 zero coupon municipal bonds. One would mature in 1999 (their daughter's freshman year); another in the year 2000 (sophomore year), a third with a maturity date of 2001 (junior year), and a fourth that comes due in the year 2002 (senior year). The bonds at maturity would provide more than enough to pay for state school tuition.

If they didn't save another dime for college during the next 10 years, and their daughter decided to go to a private school, there would be a shortfall, but a manageable one.

The chart on page 64 tells the story.

Assuming that Sarah goes to a private college, they are looking at a four-year potential shortfall of about $50,000. That is not an insurmountable problem, when your current annual income is better than $250,000 a year. And life would be swell if this was the only financial planning problem the Foxes faced.

It isn't.

The Foxes say they want to retire on $156,000 a year.

They have $340,000 in retirement assets today.

That leaves a bit of a gap.

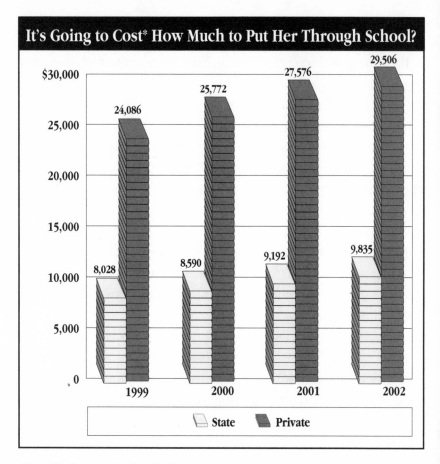

It's Going to Cost* How Much to Put Her Through School?

* Annually, for room, board, and tuition.

Let's see exactly what they are up against, starting with inflation.

The impact of inflation on retirement planning cannot be under-estimated. It increases the cost of maintaining your desired life-style while it erodes the purchasing power of fixed income payments. For example, at a 4% inflation rate, that $156,000 in today's dollars would climb to $240,000 by the time the Foxes retire in 11 years. To look at it another way, 20 years from now, $156,000 will have the purchasing power of $68,952 today.

But even without inflation, the Foxes would have a problem meeting their goals.

They simply have not saved enough.

If we assume that they will retire when they say they want to—in 11 years when Linda is 65 and Harry is 60—and proceed to draw down both principal and interest, they can spend $156,000 a year for exactly five years. After that, the money will be gone. That's not exactly the information they wanted to hear.

What happens if they live more frugally? The actuarial tables say that the Foxes will need their retirement money for 20 years. Given the money they have now, and assuming a reasonable rate of return on their investments, they can live on $59,000 a year in retirement. That's just 20% of their current income.

Why the shortfall? If you look at their resources—and it doesn't take long—it's easy to understand the problem.

In total, here's what the Foxes have going into retirement:

- Linda's Social Security (which starts in the year 2004) will produce $13,651 a year and grow at an estimated 4% annually.

- Harry's Social Security (which starts in the year 2005) will be $6,694 annually and also grow at 4% a year.

- The $340,000 they have put away for retirement should be worth $523,414 in 11 years, assuming they make no additional contributions.

When you put all their resources together, it is easy to see why they won't be able to live on $156,000 a year.

The situation is far from hopeless however. *By simply saving another $16,000 a year, every year from now until the time they retire, they will be able to live on $156,000 annually.* On a $250,000 annual salary, saving $16,000 a year for retirement is very possible.

But notice the assumptions we are building into their retirement model.

The biggest assumption is that Linda's $260,000 salary will continue for the foreseeable future. And that it may even increase. Given the fickleness of the entertainment business, that is far from guaranteed. The couple has virtually no reserve to fall back on, should she become unemployed.

And even if Linda's income continues to roll in, will the Foxes be able to save that $16,000 a year, on top of putting their daughter through a private college? It will mean cutting back a bit on their current life-style, and the Foxes have shown no inclination to do that so far.

Finally, what happens if the Foxes beat the actuarial tables? If their retirement lasts longer than 20 years, the only money they will have left will come from Social Security. It is quite possible they will outlive all their other money.

On the positive side, they have $210,000 in equity in their house, and if they decide to move to a less hectic part of the country, they will probably be able to buy a cheaper home and add much of that $210,000 to their retirement savings.

In addition, there are a couple of things they can do today to make retirement more pleasant.

For one thing, they can reduce the amount of money they are paying in taxes. Between state and federal taxes, the Foxes have a combined tax rate of 37.9%. What this means is they should be seriously thinking about putting more of their future savings in tax-free investments such as California municipal bonds. That will not impose a hardship. A California municipal bond yielding 6% will produce a tax equivalent yield of 9.66%. This decision requires some planning, however. If a substantial portion of their income comes from tax-exempt income, the Foxes may be subject to the Alternative Minimum Tax.

There is one other thing the Foxes should do as a matter of course, and that is wipe out all their consumer debt. They have a $20,000 car loan. That should be paid off immediately, either through savings, or by writing a check against a home equity credit line. Consumer interest is not deductible, while interest on home equity loans usually is, and would be in this case.

With a little bit of discipline now, the Foxes will be able to afford a very pleasant retirement. If they fail to save a relatively small amount—just 10% of their current income for the next 11 years—they will be very disappointed, once Linda retires.

"We'll have to rely on Social Security quite a bit, something I would rather not do."—Connie Schmidt

Carl and Connie Schmidt of St. Louis have an income that places them in the top 22% nationwide, but they will tell you they sure don't feel well-off. Even on a combined income of $68,500 a year money is tight, and with a net worth of just $67,000 it is hard to see how they are going to able to put two children through school.

The good news is that the Schmidts can afford to retire. The bad news is that unless they start putting away significant sums of money immediately, and/or Carl chooses to stay with his current employer for the rest of his working life, they won't be able to retire, *and* put their two children through college.

Snapshot	
Current annual income (from all sources)	$68,500
Current federal tax liability	$12,215
State income tax	$2,724
Investment Assets	$20,000
Portfolio allocation:	100% cash
Net worth	$67,000

Net Worth Summary		
Assets	Personal Assets	$145,000
	Investment Assets Portfolio	$2,000
	Other	$0
	Retirement	$18,000
Total Assets		$165,000
Liabilities		$98,000
Net worth		$67,000

Let's start with the good news.

The Schmidts say they want to live on $48,000 a year once they stop working, and as things stand now they will be able to do that, thanks in large part to the Social Security benefits they will be receiving.

Carl's defined benefit pension, should he stay with the firm, will pay him $31,112 a year, once he retires in 2017 (when he is 65), and he will be receiving $13,005 a year in Social Security. Connie's Social Security will contribute another $6,728.

That will give them a combined retirement income of $50,845.

In addition, if Carl didn't contribute another cent to his IRA, the $18,000 he has already put away—if it averages 8% in earnings and gains per year—should be worth $134,574 in 25 years.

That money is going to be needed, because the Schmidts really haven't taken inflation into account as they have gone about their retirement plans.

For example, in their second year of retirement it will cost them $49,200 to buy $48,000 worth of goods and services, assuming a 4% rate of inflation. That climbs to $51,917 in year three, $53,994 in year four, and even taking into account the income they will be earning on the $134,574 they will have by then—thanks to Carl's IRA—they will actually be running a deficit starting in year five of retirement.

The deficit is not fatal. By constantly tapping into their principal, they will be able to maintain a life-style of $48,000 a year in constant dollars, thanks in large part to the 4% annual increases they will be getting in their Social Security checks. However, they sure have cut it close.

How close? Well, if they were willing to spend every single dollar of principal, over the 20 years they are likely to live once they retire, they would only be able to afford a lifestyle of $52,500 a year.

They could, of course, make their future life a bit easier, if they'd only begin now to put more away for retirement. However, they have a more immediate problem. They haven't saved a dime for the education of their two children, and Ingrid is already eight, and their "baby," John, has just turned six.

The following chart shows the kind of tuition bills they will be looking at, assuming that college costs—which are currently $5,000 a year for tuition, room, and board at a state school, and $15,000 at a private one—continue to increase at 7% annually.

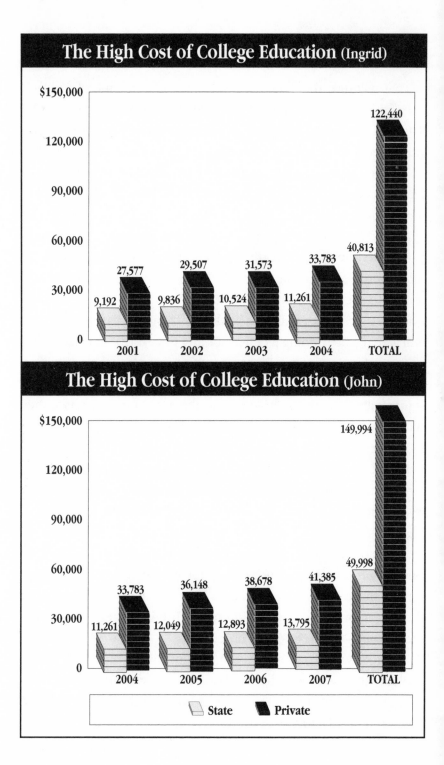

The High Cost of College Education (Ingrid)

	2001	2002	2003	2004	TOTAL
State	9,192	9,836	10,524	11,261	40,813
Private	27,577	29,507	31,573	33,783	122,440

The High Cost of College Education (John)

	2004	2005	2006	2007	TOTAL
State	11,261	12,049	12,893	13,795	49,998
Private	33,783	36,148	38,678	41,385	149,994

State   Private

As you can see, the Schmidts are woefully unprepared to pay for college. If they were able to put away $19,000 today, they could reasonably expect it would grow to $40,800, or enough to pay for four years at the University of Missouri or another state school, when Ingrid was ready to attend. (They would need to invest $57,100 today, to be assured that a private school eduction would be covered.)

The situation is a little bit better for John, since college is slightly further away for him, but the cost is still daunting. It would take a lump sum investment of $18,800 today, to assure his college education at a state school, and $56,300 to pay for private school.

There is just no way the Schmidts can lay their hands on that kind of money today.

That means they are going to have to save in stages, and they'll have to put away a great deal. Starting today they will need to save $2,600 a year, every year, to pay for a public college for Ingrid. If they decide to send her to a private university, that number climbs to $7,700 annually.

For John, they'll need to invest *an additional* $2,200 every year for public school, and $6,500 to make sure they can pay for private school tuition, room, and board.

College savings will take a big chunk out of the Schmidts' budget, a document they don't yet have.

They'll need to create one—and soon—if they hope to have more than a retirement that is adequate, and if they want to ensure a college education for their children. Otherwise the Schmidts and their children stand to be disappointed in the future.

"I'm too old to take chances."—Milton Quincy

Milton Quincy, 75, is set for life. The television packager says he would like to continue to live the way he is living now—spending and giving away on average $350,000 a year—but the fact is he can actually afford to improve his standard of living in retirement. The only concern he has is minimizing his estate taxes, which at present would cost his heirs $2.5 million, or approximately 42% of his net worth.

Milton could serve as the model for how to retire well. If Milton was willing to spend all his principal and interest over the next 15

Snapshot	
Current annual income (from all sources)	$598,200
Current federal tax liability	$139,430
State income tax	$45,400
Investment Assets	$5,140,000
Portfolio allocation:	8% cash, 24% equities, 68% fixed income
Net worth	$5,940,000

Net Worth Summary		
Assets	Personal Assets	$800,000
	Investment Assets Portfolio	$4,057,000
	Other	$100,000
	Retirement	$983,000
Total Assets		$5,940,000
Liabilities		$0
Net worth		$5,940,000

years—which is what the actuarial tables give him—he could live on $489,000 a year, 20% more than he is keeping now after taxes.

And he wouldn't suffer much at all if he decided to go the other way. Should Milton decide he wants to leave his entire net worth—nearly $6 million—intact so he can pass it on to his heirs, it wouldn't mean scrimping very much. His investments earn $270,900 annually.

To put it mildly, Milton has prepared to retire quite well. His biggest concern is estate planning.

Oh, sure. He could fiddle with his portfolio some. An asset allocation tailored to Milton would call for him to increase the equity portion of his portfolio from 24% to 30%, and raise his cash equivalents from 8% to 10%. (As a result of those moves, the fixed income portion of his portfolio would fall to 60%.) But these are not exactly radical changes and don't call for a lot of attention.

And neither, quite frankly, does his tax planning, even if it is possible for Milton to reduce his tax rate a bit.

As a wealthy resident of California, Milton is subject to a 11% state tax rate, which means his maximum combined tax rate is 38.59%. (Why isn't it 42%—the 31% federal rate, plus the 11% state rate? Because the California state tax is deductible from his federal tax return.)

Milton is currently paying a combined tax rate of 30.9%, and he could reduce it further by shifting more of his fixed income investments into California municipal bonds. Those bonds would be free of federal, state, and local taxes. In addition to reducing his taxes, investing in those bonds would probably raise his standard of living even further. Based on his combined tax rate, a 6% tax-exempt bond produces the equivalent of a 9.77% taxable yield. (Since Milton's income is high, he may be subject to the alternative minimum tax. He may be able to buy special AMT municipals, which offer investors higher tax-free yield than they would receive from regular municipals. See Chapter 16 for more information.)

With his financial house already in good shape, he has turned his attention to fine-tuning his estate planning in order to reduce the estate taxes that his heirs will have to pay. (The taxes must be paid in cash within nine months of the date of death.)

Milton has already worked diligently at this—and to solve part of this problem he has gifted part of his assets (through his annual exclusion and unified credit—see Chapter 29 for more details) into an irrevocable trust for his heirs. The trust bought a $2 million irrevocable life insurance policy that is not subject to estate taxes. At Milton's death the $2 million could be used to pay most of the related taxes and administrative expenses, and so essentially leave most of the estate assets intact for the benefit of his heirs.

Balancing present resources against future needs is the essence of financial planning. Some of the "real people" we surveyed face a savings shortfall. But they have time on their side, and can recover. Some are doing fine, with only minor spending (saving) changes needed.

CHAPTER 3

Keeping Records and Making Budgets

In earlier chapters you made a semieducated guess about how much money you'll need in retirement. ("A lot," was the answer, as you recall.) But how much do you have now?

The answer is more than a matter of ego gratification. You need to know your current net worth because it will help you plan your future. Specifically, subtracting your present net worth from your future needs will give you a pretty good idea of how much money you'll need to save between now and the time you retire.

(That's another way of saying that if you want to get where you're going, you need to know where you are right now.)

Figuring Out Your Net Worth

The key to any financial planning process, any budgeting approach, is to know your net worth.

Net worth is the total value of everything you own (your assets) minus everything you owe (your liabilities). We've included work-sheets in this chapter to make preparing your personal budget easier.

When you calculate your net worth, as you fill in the asset part of the ledger, use actual market value (net of any selling charges, if applicable) and *be extremely conservative*. Remember, if and when you put your personal possessions on the market, they'll always sell at a deep discount, whether you sell them through the classifieds, at auction, or during a tag sale. So be realistic. Put down what is the *least* amount you're likely to receive, and not the item's replacement value, which is probably much higher, especially when it comes to things like cars and home furnishings.

When you figure out your net worth, you may be pleasantly sur-prised at the value of your assets, especially if you bought a home prior to 1985. Unfortunately, that high number may be misleading. Once you've filled in the asset portion of your personal balance sheet, you have to ask yourself which of those assets really will be available for your retirement. For example, your cars and furniture can hardly be considered potential sources of retirement income. Even your home may not be a retirement asset, unless you intend to sell it and invest at least part of the proceeds for extra income, or take a reverse mortgage (as we will discuss in Chapter 23).

Not only may the value of your assets be less than they appear, your liabilities may be larger. Sometime between now and retire-ment, you may be planning to use some of those assets, to buy a second home, or pay for college.

All this explains why we have included that column on the far right of the chart, the one labeled "amount of assets available to fund retirement." After you have figured out your net worth, *realis-*

tically try to determine how much of it you will be able to touch once you're retired.

Please note: Your net worth will probably change over time. Each mortgage payment you make today decreases the principal outstanding on your loan, and you might even receive a raise, or two, between now and the time you decide to stop work.

Since your net worth statement is going to influence, to a large extent, how you go about your retirement planning, you should update the statement periodically. We suggest once a year. In the first quarter of each year, just after you have received your year-end records for things like mortgage payments, contributions to your retirement funds, and assorted tax and interest payments, sit down and figure out what you are worth.

The timing works out pretty well because this is also the time of year when you start preparing your tax returns.

Who knows? The annual blues caused by knowing what you paid (or owe) in taxes might even be offset by a yearly increase in your net worth. This could even give you a passing moment (or maybe just a second or two) of elation.

Budgeting—the Dreaded "B" Word

Some presidents back, when yet another recession was looming, the White House decided that the nation would all but fall apart if it heard its leader utter the dreaded "R" word. Not wanting to inflict such heavy psychological damage, President Dwight David Eisenhower euphemistically warned that a "rolling readjustment" was ahead.

When it comes to talking about retirement preparation, financial planners have their own version of the "R" word. It begins with "B," as in budget. And it's no wonder they are reluctant to say the word.

Budgeting is not pleasant. Constructing a budget *is* hard. Sticking to one is even harder. And in reviewing the finances of all our couples and singles, once they filled in their net worth statements, it became clear that *all* but one will have to go on some sort of budget (spend less and save more), in order to reach their goals. (Even our example of a very affluent person—one who's been planning his estate for years—still needs a budget as he spends down.)

We Interrupt Your Budgeting to Bring You a Word About Social Security

When you tackle your budget, and add up all your taxes, you'll be reminded—once more—about your Social Security outgo. To ease your tax pains slightly, you can think of FICA payments as an investment in your future.

While it's nice to think that at some point you'll be getting a check back from the Social Security Administration, you have to recognize that the check isn't the government's way of recognizing what a swell person you've been. Your Social Security check is nothing more than a refund—and probably a partial refund at that—of your tax dollars, specifically the FICA tax, which stands for Federal Insurance Contribution Act, which you paid while you were working.

Social Security, of course, is an important factor in retirement planning. In Chapter 26 we'll discuss how it can benefit you.

But who is going to tell them? No one likes to be the bearer of bad news, except maybe actors on afternoon soap operas—because it gives them more camera time.

You can see it now, can't you?

If a soap opera star had to tell Mary and Dick that they have to budget, the scene would probably play like this:

(We open on a close-up of the . . .)

FINANCIAL PLANNER [*wearing severe blue suit, red bow tie, and wire-rimmed glasses*]: Mary, Dick, I don't know how to say this, but you are going to have to . . .

[*organ music comes up underneath: Da Da DUMM!!!*]
    . . . budget.

MARY: Oh, Dick!

DICK: Mary, I'm so sorry.

[*We hear the audience gasp, as Mary and Dick hold on to each other for dear life*]

[*Fade out*]

No wonder some financial planners search for euphemisms. You'll hear them talk about "personal monetary planning," or how you must create—this is our favorite—a "spending plan." (Your major problem probably is not how to spend, it's how to save.)

Well, we have enough trouble spelling *euphemism* without trying to create one. So, this section isn't going to call a budget anything other than a budget—a fiscal plan you devise to help you establish priorities.

Instead of trying to mentally keep a budget, we suggest you sit down on a rainy Saturday morning (the day is shot, anyway) with your checkbook, and the diary you have been using to record cash expenses (more on this in a few pages), and put together a *real, written budget.* This way you'll have a tangible document to refer to when it comes time to cut expenses somewhere and put (more) money away for retirement.

Working Backwards to Your Budget

However, knowing what a budget is doesn't make doing it any easier. But if you go about creating a budget backwards it becomes a bit less painful.

Think about it this way: The reason you are finally talking about creating a budget is that you want to put some money away for retirement. That means you are going to have to adjust some of your spending habits. If all life is really a matter of choices—"Do I spend now, or save now so I can spend later?"—then the budgeting process is where you're going to have lots of life.

But you'll never know what you'll have to change in the future, until you understand *for certain* what you are spending now.

So, an analysis of your current spending is where we start, and that means gathering all your receipts, canceled checks, and the like.

The bad news is that this is just about as awful as it sounds. The good news is that you have already had a lot of practice at it. You go through this grief and aggravation every year, when it comes time to file your taxes.

Now, last April 14, or whenever you actually got around to doing your taxes, you could have sworn that nothing good would ever come from that exercise. And normally, you'd be right. *But the mere process of having assembled your records for tax purposes—* whether you put all receipts into a file folder, or plugged all the information into a software program—*puts you way ahead of the game when it comes to retirement planning.*

Tax preparation software programs are wonderful tools. Some are friendlier than others. You can organize (which means all this will be easy to update) by the month or the year your record keeping, budget making, and tax preparing.

These programs aren't solely for the computer hacks who play away at their PCs for 18 hours a day. These programs—some are more friendly than others—can be used by anyone who's reasonably computer-literate. They're particularly accessible for the small businessmen and the self-employed who use personal computers daily in their businesses.

Obviously, these software programs aren't the complete answer, whether it comes to preparing your taxes or planning your retirement. You still need to keep your original receipts and canceled checks in case the tax man comes a-callin'.

And ultimately you may still have to call on the advice of professionals: your accountant, your tax lawyer, your financial consultant.

Budgeting by the Numbers

Whether or not you use a PC, you always start out the same way.

Take out your records and divide them into two piles. In one put the stuff you are legally bound to keep virtually forever because there might be a future tax implication based on something you did in the past. (By *forever* we mean until the tax consequences are resolved.) Three kinds of transactions fit into the "forever" category: security transactions (or transactions involving any asset with a possible capital gain or loss), home ownership records, and retirement plan contributions and/or withdrawals.

Record Keeping and Budget Making: Income

	Monthly (Estimate)	Annual (Estimate)
Salary:		
wages, tips,		
bonus, commission		
net self-employed income		
Interest		
Dividends		
Investments income (gains – losses)		
Rental income		
Pension		
Social Security		
Other		
Subtotal		

Record Keeping and Budget Making: Taxes

Federal Taxes		
State Taxes		
City Taxes		
FICA (Social Security and Medicare)		
Other Income Taxes		
Subtotal		

We'll deal some more with record keeping in a few pages. For now, let's just concentrate on the daily process of having money come in and go out (too fast).

Let's start with income. This is the fun part: do it in fill-in-the-blank form at the top of page 82.

Next come the tax bites: fill in the bottom form on page 82.

Now deduct the total of the second table from the total of the first table. The difference is your after-tax income.

If only you could have this left over at the end of each month, right? Well, you don't, because of your deductions. We've provided a list on pages 84 and 85.

What this list should do is track *all* your expenses, just about *to the penny.* Given how painful it was filling in the blanks for just one month, you're probably tempted to ask if you can't take the

---

Keep These Records—Forever

This is just us talking here, but we suggest you hold on to all your key financial records forever. Yes, we know that in most cases the IRS only has three years to audit you. For the record, it's six years if you underreport income by at least 25%, and forever if you didn't file a return, or submitted one fraudulently, but as an IRS official asked us, somewhat off-the-record, "Are you actually going to admit to doing any of those things? Three years is fine except for records pertaining to the purchase or sale of a house, security transactions, and retirement accounts." (See our discussion of those things a bit later in this chapter.)

We heard what the official had to say, but holding on to all the records that make up your returns just seems to us to make sense. For one thing, it will help you see how your expenses have changed over time, and for another, canceled checks are a wonderful way of coming up with a name that you need every five years or so.

Record Keeping and Budget Making: Expenses

	Monthly (Estimate)	Annual (Estimate)
Mortgage/Rent		
Gas/Oil		
Water		
Electricity		
Phone		
Garbage pickup		
Food		
Household help/ Cleaning services		
Lawn care		
Household repairs/ Improvements		
Car payments		
Car insurance		
Car maintenance		
Gas		
Bus/Subway/Taxi		
Medical		
Dental		
Vet		
Life insurance		
Health insurance		
Disability insurance		
Subtotal		

Record Keeping and Budget Making: Expenses (continued)

	Monthly (Estimate)	Annual (Estimate)
Dental insurance		
Property insurance		
Clothing		
Laundry		
Furniture		
Child care		
Education		
Old bills (student money borrowed from your family, etc.)		
Loan & credit card interest and finance charges		
Bank, Investment fees charges		
Donations		
Books/Magazines/ Newspapers		
Restaurants		
Entertainment		
Hobbies		
Health club/ Country club		
Cable TV/Video tapes, Rentals		
Gifts		
Vacation		
Credit cards		
Cash expenditures		
Savings		
Subtotal		

easy way out—take one month's detailed analysis, simply multiply by 12, and have a complete record for the year.

Unfortunately, no.

Some of your payments—such as insurance—are probably being made on a quarterly or semiannual basis. And then there are the one-time events, such as your annual three weeks in the south of France, which produce whopping entries all in one month. That's why, we're afraid, you have to keep the list both ways, monthly and yearly.

There are a few other things to note about the list. Wherever possible we segregated expenses.

For example, you'll notice we separated gas/oil, water, electricity, and phone instead of lumping them all into one category called "utilities." The idea of putting together this budget is to examine carefully *everything* that you spend. That's why each item gets its own line. When you look at what you are shelling out for your phone bill each month, you might be tempted to write a letter every now and then. (Also, do you really *have* to spend $50 a month—that's $600 a year—on cable TV? While you're in a grousing frame of mind, look at your annual electricity costs, and ask, "Do I *really* need to leave the outside lights on *all* night?" A timer might end up saving you a decent amount over 12 months.)

Translating Plastic Charges to Real Expenses

Remember that credit cards and cash are simply conduits for buying something. So both charges or cash expenditures should be allocated back to the real purchase: clothing, entertainment, etc. It's not enough to know how much you spend (cash and plastic); it's crucial to future budget making to know precisely where the money goes. Much more on this exercise in a few paragraphs.

Finally, you'll see that we highlighted the last three items. Here's why.

Credit cards. The balance you owe on your charge cards doesn't represent one specific, nonbudgeted item. Rather, as we pointed out, you are using your credit cards to put gas in your car, or clothes on your back.

All those purchases must be allocated back to the proper category (gas, clothing), quite possibly at a premium if you are not paying off the balance of your bill each month. That $50 sweater really costs somewhere around $59 if you take a year to get that purchase off your credit card. The credit card companies are more than happy to let you have the use of their money, money that they are lending you at about 18% annual interest. (More on this in Chapter 4, "Managing Your Credit.")

Cash expenditures. There is a reason we didn't put in a category called "Miscellaneous." If you start the day with $50 in your pocket, and come home with $30, that $20 didn't buy miscellaneous. It went for coffee, cigarettes, or a cheeseburger deluxe with extra pickles.

Start keeping a diary or carrying a notebook with you and record each purchase, even if it is just 50 cents for your daily paper. Your job is to put the *cash* flow under the same microscope that you do with everything else. Who knows, you might even stop smoking as a result.

Savings. For most people this is just not an item in their budget.

What often happens when people create a budget—usually in their heads—is that they assume, in a vague way, that surplus equals savings.

When they've finished going through this budgeting exercise, they end up with something that looks like this:

Record Keeping and Budget Making: Savings

	Monthly (Estimate)	Annual (Estimate)
Total income		
minus **Taxes paid**		
minus **Expenses**		
Total		
equals **Surplus** (Savings)		

But does it? If it does, congratulations. You are doing better than most. But after you're done patting yourself on the back, start asking yourself: What kind of savings? Nonretirement investments? Good. Better yet, some of the surplus could be pumped into a tax-deferred retirement account.

If you are more erratic than you realized when it comes to putting away money for savings, then your long-term alarms should be ringing; red lights should be flashing.

Assuming you won't hit the lottery, or have a long-forgotten rich uncle think kindly of you as he shuffles off—the only other answer, when it comes to preparing for retirement, is committing yourself to a *regular* savings schedule. (Senator Lloyd Bentsen, a long-time advocate of IRAs, puts it this way: "Whenever you put money into a tax-deductible IRA, you're writing a check to yourself instead of to the IRS.") You have already committed yourself to regularly making your rent (or house) payments, and making sure you have paid the car loan each month, so just write one more check each month to yourself for savings.

We know, we know. There is a difference. When you make your car payments you're reminded each day what you are buying as you sit behind the wheel. When you make a "payment" into a retirement account, there is no instant gratification. But we assure you that there will be gratification down the road.

Save the Automatic Way

We have two possible solutions. First, when it comes to creating a systematic savings program, if your employer offers an automatic savings option, take advantage of it. Have a fixed amount of each paycheck go to purchase a savings bond, or company stock (if you think it is a good investment). And by all means take *full* advantage of their offer to take money out of your paycheck and put it directly into a retirement plan, *even if they don't offer to match any, or all, of your contribution.* (For a complete discussion of company retirement plans, see Chapter 7. In Chapter 8, on 401(k)s, we will tell why this particular retirement plan has become phenomenally popular in recent years.) Once you've automatically moved the money into a plan, or account, you also may be able to put the money to work—that is, invest it—automatically. Automation—in financial transactions—can be a wonderful thing for you and for the institution.

A second, relatively painless way of saving more systematically calls for you to reorder your budget just a bit: Move the savings component of your budget from the last line to the first. In other words, when you sit down to pay the bills each month, make a check to your retirement fund the first one you write.

Even if you can only manage to save $5.47 a day—which works out to be roughly half the cost of your car loan, or lease payment—you'll have enough to fully fund your IRA each year. (We'll show you—in Chapter 11—how that $5.47 per day, done consistently for years, and invested tax-deferred, can make your retirement quite pleasant indeed.)

If the painless way of savings doesn't work, maybe scare tactics will.

As you plow through your budget, and decide you just can't cut current spending to fund future comforts, let us remind you of the four premises that make up this book:

1. You'll probably live longer than you think.

2. In fact, you may spend as much time retired as you did working.

3. As a percentage of your future income in retirement, employer retirement plans and Social Security benefits will undoubtedly shrink.

4. Your retirement future is in your hands.

Record Keeping

Okay, by this time the records you need to prepare your budget will have all been analyzed nine ways from Sunday. But what do you do with that other stuff we asked you to put aside: the records of your stock trades, home purchase, and retirement accounts?

Let's take them one at a time.

Security and other property/assets transactions. You need to keep track of the "cost basis" of each security.

The cost *what?*

Cost *basis.* That's nothing more than a fancy way of saying what the security cost you. Normally, it's what you paid for it. If you inherited the security, your basis is the value on the day the previous owner died.

Cost basis only becomes important when you sell the security. Then it's crucial. You subtract the cost basis from the price you receive for your stock or bond when you finally sell it. The difference is your gain (or loss) for tax purposes.

What if you didn't keep, or don't know, your cost basis? All is not necessarily lost. Brokers can sometimes help by sorting through old records, but there are limits to how far back they (or their computers) can go. (They also may charge you for the search.)

Try to keep the shoe box (or shoe boxes) with your security records intact. You have to. When it comes to record keeping, the IRS has a singular point of view: *Record keeping is your responsibility.*

Home ownership. In some cases, a much-appreciated house (co-op, condominium, vacation property) may be your biggest single asset. (For potential ways of converting your home equity into retirement assets, see Chapter 23, where we will also talk about the one-time, $125,000 capital gains exclusion available to people 55 or older who sell their homes.)

You probably are already keeping your deed or mortgage in a

secure place, such as a safety deposit box, but what about the records regarding the capital improvements you've made to your home?

Whether you've added storm windows, put on an addition, or installed a new half-bath downstairs, you've done more than increased the livability of your home. You've also *decreased* your potential tax liability.

When you sell your house, the *total* cost of your house *plus the improvements* you've made that "prolong the useful life" and "add value to your home" are deducted from your sale price. What this means, of course, is that your taxable gain may be reduced considerably by the improvements you make.

As soon as possible put together a list, complete with canceled checks, of your major home-improvement projects, such as that $20,000 kitchen remodeling project you undertook a while back. But while searching for the receipts for the large jobs, don't forget to also locate the bills for the smaller improvements, such as putting in baseboard heat, or those new windows. Anything that improves the value of your home—a new rec room, upgraded plumbing, paving the driveway for the first time—can be added to the cost basis of your home, so it will pay you to keep good

---

When Is an Improvement Not?

Unfortunately, you can't add the cost of everything you do around the house to your home's cost basis. *Improvements* can be added to the cost basis of your house, but routine maintenance can't be. If you pave the driveway for the first time, that's an improvement, and so can be added to the basis.

However, a few years later when it's time to repave or recoat the driveway, you are out of luck. The repaving would be considered routine maintenance by the IRS.

---

records of what you spent. Add up all these improvement jobs—some were weekend handyman specials; in some you called in a professional for a half-day's work. They're cumulative: $50 here, $200 there, and then a year's total times 20 years (or however long you're constantly improving the home), and all these small jobs can equal, as a capital improvement, your two or three major improvements. Don't short-change yourself. If the cost basis changes, so will your taxes.

Our point here—and indeed through the entire chapter—is two-fold: (1) IRS audits are settled not with persuasive oratory but rather with hard documentation of transactions. Keeping those records is your responsibility, no one else's. (2) If you don't keep those records, you may forget to claim what is rightfully yours come tax time.

Retirement accounts. For all of these plans, keep summary, or transaction, records forever. If it's a company pension plan, your company should be keeping detailed records for you, and you'll see the all-important summary at retirement or at lump sum distribution time. If your retirement plans involve salary-deferral programs—such as a 401(k) or a 403(b), or another savings plan, or even a SEP—you should be getting statements periodically throughout the year. Remember, these accounts are salary deferrals. Taxes will be due someday on what has been deferred. That means good records are vital.

Consider IRAs. As simple as they may seem, IRAs can become confusing when it comes to resolving tax questions. Shifting laws governing the deductibility of your contributions virtually demand perpetual keeping of *all* records.

A quick example will underscore why. Just a few years ago, just about anyone could contribute $2,000 to an IRA, and deduct that $2,000 from taxable income. If you made $50,000 that year, and made a $2,000 contribution to an IRA account, you only earned $48,000 for tax purposes. The idea was that you'd be taxed on both your $2,000 contribution *and the earnings and gains it produced when you withdrew the money.*

So far so good. But later, in 1986, the law governing IRAs changed. New restrictions lessened the attractiveness of IRAs. For example, people covered by a retirement plan could still put new money into their IRA, but could no longer take the contribution as a tax deduction if their earned income was above a certain amount. Why contribute, then? Because the earnings on that contribution would still accumulate tax-deferred. You wouldn't be taxed on the earnings or gains until you withdrew your money.

Now we are still very bullish on IRAs. Whether or not your current contributions are fully or partially deductible, we still think that the trusty old IRA is the best small tax shelter retirement plan there is. (Note that we said "small." We emphasize that an IRA is available to anyone who *has earned income.* But the very best of the "larger" plans—if an employer offers it to you and if your employer is matching some of your contributions—is a 401(k) plan.)

The IRA—it *is* the cornerstone of good retirement planning, as you'll see in Chapter 11.

You need good records to keep all this—what was deductible, what isn't; what was taxed, and what won't be taxed—straight. Otherwise the IRS could assume that you paid no taxes on either your contributions or the money those contributions earned, and you are going to have a heck of a time proving otherwise. Your IRA statements, plus your tax returns (in particular, your IRS form 8606 which you may have to file each year), will be a necessity when you start taking money out of an IRA. The most important set of records are those of your basic tax filing—your returns are always the start of any audit. But a backup can be your other records. When it comes to dealing with the IRS, you are considered guilty until proven innocent. If you can't prove you have already paid taxes on your IRA contribution, you may very well be taxed a second time. To be fair, the IRS doesn't want to tax you twice. But the burden of proof, just like the responsibility for record keeping, is on you.

One direct consequence of the demand for good IRA records is that many of the 25 million people who now have IRA accounts have been consolidating those accounts over time. We think that is a good idea. Instead of having $2,000 at an S&L, another $2,000 with a broker, and a third $2,000 in a bank account, we suggest putting all your money in one place. (We say "one place"—but there may be tax advantages to keeping your IRA regular assets segregated from your IRA rollover assets. See Chapter 25.)

There's nothing wrong with keeping all your eggs in one basket, if you—like Mark Twain's Pudd'nhead Wilson—watch that basket very carefully.

Besides, having all the money in one place reduces the paperwork. By law, each IRA custodian must send you at least one summary statement a year. For your more active accounts, you might receive quarterly, or even monthly, statements. The fewer places you have your money invested, the fewer statements to keep tucked away in the bottom of your desk.

About those statements, examine them immediately! It is a whole lot easier to correct mistakes now. You want to have any problems resolved within the tax year, so you don't have any potential wrestling matches with the IRS.

Keeping good records—making a budget (and then trying to live up to it) isn't one of life's fun games. It can be downright dreary. But it can lead to sound financial planning (adjusting). You should even budget monthly "gifts" to yourself (in the form of retirement or pension savings accounts) first, rather than last.

CHAPTER 4

Managing Your Credit

There's a reason we called this book *Grow Rich Slowly*: We wanted to make it clear from the outset that there aren't any "gimmicks" or "tricks" you can use to produce a well-funded retirement.

But the title serves another purpose as well, when it comes to talking about managing credit. You are going to grow rich *extremely* s-l-o-w-l-y—if at all—if you spend more money than you need to on credit card charges, or consumer loans. Every dollar you use to pay off debt or high loan costs is a dollar that you are not going to be able to put toward your retirement.

In this chapter we are going to review some of the basics of managing credit that will help you free up more money for retirement.

Credit Cards

Why would anyone carry over any portion of his or her credit card balance from month to month? It's literally like paying from 18% to 20% more than you have to—for every single item that you charge.

Why would you willingly do that? Because the interest is tax-deductible, people used to say.

But that hasn't been true for a while. There generally is no interest deduction allowed for consumer, auto, or credit card debt.

If you are not paying off your credit cards each month, you're paying a lot more than you have to for the things you buy. Suppose you go out and purchase $1,000 worth of clothes and instead of writing a check for $1,000, or peeling off twenty $50 bills, you decide to pay off your purchase in "12 easy payments," payments that carry an annual interest rate of 19.8%, the going rate on an awful lot of credit cards. What happens? Instead of writing one $1,000 check, you write a series of smaller ones during the year. While that may sound good at first, at the end of the year you'll find that you've paid a grand total of $1,198, instead of a $1,000, for those clothes. (Actually, your interest costs would be somewhat less than the flat $198, depending on the repayment terms, since each month your loan repayment would decrease the balance.)

That extra $198 or so you've paid is almost 10% of your annual IRA contribution. Doesn't it make a lot more sense to put that $198 toward your retirement, instead of helping a bank report higher earnings?

Some Interest Is Still Deductible

Interest charges on home equity and margin loans, which we will talk about shortly, are generally deductible.

When you are thinking about ways to lower, or consolidate, your debt, look for loans that will charge you a lower interest rate, and are deductible. That means thinking about using home equity and margin loans first, and things like credit cards, or cash advances on your credit cards, last.

It's understandable how you can run up huge balances on your credit cards. It is now possible to charge everything from a ticket at the movies to groceries at your local supermarket, but you pay an extremely high price for this convenience, if you carry forward a balance on your credit card from month to month.

If you find that your credit card charges are consistently too high—and if you are not paying off the balance in full each month, they *are* too high—keep the following five things in mind:

1. **Go back to your budgeting charts.** Write down exactly what you are paying for with your credit cards. If you do, instead of saying, "I've just got to charge less," you might conclude "I've got to stop buying X, Y, and Z." If you don't spend the money, you don't have to pay it back.

2. **Consolidate.** Pay off all your outstanding credit card balances with one loan, a loan that has a lower interest rate than your credit cards do.

   What kind of consolidation loans are we talking about? You have three choices:

• **Home equity loans.** This is a concept we will talk about more fully in Chapter 23. You borrow against the equity, that is, the difference between what your house is worth today and your outstanding mortgage. Because you are pledging your house as collateral—a fact that should not be taken lightly—the interest rate will be relatively low. Obviously, you should do this as a part of a general fiscal belt tightening. Borrow against your house in order to get a low loan cost—but make sure you're slashing future credit card usage. (And make sure you *pay back* the loan.)

- **Personal loans.** You simply borrow money from the bank and promise to pay it back. Because there is little, or no, collateral, the interest rate will be relatively high, but on average it will still be 2% to 3% less than what you will be charged for carrying a balance on your credit card.

- **Margin loans.** You are borrowing money from your financial services firm, and pledging your stocks and bonds as collateral. Because your collateral is sufficient to cover the loan, should you default, the interest rate will be low, usually a point or two above the prime lending rate. It's hard to get much lower than this.

  When you take a margin loan, you can borrow up to 50% of the value of your stocks, and up to 95% of the value of government issues, such as Treasuries. Since using a margin credit line is an important financing method most often used to finance more investments, we'll delve much more into the rules of margin in Chapter 17, on investments.

3. **Stop new charges**. Don't buy anything, unless you can pay for it with cash or a check. (And using the "overdraft" loan protection available on your checking account is ex-

---

Warning Signs

Want other ways to know you are in trouble?
- Each month you only pay the very minimum due on your card.
- You are using cash advances, drawn on card B, to pay off what you owe on card A.
- You are afraid to open your credit card bills when they arrive.

---

actly the same as using a credit card, although the interest charges will probably be a bit less.) If you are going to write a check, make sure there is money in the bank to cover it.

A variation on paying cash is using a *debit* card instead of a *credit* card.

A debit card looks like a credit card, but works like a checking account or a visit to your automated teller machine. When you use your debit card for payment, the purchase price is automatically deducted from your checking account, or whatever account the debit card is connected to.

4. **Eliminate temptation.** Reduce the number of credit cards you carry to an absolute minimum. Just keep the one, or two, that you *must* carry. You might want to carry two cards. One that requires you to pay your monthly balance in full, and a second "regular" credit card that has a low annual fee and low interest rate. (Of course, if you really want to be tightfisted in credit management, an all-purpose credit or debit card—one that you can use for both traditional travel and entertainment and normal "plastic" purchases—will be all that you'll need.)

Take a scissors to the rest. And if you don't have to turn in the shreds to the credit company, turn the assorted pieces into a collage. If there is a loan outstanding on any of the cards, pay it off and return the broken card to the issuer and tell them to cancel the card.

5. **If you must keep a monthly balance on your card** . . . make sure your credit card has the lowest possible interest

rate. Not all credit card companies charge 20% interest. It is possible to find cards with an interest rate that is substantially less. Shop around.

Warning: Once you pay off the cards, make sure you cancel them, so you don't fall back into the same trap. Don't use the fact that you are out of debt as a reason to celebrate (by buying something new).

Central Assets Management

Today you can use an all-purpose financial account that lets you put all (or most) of your assets into one basket, and in effect, lets you manage the debit-credit side of the account more efficiently. Called an *asset management,* or *central assets account,* it ties a securities account to a checking account, a credit or debit card, and a money market fund. (Some of the money funds, depending on which states you live in, may even be municipal, or tax-free, money funds.)

The key to a central assets account is the use of the money market fund. Your credit balance—sometimes as low as $1—is swept automatically into the funds. In addition, you have a credit line (or margin loan capability), established against the borrowing power of the rest of your securities. When you write a check, withdraw money, or use a credit or debit card, your so-called idle money—that is, your money fund balance—is tapped first, before your credit line is used. Since loans are made on a margin basis, against your securities as collateral, your interest charges will be very close to the prime lending rate.

Refinancing

Another way to free up more money for retirement is by refinancing your existing mortgage. If you refinance, two things can happen, and both of them are good.

First, you could get a lower interest rate, which means your monthly payments will be less. That will free up money that can be saved for retirement.

Second, your house may have appreciated in value since you took out your original loan. You can now take a larger mortgage than you had before and use the additional money to fund your retirement investments.

As a general rule of thumb, any time the current mortgage rate is 2% less than your existing one, it makes sense to think about refinancing.

Thinking is not the same as doing. If the "points" that the financing institution is charging are excessive, or the fees involved—title searches, appraisals, legal bills—are particularly high, or you plan to move within a couple of years, then refinancing may not make sense. Do the math. When you know you will come out ahead, refinance.

The Importance of a Clean Record

Let's underscore the obvious: You need a clean credit history, both now and in the future. There is going to come a time when you'll want to buy (another) house, or car, or vacation home, or something else that is going to require you to take a loan. If you have a bad credit history, nobody is going to lend you the money. It's that simple.

But keeping your record clean is more than a matter of paying your bills on time. You want the major credit reporting companies—TRW, Equifax, and the like—to know that you are a good credit risk.

You are entitled to see your credit report, any time a bank or financial institution requests it (in order to see if you are worthy of a loan). Two of the largest credit reporting companies are TRW (214-235-1200) and Equifax (800-685-1111). Contact them for copies of your report. You may be entitled to one free report per year, or there may be a nominal charge, up to $10, per report. Examine each report, and if there is an error, correct it immediately. (The reporting companies tell you how to do that when they send you your copy.)

Remember, you and your spouse may have different credit histories (although the two are usually examined together in determining whether to grant a loan). Be sure to look at both. In one of the world's great catch-22's, many places will not grant you credit unless you have a history of making regular payments on your loans and credit cards. But, of course, you can't create that history unless someone gives you credit. What to do?

They Do Keep Track

If you have never seen a credit report, you'd be amazed. These companies collect data from banks and from loan, finance, and credit card companies, gasoline dealers, department stores, car dealers—just about any other place you can think of. They also keep track of the heavy stuff: mechanics' liens, bankruptcies, judgments against you, tax liens, and anything else that might affect your credit worthiness.

As long as you have active accounts, your credit history will be updated automatically. Information on paid-off, or closed, accounts is often retained for a decade or more.

Our advice, take the $2,000 you were going to contribute this year to your IRA, stick it in a bank, and then ask the bank to lend you $2,000. They'll be happy to give you the loan, since you can pledge the $2,000 you have in the bank as collateral, and you are on your way to establishing a credit history. By law, you can't pledge the IRA account itself as collateral.

By doing this, you establish a credit history, fund your IRA, and can pay off the loan, almost all in one fell swoop.

Don't forget to put the money you borrowed into your IRA by the deadline—tax-paying time, which is generally April 15. If you forget, then you've missed out on the contribution for that given year, and your retirement planning scheme has just slipped a notch.

In Case of Emergency

If you find yourself in a desperate situation, one that could affect your credit rating, you may want to think about emergency sources of funds available to you.

- You can borrow against the cash value of your life insurance.

- You can borrow against some defined contribution plans, such as a 401(k) or a Keogh (if you are not considered to be an owner-employee). There is a built-in discipline with these kinds of loans. By law, they can only be made with a fixed repayment schedule. (No loans are permitted from defined benefit plans.)

- You can suspend *temporarily* the contributions to your IRA, 401(k), or any other voluntary pension plan.

This really should be a last resort, because once you have given up making a contribution in a given year, you can never catch up. You can't put $4,000 in your IRA next year to make up for the $2,000 contribution that you didn't make this year.

Managing credit means managing debt. A central assets account can be an all-purpose financial account. Consolidating your loans, and shifting from high-interest loans to low-interest loans—such as tapping home equity or using margin accounts—helps. But even better, whittle down your spending (borrowing) habits. Just say no.

CHAPTER 5

Paying (Saving) for Your Children's College Educations

If you are thinking about how you are going to plan your retirement, *and* pay for your children's college educations—as most of our couples are—it probably won't come as much of a consolation to know that you are not alone. Millions of people—primarily baby boomers—face this concern every year.

Indeed many of them (and maybe you, too) face a third problem: How are they also going to pay for the health care expenses that their parents are likely to have?

In fact, the problem of funding retirement—while worrying about the health of your aging parents, and those looming tuition bills—has caused a new phrase to enter the financial planning lexicon. People in this predicament, and that really is the best word to describe it, are said to be facing a *"triple squeeze."*

Unfortunately, knowing there is a name for this situation doesn't make dealing with it any easier.

This chapter might.

What we are going to do over the next several pages is talk

about ways to loosen one part of the vise, the part that deals with paying for the college (and/or graduate) education of your children.

We'll start by being candid. College is going to take a lot of money. A college education will probably be the largest outlay you'll ever have to make in a four-year period. Just think about it for a minute. The average cost of a house is now $120,000, but you expect to pay for it over 15 or 30 years. Very few people plan on paying off their mortgage in four years. Yet you will probably have to pay $120,000—*and quite conceivably, a whole lot more*—to put *one child* through college in the future.

That's a frightfully large sum of money. But there are specific steps you can take now—whether your child is 5 months old, 5 years, or 15—that will ensure she'll be able to receive the kind of education you want her to have. And you'll be able to pay for that undergraduate education without jeopardizing your retirement income.

Getting Smart Later

Part of the reason why you may be facing the triple squeeze is that different segments of your life are not nearly as neatly spaced as they used to be. Let's say you married somewhat later (late 20s, or maybe early 30s) than previous generations. Then you had children somewhat later (late 30s, or even early 40s) than what we used to call "normal." As a result, your children—or rather, young adults—will be going to college later.

And, they're staying in college longer—working on postgraduate degrees. Currently, about one-third of all college students are over 25. So, no wonder you may be facing retirement and college bills all at the same time.

But before we talk about specific strategies for doing just that, let's talk about what you are up against.

What Will It Cost Tomorrow?

A lot.

Increases in tuition and fees averaged 6.6% a year at state schools, and 8.4% at private colleges and universities over the past five years. This while the average annual increase in the Consumer Price Index was about 4%.

There is no reason to think things are going to get better anytime soon. Future projections call for increases to average 6% to 7% a year. If you want to be supercautious, a rule of thumb you can use is: annual cost of college increases will equal cost-of-living increases—times two.

You have plenty on your plate to worry about—just paying for college. But for a few minutes, consider the colleges' fiscal problems. We can't ask you to shed crocodile tears over higher education's plight—but understanding what *they* are facing may give you a better perspective on *your* problem.

There are some 3,500 "institutions of higher learning"—to use the phrase of preference—in this country. In this clump are 150 full-fledged universities, some 1,950 four-year colleges, and rounding out the list, about 1,400 two-year community or technical schools. About half are private.

It's Tough Out There in Academe

Just as all of corporate America seems to be downsizing these days, we have to report that all the above 3,500 citadels of learning are having their own fiscal pressures.

Some are doing what previously was unheard of: cutting back departments, shutting down campuses, whittling down part-time instructors, even putting tenured professors out to early pasture. And many colleges are also discovering—to their fiscal sorrow—that their infrastructure is crumbling. A lot of college halls are ancient. The ivy is pretty, but it's concealing cracks.

Because the states must share costs of some federally funded mandated entitlements, such as Medicaid, higher education by default is getting a shrinking slice of state revenue. As legislatures tighten funding for state schools, so do trustees for private schools. On the private side, new endowment contributions are harder to unearth these days; on the public side, taxes aren't being raised, and so education budgets at worst are being slashed, or at best are treading water.

To their sorrow, most college and university presidents today are spending more of their time raising money or reeling in budgets than they are worrying about the broader mission of education.

What all this tale of woe comes down to is this: Since the private endowment isn't growing, federal support is dwindling, and state help is shrinking, your share of future costs surely won't be less, or even the same. Your share will be more. That helps explain why *your* share of college costs is rising so precipitously.

The following chart gives you some idea of what has been happening to the price of a higher education, and what you're likely to pay for college in the future. If you want to get nervous,

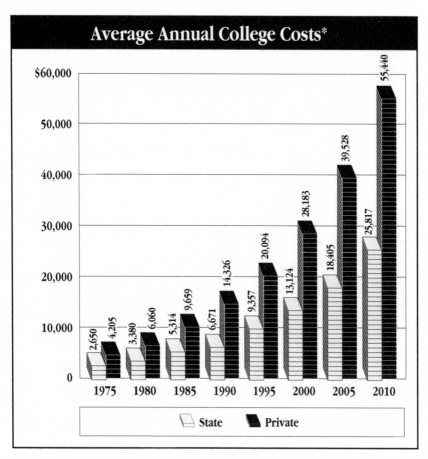

Average Annual College Costs*

State • Private

*Includes tuition, room and board, fees, etc.

just look at the last bar. If your son or daughter was born in 1992, you could quite conceivably pay well over $200,000 to put your child through school—undergraduate school, that is.

Is It Worth It?

Paying for college, and graduate school, costs a lot of money. It's a huge investment. And like any other investment, you want to know what kind of return you are going to get for your money. In this case, the answer is: a great deal.

In addition to cultural enrichment, and personal satisfaction, the value of a college education can make a *tangible* difference in the way your child will live.

Median household income for college graduates can be more than 75% higher than for high school graduates. If you add a master's to your undergraduate degree, your income should take another big jump, and a doctorate on top of a master's will produce yet another significant rise in income. Over the course of a lifetime these differences could easily top $1 million.

How Are You Going to Save the Money?

College clearly is a worthwhile investment. But how are you going to come up with the $20,000, $30,000, $50,000 *a year* that you're going to need to pay for it?

The question requires a two-part answer. First, you have to figure out how much you are going to need. (The preceding chart gave you a pretty good idea.) Then, you'll need to figure out how many years you have to get there. That's pretty easy, too. You subtract your child's current age from 18, the age at which she is likely to start college. The difference is how long you have before you have to write a check to cover freshman-year tuition. And that's just your starter—the first year's dues.

Once you know exactly what you are up against, you can start saving, and you should start saving immediately. (Yes, even if your child is still in diapers.)

There are two compelling reasons for starting early. First, the sooner you begin, the more options you'll have. Second, the quicker you begin, the less you'll have to take out of your pockets to meet college costs, thanks to the wonders of compound interest. Let's start there.

Consider a child born in 1992. We project that by the time she enrolls as a freshman, it will cost somewhere around $26,000 a year for a public college, and better than $55,000 annually for a private one.

Ode to a Doctorate

It's mind-boggling enough for any reasonably sane parent just to anticipate undergraduate costs—and we suspect that's all you can handle in one sitting. But be forewarned that years from now your proud graduate—still wearing cap and gown—may tell you excitedly that the next step upward and onward is a master's, or a doctorate. You'll obviously have to tap a much, much bigger savings source. (Some parents simply smile back, and say, "I got you here, kid. The rest is up to you.")

But if you're game for the whole route—how much does the "rest" cost? College costs at higher levels will vary, and a master's degree probably won't cost much more than the undergraduate college costs. But a law degree can cost 10% to 25% more annually, and a medical degree might jump 25% to 50% more per year over undergraduate costs.

Those are frightening numbers, and you're bound to wonder how you are ever going to come up with that amount of money *every year for four years.* And, in fact, if you had to come up with all of it at once, it might be nigh on impossible.

However, you don't have to sit idly by waiting until that first tuition check is due. Paying for school—without going broke—becomes much more of a possibility if you just put away a relatively small amount of money each year.

How small is "relatively small"? Well, let's go back to our toddler who will be part of the college graduating class of 2014. If her parents put away $1,629 a year every year between 1992 and 2010 they will have saved enough to pay the cost of *all four years* at a public college, assuming an 8% return on their investment. Private school? Saving $4,348 annually would take care of every cost (remember that tuition and room and board at a private university is projected to cost nearly $216,000 for four years by the time today's pre–nursery schooler enters college).

How can you guarantee that you'll put away enough money each year? Here's one way:

Set up a savings, or investments account, for each child and link it to a master account that is in your name. Then establish an automatic transfer program, which each month will automatically transfer a set amount from your account to your child's. The amount of the transfer? Exactly what you think you'll need to pay for college.

Here's how it would work in practice. Let's say you are the proud parents of a baby girl who was born last week. Now even though she is less than seven days old, she is already showing signs of genius, and so you're certain she is going to go to MIT, or Stanford.

114

You can't lose either way. They are both very good schools—but pricey ones.

To make sure you can pay for her education, you'd go to your bank, or the financial services firm that handles your account, and tell them to automatically transfer $362.33 (one-twelfth of the $4,348 you have to put away each year to fund her college education) to *her* account on the first of every month. (A little later we'll go into the various tax advantages that you might find in these accounts.)

So, now we've set up a way to pay for college. But where should that money be invested? Let's spend a couple of minutes with some of the most popular long-term college funding strategies.

College Funding Options

U.S. Savings Bonds. Yep. The same old bonds you got as birthday presents, at your bar mitzvah or confirmation or inside the loopy card you received from your aunt when you graduated from high school. Series EE savings bonds, which have always been exempt from state and local taxes, now offer a new tax advantage for *some* parents: bonds purchased after January 1, 1990, *may* pay interest which is federally tax-free to parents, *if* the bonds are cashed in to pay education expenses.

Why the qualifiers "some," "may," and "if"? Well, first, because the bonds must be registered in the parents' names. Having Junior listed as the beneficiary voids the exemption. But that's only a minor point.

Here's the big stumbling block. The interest is fully tax-free *only* if your adjusted gross income falls under certain limits, *when the bonds are redeemed.* In 1992, to qualify for the exemption, a couple filing jointly could have no more than $66,200 in adjusted gross income (with the interest from the savings bonds counted as part of that income). Single filers could not have an adjusted gross income over $44,150. The tax exemption tapers off above those income levels and disappeared completely in 1992 at $96,200 for joint filers, and $59,150 for single filers. The deductibility falls proportionately, as your adjusted gross income climbs. For example, let's say a couple filing jointly in 1992 had an adjusted gross income of $81,200. Since $81,200 is exactly halfway between the $66,200 floor and the $96,200 income ceiling, 50% of the interest earned on the savings bonds would be tax-exempt.

Even without the federal tax break, savings bonds are probably a better deal than you remember. The interest rate on the bonds is now 85% of the average yield on U.S. Treasury securities, and is currently guaranteed never to fall below 6%.

Zero coupons (in all their guises). Zero coupon investments give you the comfort of knowing exactly how much a fixed sum will grow to in a given number of years.

"Zeros" are sold at a deep discount to their face value, and pay all their interest, along with principal, at maturity. When you buy bonds that mature during your child's college years, you know exactly how much money you will have available when it's time to pay the bursar.

There are a couple of things to remember about "zeros," whether you buy zero Treasury bonds, zero municipals, or a corporate zero. First, while the bond doesn't pay any interest until maturity, the IRS treats your investment in a zero as if you were receiving interest annually. You are taxed on the imputed income. So, if you are buying zeros to fund your child's education, you are probably better off putting them in your children's name since their tax bracket will usually be lower. (Of course, if you buy a tax-free municipal zero, which we will talk about in a minute, you don't have this problem. There is virtually never any tax to pay on municipal zeros.)

Secondly, if you sell your bond before maturity, you are subject to market fluctuations. So don't buy a 30-year zero if your son is going to start college in 15 years. Buy a zero that matures in 15 years, instead.

Better yet, don't buy one zero, buy four: one that matures just before the start of your child's freshman, sophomore, junior, and senior years.

The advantage is two-fold. First, since the bonds sell at a deeper discount, the further they are away from maturity, the zero for your daughter's last year will cost less than the one that will pay for her first, provided that you buy both of them today.

Secondly, if you stagger—or ladder—the maturity dates, you won't have to worry about what to do with all the college tuition money, when the bonds mature right before her freshman year.

Municipal bonds. These are federally tax-exempt securities issued by state and local governments, and their agencies, to finance various infrastructure needs. The bonds are usually also free from state and local taxes.

Municipal bonds offer semiannual interest payments, and are available in a wide range of maturities—from overnight to 35 years. Again, as in the purchase of the zeros, you are better off having the bond mature just before the tuition check is due. That way, you won't have to worry about the value of your bond rising or falling before its maturity. (For more details on bonds, zeros, and their rates, see Chapter 17.)

Zero municipals. These are, as you might expect, a combination of the two things we just talked about. Zero coupon municipals are a way for investors to let their capital grow tax-free. They are offered at a discount to their face value, and interest is paid only at maturity. You don't have to worry about reinvesting the interest your bond is earning; it compounds automatically. Zero municipals are available in many different maturity ranges, so you can pick a bond that is coming due exactly when you will need the money for college.

Baccalaureate bonds. These are a special type of municipal zero coupon bond that some states issue, usually in small denominations. The bonds work like municipal zeros, but with a twist. They'll sometimes pay a small bonus—a couple of hundred dollars at maturity—if you use the money to pay for tuition at a college within the issuing state.

Prepaid tuition plans. A few states have programs that allow you to pay tuition costs today, even though your child may be 10, 15, or even 18 years away from starting his freshman year at the state schools that are covered by the program.

Generally you write one check, based on current tuition, and the plan promises to cover tuition at a state school when your child is ready to attend, regardless of the increases in college costs. If your child decides to go to college elsewhere, you generally will get your principal back, but you'll probably receive very little, if any, interest. Some private colleges have similar programs.

There is another potential problem with these types of programs. The difference between your original investment and the

118

future tuition cost could be federally taxable, when the tuition is paid.

Equities, mutual funds, and the like. Even if you decide to use equities as your primary way of funding college, you may not want to keep all your money solely in stocks until the week before the tuition check is due.

While long-term stocks have traditionally outperformed every other type of investment, in the short term the value of your stocks will fluctuate.

But, if you're saving for the kids' college costs, you have one distinct advantage over most other savings concepts. Your time horizon is fairly definite. In so many other situations you are saving for an indefinite takeout—some time in the future. In this case, the deadline, at least for the first withdrawal, is when you expect your child to enter college. The usual freshman age is 18—but your child just might be precocious, anxious to get on with it, and go on a fast track to the big campus at age 16. Or your son or daughter could matriculate a year or two later.

But let's stick with the average, and assume that 18 will be freshman beanie time. If the baby is today still in the bassinet, and you're getting an early jump on socking money away for future college, we still contend that equity should be your principal investment. *Not* the *total* investment, but the *principal* one. History tells us this.

If, however, your child is much older—say 14—then the first tuition takeout will be in only four years, so you obviously should lean more toward fixed income. Keep in mind, though, that you will probably be paying for the last year of undergraduate school eight years from now. So that time frame still calls for investing some money in equity.

How to invest in equity? If you're an experienced investor, used to picking your own stocks, continue to do so. But also consider using a professional money manager, such as a manager of mutual funds, to do the job for you. In most of these funds you'll be able to automatically reinvest your dividends—which is a smart and practical way to keep building the assets. (For more on mutual funds, see Chapter 19.)

As early as four years before your child is scheduled to start college, you'll probably want to start shifting some of your slice of equities or growth funds into investments that have fixed incomes and predictable yields. The closer your child is to starting college, the more money you should have in investments that will hold no surprises.

Should You Consider a Custodial Account or Trust?

One way to build a college fund, no matter which investment strategy you choose, is to have the investment listed in your child's name. You can do this by creating a custodial account, a concept that was established by the Uniform Gifts to Minors Act and the Uniform Transfers to Minors Act. (These accounts are commonly called UGMA or UTMA accounts.) *Each* parent, or grandparent, can give *each* child up to $10,000 a year without any federal gift tax consequences.

If your child is under age 14, the first $600 in income from the custodial account is tax-free, the next $600 is taxed at the child's rate, and income above $1,200 is taxed at your tax rate, which presumably is higher than the child's rate. After your child turns 14, *all* income is taxed at the child's rate.

Okay, those are the ground rules for UGMA-UTMA custodial accounts—but is this a good way to fund college?

It depends. The first thing to remember is that assets in a custodial account *irrevocably* belong to the child, and come under the child's control at the "age of majority," which is usually 18 or 21, depending upon where you live. So, if you are worried that the shining apple of your eye may take the money earmarked for college and run out and buy a Porsche instead, you are better off keeping the funds in your name. Consider whatever taxes you pay on the money to be the price of a good night's sleep. Or, more likely, *many* nights of sound sleep.

Secondly, you should know that if you expect that your child will be applying for federal financial aid, then a custodial account may actually cost you money.

Why? Because the federal formula currently used for figuring financial aid requires a child to contribute toward college 35% of the assets he or she has. (Parents are generally required to contribute only about 5% of their assets.)

Since all the money in a custodial account belongs to the child—remember, the terms of the account make it irrevocable—the trust will be considered part of the child's assets when it comes time to calculate financial aid. However, if you know your child won't qualify for financial aid anyway, the tax savings may make a custodial account an attractive option.

Another way to give assets to minors is through a trust, such as the ones authorized by Section 2503(c) of the federal tax code. In these types of trusts, income not currently distributed to the child is taxed at the trust's rate: 15% on the first $3,600 in income and at a 28% rate over that amount.

Until the child reaches age 21, the trustee can manage the

funds, but the beneficiary has unlimited access to both the principal and interest. (*Vroom!* Was that a Porsche passing by?) Any accumulated income must be distributed to the child at age 21. Any principal remaining in the trust may also be distributed, or it can be held in trust until a later date.

Suppose You Just Don't Have the Cash?

Even if you plan ahead, you still may not have all the money you need to put your kid(s) through college. If you don't, you're not alone.

Once you've realized you'll need some help, your first step should be to figure out what kind of scholarships and/or financial aid is available. Your high school guidance counselor or college aid counselor should be able to help. In addition, there are three books we particularly like: *Don't Miss Out: The Ambitious Student's Guide to Financial Aid, The College Cost Book,* and *Peterson's College Money Handbook.* Some magazines, such as *Money,* will periodically publish special editions on colleges—how to pick them, how to finance your tuition costs.

Think you won't qualify for financial aid? Think again. About half of all students going to college are now receiving some sort of aid, according to the College Board. So, if you need help paying for college, apply, especially if your child will be going to a private school.

Yes, private schools certainly cost more, but they also have more money available for students who need it. According to the latest figures from the Department of Education, the average amount of aid awarded to undergraduate students attending major private universities is more than $6,000 a year, while an undergraduate at a major public university receives only half that amount.

Those are intriguing numbers. As the chart on page 111 shows, private colleges generally cost twice as much as public schools. But if those schools also give twice as much aid, that means your child may be able to attend a more expensive private university, without increasing *your* share of the cost.

Note: When figuring out where the money for college will come from, *don't* count too heavily on your child being bright, or working part-time.

If your student plans to work while in college, or during vacations, you should know about the new federal formula used to calculate financial aid. Students are now expected to contribute 70% of their *after-tax* earnings from full or part-time jobs to help cover college costs, if they are receiving federal aid. That's true, even if some of the money they earned was spent on food and/or lodging while they worked.

There's more bad news. Some schools may reduce the aid they give by the full amount of a merit scholarship a child receives.

Other Ways to Pay for College

As college costs continue to rise, many parents find borrowing often is the ultimate solution to coming up with the additional money they need to pay for school. And a variety of attractive alternatives may be available, even if you're not eligible for other kinds of financial aid.

Here are four sources that we particularly like:

1. *Relatives, especially grandparents.* If your child's grandparents pay the money directly to the college or university—*not to the parent or child*—they can give as much money as is needed to cover tuition and room and board, with *no* gift tax implications.

2. *Home equity credit lines.* A home equity loan can be the best way of coming up with the money you need to pay for college, for several reasons:

First, the interest expense on loans, up to $100,000, is generally tax-deductible, while interest on other types of education loans is not deductible at all.

Second, you can usually access the money you need by writing a check for the exact amount, so you don't incur needless interest costs. You just borrow the money the day before you need it.

Third, many credit lines offer an interest-only option, so you can defer repaying the principal until after your child graduates. All these advantages are wonderful, but home equity loans come complete with one major drawback: the asset you are tapping *is* your home.

One of the—if not *the*—biggest assets you are going to have, when it comes time to retire, is this home equity. That's especially true if you prepay the mortgage as much as possible. Obviously, the more money you borrow against the house to pay for college, the less you are going to have when it comes time to retire—*unless you are rigorous in paying yourself back.*

We are not saying you shouldn't use a home equity loan for college. If you need to borrow, borrowing on the house can make an awful lot of sense.

124

What we are saying is this: *Treat the money you are taking out of your home exactly as you would any other loan. Pay it off as quickly as possible. Create a repayment schedule that calls for the money to be repaid as far in advance of your retirement as you can.*

Sure, the repayment schedule may be onerous, but remember this: you are repaying yourself. That will make writing out those large monthly checks, earmarked to repay the home equity loan, a whole lot easier to take. (For a complete discussion on how you can use your home as a source for funds, see Chapter 23, "When It Comes to Retirement, There's No Place Like Home.")

3. Government-sponsored loans. While federal programs *have* been pared down in recent years—and the likelihood is that this whittling of federal funding for education will continue for the foreseeable future because of the national deficit—the U.S. government is still the nation's largest source of financial aid for students.

The federal government offers two types of loans (through commercial lenders) that are not based on financial need. One is a loan made directly to parents (Parent Loans to Undergraduate Students [PLUS]), the other one is designed for students who are putting themselves through school (Supplemental Loans to Students).

The maximum loan amount in each case is $4,000 a year, up to a total of $20,000 for each type of loan. The interest rate is tied to U.S. Treasury bills, and has a 12% ceiling. Repayment begins within 60 days of taking out the loan, and may extend up to 10 years.

Some states also have loan programs that provide money at attractive rates.

Your child's high school guidance counselor, and the financial aid officer at the college your child decides to attend, should know what kind of income-based loans are available. Colleges in particular are beefing up their staffing in this area, since it's very much to their advantage if they're able to point you in the right direction. They want to keep their lecture halls filled.

4. *College and university loans.* As the cost of a college education has risen, so has the creativity of college financial aid offices. Among the options now available at some places are loans at below-market rates, installment payment plans that allow you to spread tuition costs over a number of months, and "guaranteed tuition plans."

The guaranteed tuition plan lets you know in advance exactly what four years of college will cost. In one common version of the plan, the college takes its current freshman charges and multiplies by four, and lets you pay the whole thing at once. This way you are protected against rising costs during the four years your child is in school. Some schools will even lend you the money to pay the bill.

College costs are increasing annually at about double the inflation rate. There are many ways—including some tax-advantaged ones—to fund a college education. If you start saving early enough for your children's (or grandchildren's) education, you may be able to put them through school and still fund your own retirement. All without going broke!

CHAPTER 6

Social Security—Part I: "The Enduring Legacy"

A British observer, surveying America's complex Social Security system, once said, "It really is an extraordinary system that America has devised—a program whereby the country's grandpaws are mugging their young."

We don't *really* ask that you should think of grandfathers as muggers, and their children as muggees. What we will do in this chapter is tell you of the past, the present, and the future of this extraordinary system called Social Security. It is a remarkable concept, which some historians have called the "Enduring Legacy" from the 1930s New Deal era.

As vital as the system is, and although the signs are that we are currently looking at a startling "surplus" in Social Security income contrasted to outgo, there will come a time well into the twenty-first century when, according to the demographers, there will be proportionately fewer young and more old people. It follows that there may be fewer workers per retiree to pay into the Social Security system. In this chapter we'll touch on the beginnings of Social Security and we'll paint its uncertain future.

But if we begin all this with a somewhat skeptical comment from abroad, let's counter with a more rosy comment from Washington:

> Before we get started explaining the program, we think it's important to answer the first question many people have about Social Security. Perhaps you've asked it yourself: "Will Social Security be there when I need it?"
>
> The simple and logical answer is, "yes it will." But that answer deserves an explanation.

And—from us—it deserves a second look.

The quote above comes from *Understanding Social Security,* a very readable pamphlet published by the Social Security Administration in October 1991. But before we start raising our questions about Social Security's future, let's see why the Social Security Administration is so confident it has a future:

> Most of the worries about the future of the Social Security result from the financial troubles the system faced in the 1970s and the early 1980s. At the time, because of high inflation and other economic problems, Social Security was in very serious financial condition. However, due to an improved economy and increases in Social Security taxes, the system now is in excellent shape—and will be for many years to come.
>
> Social Security takes in significantly more than it spends, and the extra money, called "reserves," makes up the Social Security trust funds. There have been reports about so-called "misuses" of those funds. For example, some people complain that Social Security money is used to pay for other government programs. In fact, the money in Social Security's trust funds is invested in Treasury bonds—generally consid-

ered the safest of all investments. The government, by law, has always paid back the trust funds with interest, and there is no reason to expect it will not continue to do so.

You might find this a mere nit to pick, but we find the wording interesting.

This quote comes from *Understanding Social Security*. The wording "... there is no reason to expect [the government] will not continue [to] . . ." to pay back the money it borrowed is a pretty strong guarantee.

Pretty strong. But it is not as strong as: " . . . the bonds have **always** been repaid, with interest, and you can be assured that the Government will never renege on that policy."

That quote, and the boldface, was contained in *Your Social Security Taxes, What They're Paying for and Where the Money Goes,* which was published by the government just seven months before. (In case you're a historian—or maybe you'd just like to track Washingtonspeak as a hobby—we thought we'd point out the difference.)

That reference to the "excellent shape" of Social Security is a bit of an oversimplification. Some background will help etch a more complete picture for you. For many years, Social Security worked as a pay-as-you-go program. Wage earners paid in their Social Security taxes, and the money was promptly paid out to retirees. The "financial trouble" the Social Security Administration is talking about was simply this: by the late 1970s, the ratio of workers to retirees was changing dramatically and the system was in real danger of running out of money.

In 1983 Congress solved the problem—at least temporarily. Higher Social Security taxes were part of the answer, as was a decision to gradually slow down the payout of future benefits. If

you were born in 1938 or later, you will have to wait a bit longer—
up to two years longer for people born in 1960 or thereafter—to
receive full retirement benefits. (We'll go fully into this slowdown
in Chapter 26. We'll show precisely how it could affect you.)

When a Trust Is Not Necessarily a Trust

There are a couple of other things to note about the sentence: "The
government, by law, has always paid back the trust funds with
interest."

The government has always paid back the money it has borrowed from the trust fund in the past, but this could be more
difficult to do in the future.

Uncle Sam is probably trustworthy when it comes to repaying
borrowed funds. But the following explanation of borrowing just
might destroy your initial (misguided) understanding of where all
the money you have been paying into Social Security has been
going. The money may be funneled into an account labeled the
"Social Security Administration Trust Fund," but in truth it's difficult to picture it as an ironclad trust for anyone.

Like most people, you probably pictured the money you—and
the other 135 million people who pay Social Security taxes each
year—paid in as sitting in a piggy bank somewhere, a piggy bank
that had your name on it. That money, you figured, was just
waiting for you to announce that you were tired of punching in,
or that you'd had it catching the 7:03 each morning, and it was time
to smell the roses, and start receiving some of that accumulation—
your money you had paid in Social Security taxes through all those
years.

But the only thing waiting for us in that piggy bank is an IOU. The government, despite its disclaimer, uses your Social Security taxes to expand medical research, build roads, and fund VA hospitals. Or—as some Social Security realists believe is the more correct way to look at it—the "trust" surplus simply reduces the cost of government borrowing. One way or the other the money *is* gone. In its place is "just" a government promise to repay the money when it's due.

If you find that troubling, and if the imagined picture of billions upon billions of dollars worth of IOUs stacked up in a piggy bank has caused you to have a twitch or two at night, the Social Security Administration offers you more reassurance:

Beyond the facts and figures that clearly show that Social Security is in excellent financial shape, the program's future is assured because of the broad support that it enjoys from all sectors of American society. As a nation, we recognize the need to provide a basic level of financial support and health care for the elderly, as well as for our citizens with disabilities, the survivors of deceased workers, and people with low incomes.

That goal is at the heart of the Social Security system. It's what the Retirement, Disability, Survivors, Medicare and Supplemental Security Income (SSI) programs are all about.

The numbers do clearly show that Social Security is in excellent shape—for now.

Currently the government is taking in about $1.5 billion more a week in Social Security taxes than is going out to beneficiaries. The government now estimates that by the year 2000 this "surplus" intake will increase to about $200 billion a year. No surprise there, really, for the youngest baby boomer in the year 2000 will be 36 and probably making a couple of dollars.

The turning point, of course, is that the baby boomers' older sibling(s), who could be 55 in the year 2000, will be seriously thinking about retirement just about then.

To look at outgo—in 1991 Social Security paid out some $346.8 billion, almost a billion per day. By the year 2025, the estimated payout will be ten times that, $10 billion a day.

Something Is Out of Synch

So what will happen? Here's what the best guess looks like right now, according to government statisticians. The "surplus" in the Social Security Trust Fund will peak at $9 trillion in 2027. Then, as baby boomers really retire in droves, and there are fewer workers per retiree to tax (since married baby boomers on average only have 1.8 children per couple), the size of the Trust Fund will decrease and will be completely depleted within 16 years. The $9 trillion surplus could easily turn into a *trillion-dollar-a-year* deficit by the mid-twenty-first century. The Social Security system—as remarkable and farsighted a program as it was when it was created more than a half-century ago—will be out of synch. As to that surplus, needless to say, there is constant pressure in Congress to somehow dip into it.

As it was originally conceived, Social Security was never thought to be the end-all retirement plan for workers. Instead, in its simplest form it was designed to be a sort of supplemental "insurance" to help you in retirement. Through the last half-century it has changed considerably. It has evolved into a much larger, much more all-encompassing program of benefits.

Virtually no taxpayer in America can fault the social good the benefits provide. However, when *you* think about Social Security, we'll guess that you first think of retirement programs and benefits. Indeed, some 60% of people receiving money from the Social Security Administration are getting retirement benefits.

What about that other 40%? Well, as that quote from the Social Security Administration shows, they are getting benefits because:

• They are disabled.

• They are a dependent of someone who gets Social Security.

• They are a widow, widower, or child of someone who has died.

What this means, of course, is that if you fall into one of these three categories you may be eligible to collect Social Security, and a lot of people do.

In fact about 40.6 million people—that's almost one out of every six Americans—collect some kind of Social Security benefit. Those benefits totaled approximately $347 billion in 1991.

If you are self-employed, you are painfully aware of exactly how much Social Security costs: 15.3% of the first $55,500 in income you earned in 1992—some $8,491.50—went for Social Security taxes. (If you worked for someone else, the tab didn't seem quite so big. You *only* had 7.65% of your income withheld for Social Security taxes, in the column on your pay stub labeled FICA, which stands for Federal Insurance Contributions Act—that's the law that authorized Social Security's payroll tax. But the government was still getting its 15.3% of your income. Your employer paid *an additional* 7.65% on the first $55,500 you earned.)

It sounds like $55,500 is the magic number for the elimination of Social Security taxes, but it isn't.

If you made more than $55,500 in 1991, you already know what comes next. You continue to pay the Medicare portion of the Social Security tax until your income tops $130,200. The Medicare portion is 1.45% for employers and employees each, which means that if you are self-employed, you are paying an additional 2.9% of your income from $55,500 to $130,200 to fund Medicare.

A Suggestion: Reclaim Your Future

Now all this adds up to big money, but it *still* isn't enough to fund *all* Social Security programs. General tax revenues, not Social Security taxes, are used to finance the Supplemental Security Income program, which provides monthly checks to people who are 65 or older, or disabled, or blind, and who don't own much and don't have a lot of income.

Nobody—and certainly not us—is going to question how this money is spent. Nonetheless, it is an awful lot of money, and you have to wonder how long people will be able to pay the kinds of taxes that will be required to support these programs in the future.

As we said, the Social Security Administration, which is part of the U.S. Department of Health and Human Services, does not question its own long-term viability. However, even the SSA concedes in its pamphlet *Understanding Social Security* that it cannot do it all when it comes to your retirement (the boldface is in the original):

Social Security is **not** intended to be your only source of income. Instead, it is meant to be used to supplement the

134

pensions, insurance, savings, and other investments you will accumulate during your working years.

Amen.

Now you know why this book's credo is for you to reclaim, as much as you can, your own retirement future from the hands of strangers (be they the helpful hands of *your* government, or *your* employer)—and instead, for you to self-direct your own retirement plans.

How to do just that is what Chapters 7 to 13 are all about. But much later, in Chapter 26, we will tell you about the various ways that let you tap into the Social Security benefits that are *yours.*

How Social Security Taxes Have Grown

A quick review of the amount of money people have paid in Social Security taxes throughout the years is striking.

In 1937, a worker had a maximum of $30 a year taken out of his paycheck. By 1950 it was $45; 1960, $144; 1970, $374; 1980, $1,586. And as we know, the 1992 maximum is $5,329. In all, there have been 20 Social Security tax increases since the program began. For about two-thirds of employees in this country, this present 15.3% payroll tax burden (which includes both your share and your employer's share) exceeds their annual federal income taxes. No wonder workers raise their eyebrows over the rising payroll taxes.

Some 71% of the pre-retirees recently surveyed by Merrill Lynch said they are concerned about getting out of Social Security what they paid into it. That does not strike us as an unrealistic concern.

Social Security is an extraordinary system of benefits that most working Americans will draw on. It is an "enduring legacy"—but as we move into the twenty-first century, a new reality will set in. There will be proportionately fewer young and more old. Social Security, somewhere down the line, will have to be restructured. In the meantime, think of Social Security as a "supplement"—a supplement to your other retirement assets.

PART II

Saving Systematically and Tax-Advantaged

CHAPTER 7

Everything You've Always Wanted to Know About Pensions but Were Afraid to Ask

Thanks to such lyrics as "Great ooga-booga can't you hear me talking to you," rock and roll is rarely cited when people try to answer life's fundamental questions.

Similarly, rock stars rarely serve as the source of retirement wisdom. Except in the negative. ("Hope I die before I get old.")

Still, it is a rock and roll song—admittedly written about something else—that best sums up the way we feel about pension plans: "Even bad lovin' is better than no lovin', So, I take what I can get."

If you substitute "pension plan" for "lovin,' " you'll understand our position: Even a bad pension from your employer is better than no pension at all.

Pension plans—like noses—come in all sizes and shapes. Some are huge. Some are elegant. Some are barely there. But no matter what its shape or size, it is better to have a pension plan than not.

We'd like to spend the next several pages talking about where employer pensions plans fit in, as you go about your retirement planning. In this chapter we are only going to be talking about private sector pension plans. We know there are some 17 million people who work in the public sector, who have pension coverage as well. And believe us, we are not deliberately slighting you.

However, there can be vast differences between pension plans offered by the federal government and the states, and there can even be huge differences between the plans offered by the states themselves and the tens of thousands of villages, towns, counties, and cities. Given all these differences, it's difficult to talk about public pension plans in any general way.

But here are two points about public pensions, anyway.

First, if you work in the public sector, your pension could make up a significant part of your retirement income. (Government pensions are known for being more substantial than those offered by the private sector.) Since that's true, it is vitally important that you understand the specific benefits you're entitled to. Ask your human resources department to project the benefits you will receive under your plan. (This advice, of course, also applies to people in the private sector.)

Second, most public pension plans are defined benefit plans, and the discussion later in this chapter of those plans should be of particular interest to public sector employees.

Plymouth Rock—Turkeys and Pensions

For those of you who think of a pension as virtually a God-given right, it is a bit of a shock to learn that they are still a relatively new phenomenon. True, the Colony of New Plymouth in Massachusetts had a military retirement program as early as 1626, and there are scattered reports of companies putting pension plans in place in the eighteenth and nineteenth centuries, but the fact is that even as late as the 1920s, very few—probably less than 1,000—U.S. companies, of any size, offered pensions.

Today better than 850,000 employer pension plans cover some 44 million Americans.

What changed?

Supply and demand.

Up through and including the Great Depression years of the 1930s, pensions were the farthest thing from either employers'—or employees'—minds. Demand for industrial jobs typically far exceeded supply. Unemployment hovered constantly around 25% during the Depression, and if you had a job, you worried about keeping it tomorrow. If in those dark days you worked for a company that said, and some of them did, "If you don't come to work Sunday, don't bother coming on Monday," thinking about pensions, or the lack thereof, didn't occupy a whole lot of your time.

The Farmer Goes Corporate

Farmers, then as now, have always been responsible for their own retirement planning. From 1960s on, farmers who were self-employed were able to set up Keogh pension plans (see Chapter 12), but in recent years many farmers—even small ones—have incorporated and so have been able to take advantage of a far broader range of small employer pension plans.

Boom Years Led to Pension Years

World War II, and the boom years that followed, changed that. Pent-up demand for goods forced companies to scramble for ways to find, and keep, employees. As a direct result, pension plans became a recruiting tool. Be loyal to us—by coming to work and staying for 20 or 30 years—employers said, and we will show our loyalty to you with a very direct reward. We'll give you a monthly check, sort of a reduced salary, once you're retired.

Bidding wars for employees weren't always won by offering a generous plan, but a nice retirement package sure made an offer enticing. If nothing else, all the talk about retirement packages following the end of World War II—coupled with the recently enacted (1935) concept of Social Security, which raised employee consciousness about the need to prepare for the future—got workers to ask at some point during the interview: "By the way, what kind of pension plan do you have?"

By the early 1950s, pensions had become a permanent part of the economic landscape.

For people who planned to retire during the fifties, sixties, and seventies, a Social Security check, coupled with a corporate pension, made the future seem quite rosy.

It had a secondary effect as well. Watching the way their parents lived after they retired caused people who were born in the 1920s, and thereafter, to progressively concentrate more and more on pension benefits when they joined the work force.

These people—boomers and, to a somewhat lesser degree, parents of boomers—announced that they had little interest in going down to Florida or heading off to California to play shuffleboard once they stopped working. They knew they'd be living longer, and they were in better health than their parents and grandparents, and they had no intention of living a sedentary life once they retired. Rather, they planned to take cruises around the world, attend all two weeks of Wimbledon, and play golf in Hawaii. They would finally have the chance to do all the things they dreamed of when they were working but never had the time to enjoy.

That was the plan anyway.

A Bonus or a Nightmare

Then all of a sudden these people—who are now any age from their 30s to late 50s—took a more flinty look at their retirement finances.

They began having nagging doubts about their Social Security benefits; they put their own corporate pension plan under a microscope, and they came to a sobering conclusion: "There is a very good chance that I may outlive my money. Forget golf in Hawaii, and lounging around the aft deck. How am I going to be able to pay the basic bills—and all those future medical bills—once I stop working?"

The reality of the new longevity was both enticing and frightening. Extra years in retirement promised to be a bonus—but the danger of outliving retirement assets promised to be a nightmare.

Suddenly, knowing exactly how much they would have coming to them from their corporate pension plan became vitally important.

It was about the same time that pensions became more important to Congress as well.

Prompted by scandals at several large companies—whose pensions funds either went broke and/or were looted—Congress substantially changed pension laws in 1974.

The vehicle was the Employee Retirement Income Security Act, what we fondly refer to as ERISA. Designed to curb both company and union abuse of pension plans, ERISA did more than create tougher standards. Jointly monitored by the Department of Labor and the Treasury Department, the new act became a sort of bill of rights for workers.

The new legislation sent another message. The new laws opened up more opportunities for *self-direction* when it came to the administration of pension money. The ERISA legislation made it clear that Congress believed that you were quite capable of handling your pension money yourself.

That self-direction would take three forms. First, ERISA authorized the creation of self-directed Individual Retirement Accounts. Secondly, for the first time ERISA allowed you to take your pension money with you—in the form of a rollover—if you changed jobs. (Details in a few moments.) And lastly, ERISA spawned subse-

---

A Drop in Pension Coverage

By 1980 some 50% of workers in America had some sort of pension coverage. This has dropped to an estimated 40% today. Why? Declining unionization is one factor. A pronounced tilt in this country from a manufacturing economy to more of a service economy is another.

Most of the job growth in the 1980s was in small business, and small businesses have traditionally been under less competitive pressure to offer retirement plans to employees.

And what's been happening in big business? Corporate restructuring has led to downsizing. Also, partially as a result of belt tightening—in big and small businesses—a growing percentage of the remaining employees these days are "contingent": either part-time or temporary, so few employer pension plans cover them.

quent broadening of self-direction to employer plans—such as defined contribution plans and 401(k) salary-deferral plans.

The importance of these three changes cannot be over-emphasized. Both IRAs and self-directed pensions now make up a significant portion of a well-funded retirement plan.

What Kind of Plan Do You Have?

For the longest time, there was only one answer to that question: "I have a defined *benefit* plan."

And the name described exactly what it was. The company defined what benefit you'd receive, based on your final salary—or an average of your salary over the last few years at the company—and years of service.

The longer you were with the firm, and the more money you made, the more you got come retirement. And you'd know ahead of time exactly how much money would be coming from your pension, a pension that didn't cost you anything. Your employer funded it all.

That was the good news, and there really wasn't any bad news to speak of. Oh, sure, the odds were against your pension being indexed for inflation, but that wasn't so terrible, since your Social Security benefits were.

Defined benefit plans were—and are for millions of people who still participate in them today—a great deal. They're simple, and require virtually no participation from the employee. (But as you'll soon read, fewer new defined benefit plans are being offered these days.)

In a defined benefit plan, you don't manage your retirement

money, as you do with a 401(k) plan. A company pension committee, or a pension fund manager hired by your company, does it for you. The return on the money your company sets aside for you typically is more than enough to cover your set pension.

What all this means is that if your company offers a defined benefit plan, you may be able to retire happily ever after.

The Labor Department, which monitors pension plan usage carefully, says that it is not so much a matter of defined benefits decreasing as it is that the biggest growth is coming from employee participation in defined contribution plans, such as 401(k)s. Many firms are offering defined contribution plans for several reasons. For one thing, we're living longer. Companies are somewhat more reluctant to offer defined benefits to someone who may easily live not just 10, but 20, or even 30 years after retiring from the firm. But the main reason for companies' becoming more defined-benefits-shy is the wild card of inflation. Concerns about future

---

A New Guaranty (with One Problem)

Congress has tried to make sure that you'll have a reasonably happy retirement. ERISA established a new federal agency, the Pension Benefit Guaranty Corporation, to insure benefits to workers with a defined benefit plan, should their private pension fail. (Defined contribution plans, however, do not qualify for PBGC insurance.)

The PBGC is funded by an annual assessment to employers to cover their active workers.

The problem is, the current assessment isn't raising enough money.

Because some major corporations have slid into bankruptcy in recent years, the PBGC in 1992 faced losses of at least $20 billion. All during the recession of the early nineties this deficit mounted, and some estimates have the true future deficit topping $50 billion.

Undoubtedly Congress will be asked—one way or the other—to come to the rescue of the PBGC.

---

inflation mean that companies are not as comfortable with assumptions about how much must be put aside for future benefits.

To reduce their liability to a manageable—and finite—number, companies starting in the late 1970s and then throughout the 1980s began shifting some of the burden of an employee's retirement onto the back of the employee himself. Good-bye entitlements; hello self-help.

In addition to setting aside a fixed amount of money for their employees' retirement, companies began asking employees to join salary-deferral plans, such as 401(k)s. In a 401(k) plan you set aside a certain percentage of your salary—6%, for example—and a lot of companies say "we will match you $1 for every $2 you put in."

In the following chapter we'll tell you how a 401(k) plan works. It has been avidly adopted by big business; some 95% of the largest companies in America now offer them. Nonetheless, it has resulted in a clear shifting of much of the retirement responsibilities from employer to employee. It is an important cog in your total retirement planning—and so we'll tell you why you should embrace it to the hilt.

If you are lucky enough to work for an employer who will match some of your contribution, such as in the previous example, that's a good deal—after all, where else can you earn a guaranteed 50% on your money—but ERISA made it even better. Both your contribution and that of your employer grow tax-deferred. There are no taxes due until you actually withdraw the money.

As if those advantages were not enough, the government gave you one more. Your contribution can be made in *pretax* dollars, dollars that in essence would be subtracted right from your W-2.

All in all, this is a pretty nice carrot.

The stick? Some companies—once they offered a 401(k) plan—began cutting back, or even eliminating, other retirement plans.

Two Kinds of "Defined" Plans

Let's step back and explain the key differences between defined benefit and defined contribution plans.

In a defined contribution plan, rather than guarantee you a certain benefit upon retirement **(a defined benefit),** your employer may make a certain *current* annual contribution **(a defined contribution)** to cover future retirement costs. This contribution may be tied to your salary level, and your years of service, but then again it may not. It may just be a fixed amount. ("We'll match $1 for every $2 you put in, up to 6% of your salary," your employer might declare.)

But no matter what form that contribution takes, how much you'll receive from this plan when you retire will be based on how much your employer contributes, how much you contribute, and how well your investments fare, based on the decisions *you* make.

That's a point worth exploring. In a defined benefit plan, your employer, or his investment adviser, worries about the management of your pension assets. In a defined contribution plan, the worry is usually yours.

Many employers now mix the two types of plans. They may offer a defined benefit plan as a way of providing a basic (that is, small) pension, but they'll encourage you to use defined contribution plans, such as 401(k)s, and employee stock plans, to supplement it. And a few companies with overfunded defined benefit plans have taken to reclaiming the excess funding for corporate purposes and then distributing the remaining pension assets to vested employees, usually in the form of annuities. Then they may well turn around and open new, defined contribution plans to handle future retirement costs.

However, the trend is clear. Defined benefits will be less important in providing retirement benefits; defined contributions will become more important.

What Can You Invest In?

Your company will generally offer you a limited menu of choices for your defined contribution plan. A handful of mutual funds, either equity or fixed income, a money market fund, and a guaranteed investment contract are representative of the options you'll have. You'll probably be able to change these investments from time to time. In fact, you can even create an asset allocation strategy for your own self-directed plan. Managing your own pension money is not much different from managing your own 401(k) or IRA. It's pretty straightforward, yet some people panic when they hear that their company is going to switch from defined benefits to defined contributions. There really is no reason to.

How much you panic seems to be directly related to how old you are, according to the latest Merrill Lynch retirement survey. Baby boomers, it seems, are becoming increasingly comfortable with taking responsibility for their pension money. Some 92% of them said it is important to them to be able to pick the investments that are in their retirement accounts. (However, about a third of those people said that although they *want* to run their own accounts, they are worried they *aren't yet* knowledgeable enough to confidently pick from the investment options offered.)

Many companies these days are resorting to educational seminars to teach their employees the basics of how to manage their own retirement plans.

Instead of lamenting a switch from defined benefits to defined contributions, you should be celebrating. Why? Because of what happens if you change jobs.

Under a defined benefit plan, if you leave the company before retirement, you are entitled to whatever pension benefits you have earned up until that point. *However, in almost all defined benefit plans, you won't see that money until you reach your former employer's retirement age.* There is seldom a lump sum, or rollover provision. (Details on how those things work in a few moments.)

Plus, the benefits you receive will probably be frozen at the level they were at when you left the company. So if you had earned a $400-a-month pension by the time you quit, then that's what you are going to receive when you reach your former employer's retirement age, even if $400 is then worth considerably less in today's dollars.

However, things are different if you have a defined contribution pension plan, and decide to leave your company.

When you leave, you'll probably be offered "a lump sum distribution," that is, all at once you'll get all the money you're entitled to. If you're thinking long term, have your employer transfer the distribution directly to an IRA (so that you're not hit with a withholding tax). Once it's safely lodged in your IRA, you continue managing the money tax-deferred yourself.

If you're thinking short term, you can take the money, pay the taxes due (remember, both your contribution and your company's have been growing tax-deferred), and go out and buy a Rolls-Royce or whatever else you want. (Deciding whether or not to take a lump sum distribution often comes down to tax [and penalty] considerations. In Chapter 25 we'll give you the pros and cons.)

So, What Does All This Mean?

Once upon a time, when the world was young, retirement planning was pretty simple. You'd get a monthly check from Social Security, and possibly a small monthly pension check, and retirement life was fine.

Retiring today? You'll undoubtedly still get Social Security. But after that . . . Well, after that it's up to you.

While the shift toward defined contribution plans means it is much more difficult to project *exactly* how much money you'll have once you retire, you should be able to come up with a ballpark figure (see Chapter 2). In fact, one way or the other you'll have to make a projection while you are still working if you want to have a handle on how much additional money you'll need in order to have a comfortable retirement. To help you do this, go to your financial services firm. Many have various software programs—usually free—at their fingertips that can produce projections for you based on the raw data you supply.

If your company has a defined benefit plan, its human resources department can give you a pretty good estimate of what benefits you'll have coming to you at retirement. Specifically, they'll be able to tell you what benefits you have accrued to date, and what portion of them are vested. Plus, they should be able to project ahead and give you a pretty good estimate of what you will receive should you stay with your employer until retirement.

If your company offers a defined contribution plan, you'll automatically receive statements—either quarterly, semiannually, or annually—that tell you how much you've contributed to the plan, how much your employer has put into the plan, and how well your total investments have done.

If you are invested in more than one choice, the statement will also reveal how each of your investments is doing. (This detailing will help you to decide whether or not to change investments, and how to allocate your money in the future.)

Finally, the statement will show how much of your employer's contribution is yours to keep, that is, what percentage of that contribution is vested.

Vesting

Vesting refers to the rights you have to the money your *employer* contributes to your retirement plan. If your employer has contributed $1,000 and you are 20% vested, then $200 of that $1,000 is yours to keep (plus 20% of the earnings on the employer's contribution), should you leave the company tomorrow.

Any money that you yourself have contributed—plus whatever your contribution has earned—is always 100% yours. It's yours from the day you put it in until the day you take it out. As far as your contribution is concerned, you are always 100% vested.

Prior to ERISA, it was common for companies to require you to work for many years before you were entitled to *any* of the pension money that had been earmarked for you. Some companies might have required you to work for 10 years or more before you became vested.

Some companies had *no* vesting schedules. In extreme cases—the kind of horror stories that prompted Congress to act—an employee might have planned to retire after working for a company for 35 years. If his company went under just as he hit his 34th anniversary, his pension benefits might—in the old days—have been wiped out.

As a result of ERISA, and subsequent pension law change, definite vesting schedules were set. Vesting time was decreased, and generally companies were given two choices when it came to creating vesting schedules.

For example, your employer can offer you a "cliff" option, so named because you either climb over the cliff—and become completely vested—or fall off it—you leave before you get anything at all. There is no middle ground. If you work for a company five years and that company has chosen a five-year cliff vesting schedule, you are fully vested. If you leave before your fifth anniversary, you fall off the cliff. You receive nothing.

The other choice is a "gradual" vesting schedule. After three years, you begin to own some of the money your company has set aside for you. By your seventh anniversary you're totally vested.

The bar graph on page 154 shows how the plans stack up head-to-head.

From the Primer to the Specific

Okay—your first lesson in the changing world of pension plans is over—and, we hope it wasn't so bad.

Let's leave this primer and move on—over the next five chapters—to a very detailed examination of other retirement plans:

401(k)s
403(b)s
Employee Stock Plans
IRAs
SEPs
Keoghs

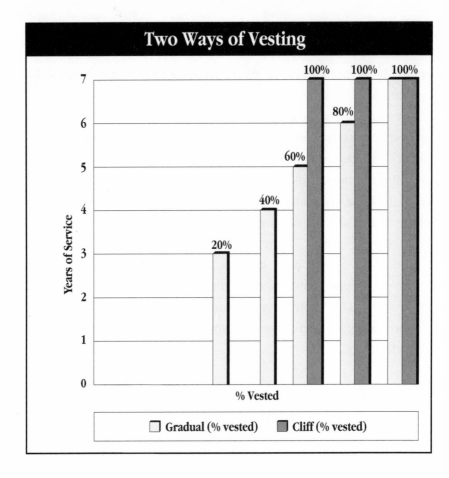

At first glance this list may look like a crazy quilt of alpha-numeric mystery codes—but we promise they will soon make sense.

They have much in common. All are designed to invest savings dollars systematically for you (to make it easier on your budgeting); all are tax-advantaged; and finally, most of them can be self-directed, which means you're given a golden opportunity to save smarter.

We end this chapter where we started. Any employer pension plan is better than no plan at all. But no matter what kind of plan your company offers, get to know it. Understand the benefits, and the limitations on those benefits.

More important, determine exactly what percentage of your retirement income will be coming from your employer pension, and then you can decide—assuming you find there is a savings shortfall—on the next step: figuring out which additional retirement plans are best for you.

CHAPTER 8

401(k) Retirement Plans

While the idea of providing a company pension for retired employees really started to take hold following World War II, it took until the early 1980s for the most popular retirement plan of all time to be introduced. Named after the section of the Internal Revenue Code that governs it, the 401(k) quickly swept through the *Fortune 1,000*.

Today more than 95% of companies with 5,000 or more employees offer a 401(k) plan to their employees. And more and more smaller companies are adding it as a corporate benefit every year. (Even the smallest of companies—those with 25 or fewer employees—are able to employ the basic principles of the 401(k) salary-deferral concept through yet another retirement plan, the Simplified Employee Pension plan. SEP is a very specialized retirement plan, which we explain more fully in Chapter 12.)

Back in Chapters 1 and 2, we outlined case histories of five couples and two singles who had concerns about retirement. One of our examples—Martha Skylar of Atlanta—was not taking full advantage of a 401(k) plan offered her (pages 30 and 52–56).

Throughout this chapter, we'll use Martha as an example of the way a 401(k) can help to bridge the retirement savings gap.

But first some background.

Something Everyone Loves

How do you explain the phenomenal popularity of the 401(k) concept? It's simple: 401(k) plans benefit both employers *and* employees.

Employers like the plan because it helps limit their costs of retirement contributions. Unlike defined benefit plans, which call for a company to keep paying out benefits for as long as the retired employee is alive, companies know in advance exactly what a 401(k) plan will cost. With a 401(k) plan, the employer has shifted some of the retirement benefit costs to the employee. (And in extreme cases, *all* may be shifted to an employee.)

From the company's point of view, there is a second benefit as well. The plans usually require employees to *actively* participate in the administration of their retirement benefits. Employees are forced to take responsibility for their own financial future. Employees, and not the company, decide how all the contributions to a 401(k) will be invested. Just as you self-direct your IRA, you may now be able to self-direct your 401(k).

This is probably a good time to try to clear up the confusion some people have between 401(k)s, and company pension plans. Although they can be interrelated, they are *totally* different things.

Your company, and your company alone, funds your pension. You are neither required, nor permitted, to make contributions to your pension plan. Your company, and not you, decides how big that pension will be. (Generally your pension will be determined on the basis of your salary and how long you worked for the company.) But no matter how big, or small, the size of that pension—as we discussed in the previous chapter—is something that your company decides unilaterally.

Your 401(k), as we will see, is a *partnership* between employer and employee. (Most of the funding onus in a 401(k) is clearly yours—although some employers will "match" your contributions to a certain extent. More on this—in just a few pages.)

Now even though pensions and 401(k)s are separate things, they can be intertwined. For example, your company can decide to base your regular pension on your salary either before or after your contribution to your 401(k). So in our example, Martha's pension could be based either on her $50,000 salary (her wages before her 401(k) contribution) or $47,000 (the amount of money on which she'll pay income tax).

Also, some companies have started to cut down on the amount of money they put into their regular pension fund, as a way of offsetting the cost of matching an employee's 401(k) contributions. In effect, they are using the 401(k) plan as a supplement to their "regular" pension plan. And other companies, deciding that escalating benefit costs, including pensions, have gotten out of hand, have even terminated their existing pension plans, distributed the vested pension rights to employees, and then have established new 401(k) plans, limited solely to employee salary-deferral contributions.

It *is,* increasingly, a cold world out there.

Employees love the 401(k) plan because they get a chance to contribute *pretax* dollars to a retirement plan that allows not only their contributions but the dividends, interest, and capital gains those contributions earn to accumulate tax-deferred. We'll see how this works, as we walk through a typical plan. We'll use Martha Skylar's 401(k) as our example.

When Martha's company started the plan, she was asked how much money—if any—she wanted to contribute to the company's 401(k) plan. The option is always the employee's. *You,* not your company, decide how much of your *pretax* salary to contribute to the plan, how much salary you want to "defer"—that is, defer until you take it out, and taxes come due. Usually, the company will give you a range of choices, say between 1% and 15% of your salary.

There is a maximum that is established by law. In 1992, you could defer the lesser of 20% of your gross salary or $8,728. (That number is adjusted each year to account for indexed inflation, and will increase over time.) This amount may be reduced if your employer made other contributions to the plan on your behalf.

Once you establish your contribution, the money is automatically deducted from your paycheck every payday, and deposited in your 401(k) account. Periodically, you will be offered a chance to increase, or decrease, the amount of money you contribute to your 401(k). You'll also receive regular (at least annually, and possibly semiannually or quarterly) statements that will show how your investments are doing.

Contributing to a 401(k) is a truly wonderful idea, for five specific reasons:

1. **It may be your only "pension."** If you change jobs frequently, 401(k)s are vital. You may not stay at any one place long enough to qualify for a significant benefit from a traditional defined benefit plan. Similarly, you could

spend your entire working life at companies that provide either very small pensions or no pensions at all. If you fall into any of these categories, your 401(k), along with your IRA and any other retirement account you set up for yourself, may be, along with Social Security, the only major sources of retirement plan money you're going to have.

2. **It's eminently portable.** Your contributions are always yours alone, and once you become vested in your employer's contributions (if any), you will never forfeit these benefits. You usually will be able to take them with you.

3. **It reduces your reported income and thus current taxes.** As we've seen, Martha Skylar made $50,000 last year, and set her 401(k) contribution at 6% of her income. That means $3,000 of her *pretax* salary was put into the company's 401(k) plan.

   For federal income tax purposes, that $3,000 is treated as deferred compensation, though the contribution is not free of Social Security taxes. So when it came time to fill out her tax returns, Martha was taxed on just $47,000, which is her salary minus her 401(k) contribution. The $3,000 is deferred from federal and state taxes. What's even more important, over the next several decades, is that *all* her earnings in the tax-sheltered plan—the 401(k)—would also be tax-deferred. (Incidentally, not all states will allow salary deferral in terms of their own income taxes.)

   Now, is that $3,000 contribution free of federal taxes forever? Martha will be taxed on that deferred amount when it is actually distributed to her, which will probably happen once she's retired, or she may decide to roll the money over to an IRA, and keep the tax deferral going.

(We'll handle the question of early withdrawals from a 401(k) account in a minute.)

But, sometime, taxes will be paid. These plans are tax-deferred, *not* tax-free.

4. **Not only is the contribution tax-deferred, so are any interest, dividends, and/or capital gains that it earns.** Again, all the money in the 401(k)—the contributions, plus the money those contributions earn—accumulates tax-deferred. Just as in the case of Martha's contribution, she will be taxed on the money her contributions earn only when she ultimately receives it.

In a few moments we'll show you what Martha Skylar is doing with her 401(k). But first, let's look at a typical example of the power of compounding in a tax-deferred account.

Suppose you save only $2,000 annually in your 401(k), and your employer is *not* contributing. In 15 years, if you're earning 10% compounded annually, your money would grow to $69,899. You have contributed, pretax, $30,000—and the total earnings or gains, also tax-deferred, gave you an extra $39,899.

Suppose you *really* think long-term, and you continue putting in $2,000 a year for 15 more years. At the end of the 30 years, your contributions will have totaled only $60,000—but because of the power of tax-deferred compounding, your earnings at 10% would amount to $301,887—for a total of $361,887. (This is when you're entitled, in our view, to shout "Bingo!")

5. **If the company matches all, or part, of your contribution, that money is also tax-deferred.** Let's spend

some time on the company matching idea, because it is, quite frankly, the easiest money you will ever make.

In a typical plan, an employer will match your 401(k) contribution to some degree, say 50 cents for every dollar you put in, up to 6% of your salary. In addition, the employer will also typically limit your overall contribution to a maximum of 15% of your salary. And that is exactly how it works in Martha's case.

So, Martha put $3,000 into the 401(k), and her employer promptly contributed $1,500 on top of that. (By the way, some employers also limit their 401(k) contributions to a dollar-amount cap—perhaps $1,000 or $2,000.) What this means is that Martha has earned a *50% return on her contribution to the 401(k) (or, a minimum of a 50% return on her contribution as soon as she is vested)—even before she decides where that money should be invested.*

And what makes this an even better deal is that this employer contribution, just like the money he put in, is tax-deferred as well.

Always, always, always take full advantage of your employer's matching offer if you're lucky enough to get one. You can't afford not to earn a 50% (or more) return on your money—that is, your contribution.

And that brings us to an intriguing question. Do you fund your 401(k) beyond the point where your employer's matching stops? In Martha's case, her employer is matching her $1 for every $2 she puts in, but the company contribution stops once she has contributed 6% of her income, or $3,000. But should she keep funding her 401(k) up until the limit anyway?

Our answer is yes.

Our guess is, at first blush Martha put in only 6% of her income because that was the ceiling her company established for matching. She figured, rightly, that she would make sure she got every cent her company was willing to provide. Then she quit funding her 401(k), even though under the plan she still could have contributed another $4,500 (the difference between the $3,000 she already put in and the plan limit of $7,500).

Now, Martha's decision not to add to her 401(k) is clearly defensible. Since the company won't match any additional contributions beyond the $3,000, there is no guarantee that she is going to make 50% on any additional money from her own pocket. It fact, the odds are that she won't. Still, putting more money into her 401(k) is a good idea.

Why? Because of the inherent nature of 401(k)s.

That additional $4,500 could have been invested tax-deferred, since it would be deducted from her taxable income. She would have paid federal taxes not on $50,000 (her salary), or $47,000 (her taxable income after her 6% contribution), but on $42,500. And, again, her state and local taxes will also be reduced.

Plus, all the dividends, interest, and capital gains she will be earning on that additional contribution won't be taxed until she actually receives it.

So even if the company won't match that additional contribution, fully funding Martha's 401(k) is still a good deal.

Who Owns All This Money and When?

We've told you to put a lot of money into your 401(k), and we've explained how an employer's matching program works. A logical question right about now would be: Who does that money belong to, and when?

Any money you contribute—$1 or $3,600—to a 401(k) plan is yours forever and ever. It's yours whether you're in the plan for one week or for 10 years. Similarly, any interest, dividends, or capital gains that your contribution earns is also 100% yours, from the moment you start funding your 401(k).

However, the same cannot necessarily be said of your employer's contribution.

If your employer is matching your contribution, you'll probably have to wait a certain period before you are entitled ("vested") to that money. A typical plan would call for you being vested after you've worked for the company for five years. The vesting schedule could be divided into steps. The company could say you are 50% vested in their contributions after three years of service, 80% after four, and all the company's contributions to the fund are 100% yours after five years. (In the preceding chapter on employer pension plans, we discussed at greater length the examples of the two basic types of vesting schedules, cliff and gradual, for employer contributions to pension plans.)

If you change jobs, you usually get to take all the money that is yours—your contribution, plus the money it has earned, plus the portion of the company's contribution that is now vested in you, plus the money it has earned. This question of whether or not to roll over is so important—and the tax impact can be so *significant*—that we've devoted an entire chapter, Chapter 25, to the rollover nuances. In that chapter we'll also lay out for you the stringent rules concerning withholding, tax penalties, and time deadlines that govern rollovers.

Where Do You Put All This Money?

We've been stressing how important it is for you to fund your 401(k), but we haven't talked about where those funds should be invested. Now in this section, we will.

While you can put your IRA investments into just about anything you want (see Chapter 11), you are much more limited with what you can do with your 401(k) money. You can only invest in a preapproved menu of choices your company provides.

That makes sense, since the company is administering the plan. They want to keep life simple.

In a typical 401(k), you will be offered anywhere between four and six investment choices. The Department of Labor suggests that employers should offer at least three different choices—and some of the latest plans offered have included up to ten choices.

Among the choices you'll usually find:

- **Guaranteed investment contracts (GIC).** That's a fancy name for what is a pretty simple idea. In essence, this is a contract between you (or your plan's trustee) and the issuer, generally an insurance company or a bank. Since you are, in effect, a lender to the financial institution, it's important that the bank or the insurance company is financially sound. Under the terms of a GIC you will receive your original investment plus a specified rate of return over a specific time period. The maturities of the investments could range from a matter of months or years—up to four or six, or even eight years. You'll know ahead of time exactly how much interest you'll be earning in a GIC.

- **A stock fund (or trusts).** Typically, your company will offer a choice of investing in a mutual fund or perhaps a unit investment trust, which invests primarily in stocks. The company might offer a growth fund, an income fund, or a growth and income fund (which could include bonds). It may even let you invest in one, two, or all three.

- **A bond fund.** Another fund might concentrate solely on corporate bonds. Its primary objective would be income, but a secondary objective could be growth as the fund would buy or sell bonds in the hopes of taking advantage of economic and market conditions.

- **Company stock.** (In Chapter 10—on employee stock plans—we'll go into pros and cons of employees' slowly but surely building up equity in their own company.)

- **A money market fund.** These are mutual funds that invest in short-term debt securities and seek to maintain a constant value of $1 per share. Since these are considered to be virtually the equivalent of cash, there is a high safety factor here, but an investment in the fund is not insured or federally guaranteed. Although you would probably always want some money in money market funds, consider them as a "parking" place. It is wise to keep some money here as part of your asset allocation strategy—but the majority of your retirement assets should be elsewhere.

These are the usual choices. As we said, some employers could end up offering you as many as 10 different options, but in all cases—with the exception of allowing you to invest in your own company's stock—you'll have to buy units or shares of one of the investments offered. You won't be able to buy a specific stock, or specific bond. You'll have to buy into a fund, or funds. That may seem to you to be restrictive but remember—your employer is offering you several different investments for a very sound reason: diversification. Also, in a mutual fund, professionals will manage the investments, and secondly, you can be assured that your investments—in a mutual fund—will be diversified.

When you buy a fund, all income, dividends, or capital gains distributions are automatically reinvested in additional shares of the same investment choice. Also, when you are contributing a specific dollar amount from every paycheck, you automatically buy more shares of the fund (or your company stock) when the price goes down, and fewer when the price goes up.

Of course, the price of the funds or stock will vary over a year. The best way to look at dollar cost averaging in a 401(k) is this: in a rising market your average cost for each share you've purchased over a twelve-month period may be lower than the average market price. (In just about every scenario we can think of—whether you're investing in tax-advantaged retirement accounts or nonretirement taxable accounts—we're a strong advocate of the two staples of long-term investing: dollar cost averaging and automatic reinvestment of dividends. These ideas are simple, and they are efficient. These "automatic" features are important enough for us to devote an entire chapter, Chapter 13, to them.)

On the positive side of the limited investment menu, you'll have the choice of dividing your investments up among the choices offered. You'll invest each payroll deduction by allocating percentages rather than dollars; that is, let's say you put 60% in a growth fund, 30% in a bond fund, and 10% in cash, or the money market fund. All you have to do is make sure your allocation adds up to 100%.

A Betrothal Doesn't Mean an Eternity

And no matter what investments you choose, you won't be stuck with them forever. You're not married to them. Periodically—perhaps daily, or once a month, once a quarter, once a year (your company decides how often)—you'll be able to change your current funding choices. So, as your investment objectives change, or economic conditions shift, you'll be able to move your money around.

Okay, now that you know what your options are, where should you put the money?

Let's start with something we've stressed before: The "safest" investment may not be the best investment.

People tend to be too conservative with their retirement investments. They figure, and rightly so, that 401(k)s, IRAs, and the like will make up a big part of their investment portfolio once they're retired, and they want to make sure nothing happens to their retirement money. As a result, they opt for the "safest" investment they can find. Preserving your assets in retirement is a praiseworthy goal, but if you're too conservative you may actually do the opposite, and end up losing ground, because of inflation.

You see that with 401(k)s. Until recently, the majority of the money invested in 401(k)s had been in GICs. This is probably a mistake, unless you are very close to retirement. It's also a mistake—we believe—to put everything in fixed income investments, or in cash or money market funds. As we've said, over long periods of time stocks have historically provided a better return than any other investment you can find. In investing, the idea is to minimize the risk, and maximize the return, and over the long haul, investing in stocks has achieved those goals quite well.

Since we are steadfast in the belief that over the long term equity will outpace just about everything else, we will pepper you with several examples. Here's one historical comparison—from 1925 to 1990:

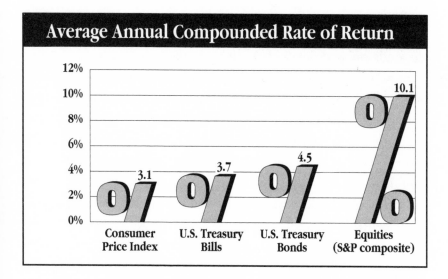

But maybe stocks are not for you.

We can talk until the cows come home about how there are risks with *everything* you can do with your money—even sticking it under your mattress. (Your money can literally go up in smoke if there is a fire, or you can be robbed, and even if those awful things don't happen you risk losing your purchasing power because of inflation.) However, if putting all of your money in a stock fund, or even a bond fund makes you nervous, don't do it. Diversify instead. Spread your assets among several different investments.

The very fact that the trend today is for employers to add more choices to your 401(k) investment menu is testimony to the wisdom of diversification. Since you're in charge of your own 401(k) portfolio, our counsel: Take advantage of the expansion of choices that may be offered to you, and diversify.

If you do diversify, your overall return will be a weighted average—a mixture—of the returns of all your investments. So, a bad performance by one may be offset by a good performance of another.

How should those investments be weighted? That, of course, depends on your level of risk tolerance.

In any investment account you control, we advocate that you allocate assets—that is, that you vary your investment choices within the three basic categories of bonds, equity, and cash—in order to reduce portfolio risk, preserve assets, and improve total return. You face some risks in every investment. With cash you face an inflation risk; with bonds, credit risk; and with equity, market risks. But all risks can be moderated through diversification.

The precise allocation for you will also depend on personal factors—such as your age, your expected retirement date, your other retirement assets, and finally, your tolerance of risk. This theory is so central to our thesis of "investing smarter" that we offer you two chapters, 15 and 16, devoted principally to the exploration of asset allocation and risk tolerance.

Suppose You Want to Get to Your 401(k) Money Early?

Don't.

At least, don't if you can possibly avoid it. Withdrawing the money early—before you're 59½, or before you actually retire—is almost always a very expensive proposition.

First of all, your plan may limit withdrawals. If it does allow them, you have to pay taxes on the money you withdraw. Remember, the money was being treated as deferred compensation. Once you take it out, the money is added to current salary and treated as ordinary income. Secondly, there could be a 10% penalty tacked on, over and above the tax, if you withdraw the money before you are 59½.

And finally, taking money out early from a retirement account is just *not* a good idea, if you want to have a long, happy, financially secure retirement.

A better idea—if you have an emergency—would be to *borrow* from your plan. Not all employers allow loans (and if you are permitted to borrow, you'll probably have to repay the loan within five years). Check with your employer to see what's permissible.

Always, always, always fund your 401(k) to the maximum. If you end up changing jobs frequently during your career, or work for companies with little or no other retirement benefits, the money you put away for yourself may be the only significant "pension" or retirement nest egg you will have come retirement.

CHAPTER 9

403(b) Retirement Plans

This is similar to a 401(k) plan—but one with a twist: It's a personal retirement plan designed for people who work either for certain nonprofit organizations or for school systems. These plans may also be called Tax-Deferred Annuities (TDAs). While the similarities are many, there are also considerable differences, as you'll soon see.

Employees of not-for-profits and educational institutions are not eligible for 401(k) plans. All institutions that are considered tax-exempt under Section 501(c)(3) of the Internal Revenue Code are prohibited from offering 401(k) plans, from ambulance corps to zoological societies. (Some nonprofit organizations have been grandfathered in by the Tax Reform Act of 1986. Most, however, have not.)

Like the 401(k), the 403(b) is named for the applicable section of the Internal Revenue Code, and the similarities don't stop there.

The similarities between the 401(k), and a 403(b):

1. Contributions are pretax. This reduces your current income for tax purposes.

2. Contributions can take the form of payroll deductions.

3. Dividends, earnings, interest, and/or capital gains are tax-deferred.

4. Your employer can match some of your contributions.

5. The plan may be the only pension you are offered at work, or it may be supplemental to another plan (or plans).

6. Both plans—403(b) and 401(k)—may allow loans.

Now the differences:

1. Investments in a 403(b) by law are limited to two categories: annuities (see Chapter 18) and mutual funds (see Chapter 19). This makes sense. In a 401(k), among other investments, you may be able to invest in your company's stock. But if you're employed by a nonprofit, or a school, you don't work for a company, so there is no company stock to buy.

    But while you are limited to two *types* of investments, the *choices* within those investment categories can be very broad.

Not All Nonprofits Are "Charitable" Nonprofits

Most local, state, and federal employees—although they obviously work for nonprofit entities—are not eligible for 403(b)s. They have their own pension plans, as we have discussed earlier. To be eligible for a 403(b) plan, you have to work for either an educational or "charitable" organization which is tax-exempt under section 501(c)(3).

In a 401(k), your employer—for ease of operations—will typically limit you to a handful of investment choices. A usual array would include a money market fund, a guaranteed investment contract, and two or three mutual funds. Objectives of the mutual funds might range from income to growth, or a fund could even be balanced between stocks for growth and bonds for income.

In a 403(b), your employer selects the plan vendor. You may have hundreds of different mutual funds to choose from. That, of course, makes it much easier to find a fund that will exactly fit your needs.

2. The annual salary deferral limits are slightly different. For the 1992 tax year, for example, the regular maximum 403(b) contribution was $9,500, or 20% of compensation, while, as we said, it was $8,728 or 15% for 401(k)s.

3. Certain eligible employees may be able to make a "catch-up" contribution. There are a number of provisions in the regulations governing 403(b) plans that allow participants to "catch up" for previous years of service in which contributions were not made at a maximum rate.

   This "catch up" is a wonderful idea. Here's generally how it works. Unlike 401(k)s, where the 15% limit on your contributions applies to this year's pay, for 403(b)s, the 20% limit is based on your salary adjusted for all the years you have worked for your employer. You have to reduce this total by any tax-deferred contributions you or your employer have made over this time, but, if the contributions have been low in years past, you may be able to contribute more than 20% of any year's salary until you "catch up."

An additional "catch-up" provision allows education, hospital, church, and some health and welfare service workers to raise the $9,500 limit to as high as $12,500 after 15 years with an employer.

Let's say you have worked at least 15 years at a tax-exempt organization, one that does not provide another pension plan. You're understandably nervous about retirement, and while you could kick yourself for not contributing to the salary-deferral 403(b) that has been offered to you over the years, the plain fact is that you haven't.

The "catch-up" provisions are one of the very few opportunities in life where you get a second chance.

Under special provisions in the law, there are substitute contribution calculations and special limits for church workers and for workers in their last year of service. In your last year of service with your employer you may be able to make a "catch-up" contribution of up to $30,000—if your employer agrees. So, if you make $30,000 a year—and you want to catch up as quickly as possible—every single dime you make that year theoretically could go into the plan. (This, of course, would be most unusual. We concede you might starve that one year, if all your income were to go to the "catch-up," so you may want to spread the "catch-up" over several years). As happens so many times with pensions, the formula that governs 403(b) "catch-up" contributions is complicated, so see your tax adviser (and also read IRS publication 571) for complete details of how it works. We emphasize that your employer *does have to agree* to this catch-up provision.

Many employees who work for schools—whether elementary, secondary, or universities—have 403(b) plans offered to them as supplemental retirement plans. They typically have essential retirement coverage through a state pension plan, and then they are offered a 403(b) plan as a voluntary way to supplement that pension.

Our advice? Even though there is other retirement coverage, fund that 403(b) to the maximum, if it is humanly possible. As in a 401(k), your employer may be matching your contribution—$1 for every $2 you contribute is common—and any time you can get a *guaranteed* 50% return on your money, take it. (Also, as in 401(k) plans, your employer may limit his 403(b) contributions to your plan.)

There is one other point to make about 403(b)s. It is not uncommon—especially among college professors—to change jobs. If you have a 403(b), the money can tag along with you to your new job. You may simply take it out of one 403(b) and put it in the program offered by your new employer. Changing from one 403(b) custodian to another is allowed by law, but your former employer has the option not to approve it. For many years changing 403(b) custodians was somewhat restricted, but in recent years employers have been more generous in allowing transfers.

A 403(b) plan is for employees of not-for-profit organizations—primarily those that are charitable or educational.

These plans are similar to popular 401(k) plans—but the differences are considerable. One major distinction: your investments are limited to mutual funds or annuities. A 403(b) plan might be supplemental to another retirement plan, or it might be the only plan offered to you.

CHAPTER 10

Owning Your Company Stock

Of all the various kinds of retirement investments, employee stock plans are particularly beloved these days—by both employers and employees. And it is easy to see why. Stock plans are usually a win-win for everyone. (An early word of caution about employee stock plans: no matter how wonderful a deal they are, be careful that you don't overload on your company's stock. When it comes to your retirement assets, diversification should be the rule.)

Let's look at employee stock plans from the employee's point of view first. Many stock plans are part of qualified retirement plans, meaning that they are tax-advantaged. But to our minds, even if your specific stock purchase plan is not tax-advantaged, it should be considered part of your retirement portfolio, if you'll be buying the stock as a long-term investment.

From the corporate point of view, stock plans can be a smart way to increase employee pride and productivity. Owning stock in your company encourages you to think and act like an owner.

If you are a part owner of the place, you'll go out of your way to watch expenses. You'll turn out the lights when you go home. (After all, it's *your* money you're saving.)

Plus, offering stock in the company is a way of attracting, and retaining, valued employees. The National Center for Employee Ownership estimates that more than 11 million employees are currently covered by some 10,000 employee stock plans.

How You Might Get to Own the Stock

If any stock is *given,* at no cost, to you by your employer, there is no decision to make. Take it, and be grateful, unless it's given—as will sometimes happen—as a part of a salary- or wage-reduction plan.

Troubled companies sometimes do this. This extreme action can be part of an overall bargaining agreement to cut wages and benefits. The alternative may be bankruptcy, or simply shutting down.

In this case, accept the stock, and hope for the best. (And, of course, you may have to pay taxes on any stock that comes your way.)

There are other ways you might be offered company stock.

Options. The name says it all. You're given an option to buy (usually a set number of) shares at a fixed price. That price is generally equal to the current market value when the option is granted. The option has an expiration date. It could be one, five, or even ten years hence.

In some cases, the option will be forfeitable if you leave the company before the option's expiration date. In other cases, even if you leave the company, but are vested in the stock options, you won't forfeit them.

Your decision on whether or not to exercise the option is simply a matter of value. Will you make a profit when you exercise the option? That depends on whether the market value of the stock is higher than the option price. If it is, you'll make a profit if you exercise your option. If it isn't, you simply don't exercise the option. (Sometimes it's possible to exercise the option, that is, buy the stock, and then turn around and sell it—all on the same day.)

Restricted stock plans. Some plans will give you the stock, at no cost to you, at the end of a fixed term, say, three years from now, provided you are still with the company.

This type of plan usually goes by the much more descriptive name of a "golden handcuff."

Your employer is looking for a way to guarantee that you'll stay with him for a long period of time and figures this may be the best way to do it. If you have a lot to lose by leaving, he figures you won't leave. (Think of this deal as a deferred, contingent bonus.)

Stock purchase plans. You may be offered the right to purchase company stock periodically (generally every quarter) at a cost that is less than the current market price. (A typical discount would be 15%.) The plan usually gives you the right to invest up to a fixed dollar amount that is usually tied to some percentage of your salary.

Once you've bought the stock, it's yours to love and cherish, or to sell instantly (to make a quick profit—taxable, of course—on that 15% discount. Although, as always, we would suggest you think long term, even if the stock is not earmarked for your retirement account).

Buying stock in a retirement plan. Although in recent years many corporations have been vigorously cutting their benefit plans, some of the most highly regarded *Fortune 1,000* companies—those known for providing employee perks ranging from extensive health and fitness plans to sabbaticals—have been adding corporate stock purchase plans to their retirement benefits menu.

The opportunity might be offered to you as just a stock purchase plan, or it might be presented through another qualified program such as the company's defined contribution pension plan, a profit-sharing plan, or a salary-deferral, i.e., 401(k), program.

What is particularly significant is that many employers in this top tier are matching whatever contributions their employees make.

Let us give you a couple of examples of how this matching works. In both cases we'll assume your annual salary is $50,000.

Company A. You are allowed to contribute up to 10% of your salary, and the company will match 50% of whatever you contribute.

Say that you go for the max, and decide to put $5,000 into the stock. (The contributions will be coming through a payroll deduction, so, in effect, you will be dollar cost averaging your stock purchases throughout the year. When the price is up, you're buying fewer shares, and when it's down, you're buying more. See Chapter 13 for a full explanation of how this long-term investing strategy works.)

The company contribution of $2,500 (50% of your $5,000) means that you have an instant 50% return on your $5,000 investment.

Here's what the situation looks like at the outset:

Owning Your Company Stock

Cash Contributions	
From you	$5,000.00
From your company	2,500.00
Total	$7,500.00
Investments	
Company stock	$7,500.00

Company B. Here the rules are that you can contribute up to 5% of your salary to the plan and the company will match 75% of what you put in.

But this plan, by design, is more complicated than it first appears. Of the company's match, 25% is in the form of company stock. The rest of the company's match plus your contribution is invested by you, in one or more of several different mutual funds that the company makes available as part of its range of retirement investments.

Here's what that situation would look like:

Owning Your Company Stock

Contributions	
From you — cash	$2,500.00
From your company — cash	1,406.25
— stock	468.75
Total	$4,375.00
Investments	
Company stock	$468.75
Other investments	3,906.25
Total	$4,375.00

Buying It Today Doesn't Mean Holding It Forever

Just because you have bought your company's stock doesn't mean you have to hold it forever. As in virtually all investment accounts, once you've bought shares through an employee stock purchase plan you can sell them at any time. But if you're buying the stock within a qualified plan, such as a 401(k), once you sell the stock there may be a limit on the number of times during the year when you can reinvest the sale proceeds in other investments, other than in money market shares. (Limitations of once a quarter for the other investments are typical.)

Similarly, just because today you are putting a fixed percentage of your retirement investments in company stock doesn't mean you are stuck with that percentage forever.

Suppose you are currently using 25% of your 401(k) contribution to buy company stock. At some point in the near future, you might decide you have enough—remember, you want to be diversified—and you might stop buying for a while. (You would still contribute to your retirement account; you'd just put the money into some other 401(k) investment, such as one of the equity or bond funds your company is offering.)

Or you might well decide to do the opposite. You become extremely bullish on your company, so you switch out of your equity fund, and decide to put half of your corporate retirement account into your company stock.

The Pros and Cons of Buying Company Stock

We certainly understand why a company would welcome your investment in its stock. In addition to making you feel like an owner, it may help to insulate the company from takeover threats.

But what about it from your perspective?

You should look at the potential investment in your company's stock as you would any investment. It is all very good to be loyal to the company, but it is *your* money, and not the company's, that we are talking about.

Your company stock, compared to the investment options in equity (such as a fund), may have a higher risk of price fluctuation and loss of principal. This is because each of the other equity investments in a retirement program will probably be a diversified portfolio of stocks, whereas your company stock is just one issue. But by the same token, your company stock may well have the highest potential among the investments for increasing sharply in value. So if you have the patience for riding out the inevitable swings—the volatility of any one stock—you may be rewarded.

Across this country, there are some employees who eventually retired as millionaires because they got company stock, and held on to it.

It Works on a Big Scale

A few of America's largest companies—with 100,000 or more employees—have been so adept at offering various stock plans to their employees that up to 25% of their stock is in their employees' hands.

On the con side, whatever your company's prospects, if you have already accumulated a sizable number of shares—perhaps through options, possibly through a pension plan—look again at the wisdom of buying another hunk of stock. Remember the need to diversify. Use the same evaluation techniques that you would apply to *all* your other holdings. You shouldn't be overloaded with one stock, even if it belongs to your company.

Don't be blinded by your proximity.

If you're one of the trees, it is hard to see the forest.

On the pro side, you do know a lot about your company. You know its strengths, its weaknesses. You know the industry, and its trends. You may well know the company's long-term plans. All this puts you ahead of others. After all, a fundamental rule of investing is to know what you are buying.

If you're basically impressed with your company's management (you may even be part of that management), you might conclude that the company's future is your future, and buy (a lot of) the stock.

> *Putting company stock into your retirement portfolio can be good for you, and your company. It helps you think and act (and share in the company's success) like an owner. Just make sure it's all part of your general diversification strategy.*

CHAPTER 11

IRAs:
Everyone's Retirement Plan

There are all sorts of ways to measure the importance of Individual Retirement Accounts. You can count the number of people who have an IRA: 25 million.

You could point out how quickly money has poured into IRAs since they were created in the mid-1970s.

You could even tally the total amount of IRA assets now held nationwide: $647 billion. (IRAs were created in 1974, as a part of the Employee Retirement Income Security Act [ERISA], and money began dribbling into the doors of a few financial institutions in 1975. However, the real growth occurred in the 1980s. Total IRA assets were $26 billion in 1981. They had grown to $647 billion a decade later, an increase of 2,490%.)

But our own favorite benchmark doesn't involve numbers, but TV. We knew IRAs were important when on a clear, cool April night back in the 1980s they were immortalized on prime time in "Hill Street Blues."

Remember that Emmy-award-winning police drama? The show always opened each week with the grizzled sergeant giving his troops the warnings of the day. That opening scene always ended the same way, with the sergeant's plea to "be careful out there." But on that pivotal spring night, just before the sergeant delivered the line that would cause the opening credits to roll, the camera panned across the beat-up blackboard in the squad room, and there—in a bold chalk scribble—was the charge:

Well, we concede it was just a flicker, and we may be the only people in America who saw it that night, but it will *always* be a milestone to us.

As the psychologists tell us, television can teach, and that's certainly true here. Do "be careful out there," and, definitely, do open your IRA today.

The Best Small Tax Shelter

As we've said, IRAs are still the best small tax shelter there is. (As we've also said, when you consider larger plans, 401(k)s are superior.)

An IRA is really an extraordinary savings device for a passel of reasons:

- An IRA is a tax-deferred savings account.

- An IRA—particularly a rollover—is an important adjunct to estate planning.

- An IRA is a perfect account for high-income investments— since income taxation is deferred.

- In an IRA, there's great flexibility to contributions in that, for whatever reasons, you can skip a year—if you have to— and resume contributions the next year.

- In an IRA, there's great flexibility in taking out the money between ages 59½ and 70½.

More explanation on all of the above points throughout the rest of the chapter.

Until recently, many people had forgotten how basic the IRA is. Prior to the Tax Reform Act, which became effective in 1987, an individual, subject to a couple of restrictions, could contribute up to $2,000 a year to his IRA. Whatever he contributed would be deducted—dollar for dollar—from his reported income. The tax deduction, in effect, worked as 401(k) contributions do now. After the 1986 Tax Reform Act reduced the eligibility for tax-deductible contributions, there was a sharp falloff in IRA contributions over the next few years.

However, recently IRAs have started to come back into favor. There are two reasons for this renewed growth:

First, people are becoming more aware of the aging of America.

They understand that since they are going to live longer than ever, they will need every source of retirement income they can get their hands on. When you start thinking like that, you understand that IRAs can serve as a vital supplement to your retirement income.

Second, people are beginning to realize that even if they can't get a tax deduction for their IRA contributions, the money in their IRA accounts still grows *tax-deferred.* As we will explain in detail later on, all the dividends, capital gains, and/or interest produced by your IRA investments are not taxed until you withdraw the money.

First, though, the basics.

IRA Class 101

Here's why an IRA should be the cornerstone of your personal savings program: it's just about the only retirement savings plan that you, and you alone, have complete control over.

As long as you have earned income of at least $2,000, you can contribute up to $2,000 a year to an IRA. That money is 100% vested from the moment you put it in. It's all yours. You direct it. You decide what it should be invested in. You decide how it's going to grow.

You might work for one employer for 30 years, and you may be lucky enough to have a superb pension plan. Or over the course of your life you may work for many different employers. Or you might be self-employed. Your employer pension plans might be good, indifferent, or even worse, nonexistent. It doesn't matter. *You should have an IRA.* Why would you even think of passing up an opportunity that at worst lets your retirement savings grow tax-deferred, and at best is tax-deductible as well?

How to Tell If Your IRA Is Deductible

Here are the current rules on whether or not your IRA contribution is tax-deductible.

If neither you nor your spouse is an active participant in an employer-sponsored plan, then you can take a full tax deduction—up to $2,000 per year *for each of you*—as long as each of you has earned income of at least $2,000.

This is tricky—because the IRS may consider you to be an *active* participant in a plan even if you're *not yet vested.* However, if—for whatever reason—you or your employer make no contribution to the plan for you in a given year, and you receive no other allocation or forfeiture in the plan, then you're entitled to a full IRA tax deduction for that particular year. (In this particular case, the IRS says you weren't "covered" by the plan that year.)

What plans are they talking about? Basically any qualified pension, profit-sharing, or stock bonus plan. That would include 403(b) and 401(k) plans, and even some government-sponsored retirement programs.

But even if you, or your spouse, are considered "active participants" in a plan, you're still entitled to take a full or partial deduction if your modified adjusted gross income (MAGI) is less than $50,000 combined, for married individuals filing jointly, or less than $10,000 for each spouse, when married individuals file separately.

If you are single, you can take a full or partial deduction *even* if you're covered by a qualified retirement plan, as long as your modified adjusted gross income is below $35,000. If you're single and *not* covered by any plan, you can take a full IRA deduction regardless of your income.

Okay, you want to know how you go about figuring out your modified adjusted gross income, in order to determine whether you qualify for a full tax deduction. (We'll talk about partial deductions in a minute.)

Here goes:

How to Figure Your Modified Adjusted Gross Income

1. Using your IRS form 1040, enter:	
a. Your total income	$
b. Deduction for self-employment tax	$
c. Self-employed health insurance deduction	$
d. Keogh retirement plan and self-employed SEP deduction	$
e. Penalties on early withdrawals of savings	$
f. Alimony paid	$
2. Add items b through f:	$
3. Subtract line 2 from your total income (Line a.)	$

The remainder is your modified adjusted gross income.

This *is* going to be confusing. Sorry, but we are talking about an IRS regulation. There is one thing to note going in: the formula that you, or your accountant, use for determining your adjusted gross income for income tax purposes is different from the modified adjusted gross income formula needed to determine your IRA deduction. Let your accountant sort out the differences.

What happens if you are making too much money to qualify for a full tax deduction?

It depends. If you are married and filing jointly and your combined adjusted income is more than $50,000 and one of you is covered by an employer plan, you are out of luck. There is no deduction. Similarly, there is no deduction if you are single and your modified adjusted gross income tops $35,000.

However, if you are married and filing jointly, and your modified adjusted gross income is between $40,000 and $50,000, or you are single, and your MAGI is between $25,000 and $35,000, you qualify for a partial deduction.

The following table tells you how large that deduction will be:

Partial Deductions—IRA

Single Filer	Filing Jointly	Maximum Taxable Deduction
Income up to $25,000	Income up to $40,000	$2,000 *
26,000	41,000	1,800
27,000	42,000	1,600
28,000	43,000	1,400
29,000	44,000	1,200
30,000	45,000	1,000
31,000	46,000	800
32,000	47,000	600
33,000	48,000	400
34,000	49,000	200
35,000 +	50,000 +	0

* Per account

Reminder: If you, as a single, or if you and your spouse, are not active participants in an employer retirement plan, a full deduction is allowed regardless of your Modified Adjusted Gross Income or your income tax filing status.

Breathing Room

One of the nice things about IRAs is that if you, like most people, are a calendar-year taxpayer (that is, your tax year ends December 31), you are given some breathing room when it comes to opening your IRA and making your IRA contribution.

Even though, for most other purposes, your tax year ends when the year does, you can still make your IRA contribution up until your tax filing deadline, usually April 15.

In essence, the government is giving you a three-and-a-half-month grace period in which to make a contribution to your Individual Retirement Account. There is no need to go scurrying around on December 31 to either open or fund your IRA.

Taking the Maximum

We know of some working spouses who have high incomes—$100,000 or more—and are not covered by any plan, who will take the full deduction for their own IRA, and then encourage their spouse, who is essentially nonworking, to earn at least $2,000, in order to take that $2,000 as deduction.

The perfectly legal result is that when it comes time to file their joint return, the couple reports $102,000 in income and takes a $4,000 tax deduction—$2,000 for him; $2,000 for her.

You can even open your IRA and fund it after you've filed your taxes.

Suppose you know you're going to get a refund. Like most people, you'd file your 1040 as early as possible, say February 1. But let's say that as of February 1 you still haven't made your IRA contribution for the previous year. No problem. The IRS will let you take a credit for your contribution, as long as you actually make the contribution by April 15.

One note of caution: No extensions on IRA contributions are permissible, even if you obtain an extension for filing your taxes. April 15 is the very last day on which you can establish or contribute to your IRA.

But just because the government gives you the extra time doesn't mean you should take it. You shouldn't. The power of tax-deferred compounding should compel you to make your contribution as early in the year as possible. You want your money working for you tax-deferred as long as possible.

The following table gives you a quick look at what happens if you contribute $2,000 to your IRA on January 1 of your tax year, as compared to what happens if you make that $2,000 contribution on the very last day possible: April 15 of the next year, some 15½ months later. In both cases, of course, you'd receive the tax deduction, if you are entitled to it. However, contributing early will make your IRA worth a whole lot more.

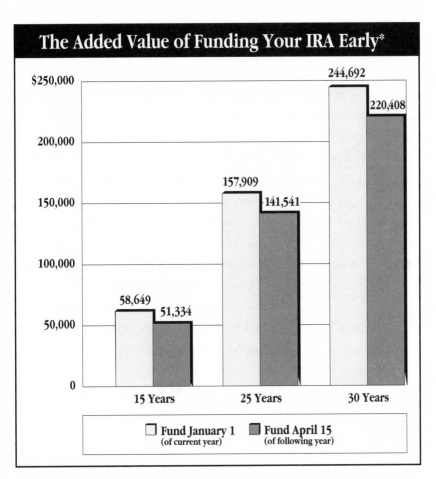

The Added Value of Funding Your IRA Early*

* Assuming a $2,000 contribution each year, and an 8% return on the investments.

Turning $5.47 a Day Into Tens of Thousands

Given that IRAs are one of the very few tax breaks still available, we strongly recommend you be systematic in funding your IRA account. We've found it's easier to do that if you consider your IRA as a fixed obligation such as your house or car payment. Make funding your IRA part of your budget obligations. Put $2,000 ($166.66 a month) into your IRA this year, and next, and the year after, and keep the string going until you retire.

If you stew about the big ticket of $2,000, and even if the monthly tab of $166 seems like a lot, then why not adjust your thinking down to a daily IRA bill of $5.47? You say you can't possibly cut your spending $2,000? We dare you to claim—with a straight face—that you can't somehow cut your daily spending by $5.47. To prompt your penny-pinching, we suggest that all you have to do is think ahead to retirement—years or decades from now—when the $5.47 will have compounded to tens or even hundreds of thousands of dollars. (In just a moment we'll give you some dramatic examples of how the $5.47 does compound.)

That's our advice. But in truth, you don't have any legal obligation to follow it. Since IRAs are voluntary retirement plans, you are not legally required to make an annual contribution, once you've opened an account.

Since your IRA is voluntary, you can be erratic in funding it, for whatever reason. In most employer pension plans, pension contributions can't be ignored just because the company had a bad year, or doesn't feel like contributing. The employer *must* fund the plan, or possibly face the wrath of the Labor and/or Treasury Department.

If, for whatever reason, you wake up at tax-paying time and realize that no money has gone into your IRA during the past year, what should you do?

Our first advice is to borrow the money elsewhere. (Remember, there is no extension allowed when it comes to IRA contributions.)

One strategy that might work well for you is borrowing on the house (see Chapter 23). Write a $2,000 check against your home equity credit line. This way, you'll be able to make your $2,000 contribution *and* the interest on what is in essence a loan to yourself will be, in most cases, completely tax-deductible. (Of course, you should pay the loan back eventually—you're paying yourself back.)

Our second suggestion: Fund your IRA to the extent you can. Put in $1,000, or even $500. Something is better than nothing. (It's your retirement we're talking about.)

If you honestly and truly can't contribute anything—there is no money available from any source—then, with great reluctance, skip that year, with the understanding that you'll make the full contribution the next year, when you are in better fiscal shape.

Now discussions—in the abstract—about the need to save money are not convincing. So let us give you a graphic example of why you ought to be funding your IRA to the maximum.

Let's say that in 1993 your IRA is worth $20,000, and we'll assume you're going to add the maximum contribution of $2,000 per year for the next two decades.

The chart on page 198 demonstrates what the power of time and compounding can mean to you. We show what happens if you earn, over the next two decades, 6%, 8%, 10%, and 12%.

Earlier we said it's more important long-term to have your money grow tax-deferred than it is to get a yearly tax deduction. Note that in this projection if you are earning 8% annually from 1994 on you are earning more in tax-deferred interest, dividends, and gains each year than you are actually contributing. In fact, by the twentieth year, your annual tax-deferred earnings of $14,000-plus are some seven times your annual $2,000 contribution.

It may not seem too dazzling to move up from 6% to 8%, but it

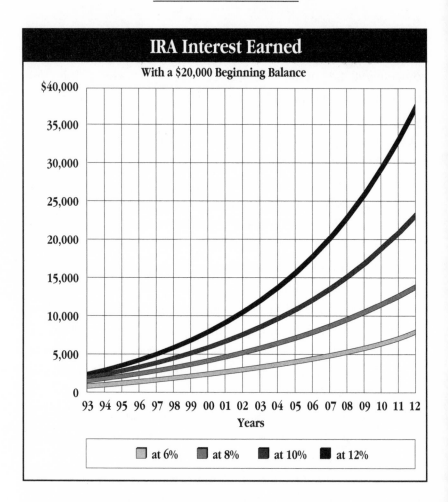

IRA Interest Earned

With a $20,000 Beginning Balance

is considerably harder to move from 8% to 10%, and the last incremental move in this scenario—from 10% to 12%—will be much, much harder to pull off in terms of consistent investment performance over the two decades.

Taxable Returns versus Tax-Deferred Returns

For our next example, let's say you're starting a brand-new IRA. What follows is a table that shows how a $2,000 annual investment in a tax-deferred IRA grows faster than the same amount in a taxable investment. (We're assuming that you're in a 31% tax bracket, and we're also assuming that you're not eligible to take any part of your IRA as a tax deduction.)

This example makes clear what the tax bite does to you.

As you can see from the chart on page 200, after 30 years of earning 8% in the IRA, the $2,000 annual investment has grown to a nest egg of $244,692. After 30 years at 8% a taxable investment would have grown to just $153,401. By compounding tax-deferred in the IRA you would earn $91,291 more.

And while you're contrasting taxable and tax-deferred returns, also take a last look at the difference that the increased earnings hikes of 2% can produce over the three decades in your IRA:

8%	10%	12%
$244,692	$361,887	$540,585

What Are IRA Age Limits?

Can you be too young, or too old, to contribute to an IRA?

No and yes.

You can't be too young, as long as you have taxable earnings.

You can, however, be too old. You can continue to put money into your IRA, provided you have earned income, until you turn

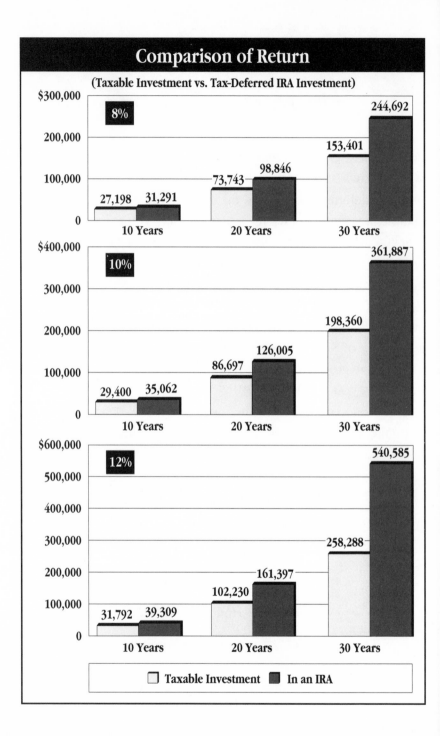

Comparison of Return

(Taxable Investment vs. Tax-Deferred IRA Investment)

8%

	10 Years	20 Years	30 Years
Taxable	27,198	73,743	153,401
IRA	31,291	98,846	244,692

10%

	10 Years	20 Years	30 Years
Taxable	29,400	86,697	198,360
IRA	35,062	126,005	361,887

12%

	10 Years	20 Years	30 Years
Taxable	31,792	102,230	258,288
IRA	39,309	161,397	540,585

☐ Taxable Investment ■ In an IRA

70½. To be precise, if you haven't hit 70½ by the end of the calendar year, you can still fund your IRA. You are not allowed to add money after that. (Although you can continue to fund your SEP and Keogh plan virtually forever, as long as you have earned income, there may come a time when you are both putting money into and taking money out of your SEP or Keogh—all to your tax advantage. More on this in the next chapter).

Spousal Accounts

In two-income families, both the husband and wife can have an IRA, and both, as we've said, can contribute up to $2,000 a year into their accounts.

But a spousal IRA can also be opened for a nonworking spouse. The law says that between the working spouse and the nonworking spouse, the two accounts can be funded to a maximum of $2,250 per year.

You can split up the money any way you like, provided that not

---

Even a Baby (with Earned Income) Can Have an IRA

Children who are 12 years old and have a paper route can—and do—have IRAs. Children who are 15 and take a summer job in a fast-food shop have IRAs.

The youngest IRA believer that we know about is six months old. (Talk about long-range planning!) The infant "works" as a model, is naturally filing a tax return, so her parents set up both an IRA and a Keogh plan for her. (If the minor's IRA is a self-directed account, allowing the minor to buy stocks or bonds, a guardian, usually a parent, will actually have to open the account for the benefit of the minor.)

201

more than $2,000 goes into either account. You can put $2,000 in your IRA, and $250 in your nonworking spouse's account.

That's the traditional way. But you don't have to be bound by tradition. You could divide it equally: $1,125 in each. (Remember, under the law, you can't own IRAs jointly. You and your working or nonworking spouse *must* have separate IRAs.) You can even put $250 in your account, and $2,000 in your spouse's.

"Why on earth would I do that?" you say. "I earned that money. It should go into *my* account!"

We understand that position, but assuming that you and your spouse plan to spend the rest of your days together, giving her (him) most of your annual IRA contribution *makes sense.* Instead of having your IRA pass to your spouse at your death, you are giving the money to her now. And it can be a lot of money.

Let's assume that for 20 years you fund *your* IRA with *only* $250, and it earns 10% over that time. This small IRA will be worth $15,750 two decades hence.

However, that nonworking spousal account you've so generously been funding to the tune of $2,000 a year for 20 years, will be worth—assuming that same 10% rate of return—$126,005. Giving the money now is something to think about.

It's even possible to add to an IRA spousal account after you have died. This may seem ghoulish—but here goes. You're the working spouse, and let's say you have the bad luck to die on February 1st (but had earned at least $2,000 by then). Your nonworking spouse (widow or widower) could then put the $2,000 contribution you would have made based on your earned income up until your death into his/her spousal account up until taxpaying time (let's say, April 15th next year). The contribution may or may not be deductible—but the important thing for your beneficiary is the fact that the IRA just keeps on chugging along, even if you're no longer on the train.

Loans? No Dice

Unlike some retirement plans—such as a 401(k), 403(b), or (more rarely) in a Keogh—you *cannot* borrow from your own IRA. You can't even pledge a part of it as security for a loan.

If you were to try to borrow against your IRA, the portion used as security would be considered a distribution. That might trigger a 10% premature distribution penalty, plus a 15% excess distribution tax. And that's just for starters. If the IRS really decided to get nasty, it could take another 5% as a penalty against prohibited transactions, and there are even laws on the books which allow the government to hit you with a 100% tax if you don't correct or rescind the transaction.

It doesn't get much clearer than this: *Don't even think of borrowing from, or against, your IRA.*

Picking Your Investments

Now that we've covered the mechanics, on to the good stuff. What kind of IRA investments should you have? Remember, this is a *self*-directed retirement account. You pick and choose among the literally thousands of investment choices out there. Unlike your investments in a 401(k) or 403(b), you aren't going to be limited to a handful of choices. Your investment horizon is virtually unlimited.

In a moment we'll tell you what you *can't* do, but first, here's what you *can* invest in.

Just about any stock or bond that's publicly traded can be bought and held in an IRA. Of the 3,500 (and growing) mutual funds and hundreds of unit investment trusts, almost all work in an IRA.

You can also pick and choose from preferred stocks, convertible bonds, collateralized mortgage obligations, zero coupon bonds, certificates of deposits, U.S. treasury bonds, and commodity funds.

In a few IRAs, you can even hold mortgages.

In short, the sky is the limit. Almost. There are a couple of things to note about this. Just because the law says you can invest in all these things, that doesn't mean you are going to have all these investment choices open to you through all IRA accounts. Some custodians—for ease of operations—will only permit you to invest in their products. The range they offer may be very limited.

For your protection, the law specifies that the trustee or custodian of an IRA must be a bank, federally insured credit union, savings and loan association, or another financial institution—such as an insurance company or stockbroker—which has been

---

Don't Be Redundant

Investments that are not suitable are tax-advantaged funds that invest in tax-free municipal bonds. A rule of thumb: It makes no sense to invest in tax-frees in a tax-deferred account.

First, it's redundant. Earnings in IRAs by their very nature are tax-deferred, and contributions can be, as we discussed, tax-deductible as well.

Second, when you inevitably take the money out of an IRA, all the interest, dividends, and capital gains your investment produced *will* be taxed—no matter what it was invested in. That's just the law.

approved by the IRS. The assets must be segregated, and custodians must meet strict IRS rules regarding the safekeeping of your investments and how they account to you.

Even given all those restrictions, some custodians go further. They may only want to hold assets that fit into their own operational capability. That's why, for example, most custodians won't hold real estate mortgages. It's not a legal question: they just aren't comfortable, for example, with the IRS requirement that they value the holdings—in this case, a piece of real estate—each year.

Sorry—No Rembrandts Allowed

What can't you buy? Our lawmakers became very heated and very specific on this.

After IRAs became all the rage in the late 1970s, Congress was appalled to see that some custodians were a little overzealous—to be kind—in their promises to prospective IRA customers. Ads shouted that holding diamonds, for example, in an IRA would practically guarantee you a 30% or 40% (or higher) annual rate of return. Congressional eyebrows went up—and as a result of those claims a new law was passed prohibiting holding "collectibles" in an IRA.

By collectibles, the law specifically outlaws IRA investments in artwork, rugs, antiques, precious metals (such as gold, silver, or platinum), postage stamps, gems, and coins. (There's always an exception. You *can* invest in certain gold or silver coins *minted by the U.S.*, or states, such as the American Eagle gold coin.)

A House Full of Records

IRAs are available at every street corner in the country. Well, we exaggerate slightly, but they are available at virtually every financial institution: banks, savings and loans, credit unions, insurance companies, mutual funds, and stockbrokers. We are talking a lot of street corners.

When IRAs first became popular people tended to open their initial IRA at a bank and bought a CD because interest rates were so high. Then the next year, when a higher-paying CD was available down the street, they'd open a second IRA at the S&L. In the third year, when it came time for their IRA contribution, yet a third IRA account would be opened. This is fine; there's nothing wrong with shopping around for the best deal. But the more IRA accounts you open, the more IRA accounts you have to manage.

Let's say you stopped with three. At the least, you'll be getting three annual statements explaining how well your accounts are doing, and it is quite possible that you might be getting statements quarterly, or even monthly.

If you are on a monthly basis, you're now getting 36 statements a year, and before long, you're not just keeping an IRA file, you have an IRA filing cabinet.

"Why worry," you say. "When the pile gets too high, I'll just toss 'em in the circular file."

The problem is, as we discussed in Chapter 3 on keeping records, you might have to keep the records forever, or at least until you pay the taxes due on your IRA distributions. As the IRS bluntly reminds us—and these are their words—"You cannot keep funds in an IRA indefinitely. Eventually you *must* withdraw them." And when you do take out the money, all those taxes you have been deferring are due.

In Chapter 31, we'll discuss the rules on IRA takeouts, but what it boils down to is this: you're going to have to prove what portions of your IRA contributions were deductible or were non-deductible. If the government has already taxed you once, that is, your contributions were nondeductible, and because they were made *after taxes,* the government honestly doesn't want to tax you twice, but the burden of proof is yours. And the only proof the IRS is going to accept are your old tax returns *and* your IRA records.

This can add up to an awful lot of record keeping. For example, if you make a nondeductible IRA contribution, the IRS requires you to file Form 8606, along with your normal income tax report, for any year in which you either take a distribution or make a nondeductible contribution. Although the IRS doesn't absolutely demand that you keep your IRA records forever, it's pretty clear that years—or decades—from now when you are harvesting your IRAs, all those records will be handy, if not vital, in explaining what you did and when.

Watching all those pieces of paper pile up is like a bad dream. Ten, twenty, thirty years from now it is easy to imagine that you'll have a room—and maybe even a whole house—filled with financial records.

Consolidate Your IRAs

You don't have to let the nightmare become a reality. There is a way to avoid the paper surfeit. Consolidate your IRAs. Put all of your IRA money into one account—an account that gives you myriad investment choices. (However, you'll probably want to keep your regular IRA assets separate from your rollover IRAs. See Chapter 25 for more information.)

By doing this, you gain three distinct advantages, in addition to reducing the paper glut.

1. Your money is easier to manage. You can tell at a glance how well your IRA investments are doing.

2. Your custodial costs should be lower, if you're paying one fee instead of several.

3. The strongest reason for consolidation may be a psychological one. If you have a $2,000 IRA here, a $4,000 account there, and another couple of accounts somewhere else, you tend to think of them as little savings accounts, and you might not pay a whole lot of attention to them.

We have nothing against "saving" (indeed, this whole book is a plea for saving more), we just think that you should think of your IRA savings accounts as *investment* accounts.

Roll up all these small accounts into one—and suddenly you'll see the big picture. You don't have one account of $4,000, another of $9,000, a third of $5,000, and a fourth with another $4,000. Now you have one *$22,000* account.

Consolidating your miscellaneous IRA investments tends to focus *you*. The very size of that one account makes you pay attention to it. It makes you want to be smarter in the way you manage it.

There are two ways to move assets from one IRA account to another.

Transfer. This is the cleanest way. No reporting is done to the IRS, because your assets are sent directly, or transferred, from one custodian to the new custodian. There is no limit on the number of transfers you can do a year.

Rollover. If you receive the assets yourself from the old custodian, you're given up to 60 days to roll over the assets to the new custodian. *Warning:* Only one rollover is permitted each year per IRA account, and the distributions are reported by the old custodian to the IRS, and then later the new custodian reports the receipt of the assets. Obviously, a transfer is better than a rollover.

Coming Up: Rollovers, Lump Sums, SEPs, and Keoghs

In this chapter we've focused on the use of IRAs as a way to save for retirement.

But there is another, much more exotic, use of an IRA: it can receive rollover distributions.

These distributions—generally called *lump sum distributions*—come from qualified retirement plans, such as pension or profit-sharing plans, stock bonus or annuity plans, Keoghs, 403(b), or 401(k)s.

Since these distributions can be a major slice of your retirement assets, we've given them a section of their own, Chapter 25. (In that chapter we'll give you a full examination of the pros and cons—the tax ramifications—of rollovers.)

And as long as we are talking about variations on the IRA theme, let us mention one more: *Simplified Employee Pension (SEP) IRAs*.

A SEP, to use the IRS verbiage, is a "special IRA." We prefer to call it an "elongated IRA," because you may be able to put up to

$30,000 of earned income a year into it, as opposed to a maximum of $2,000 into a plain vanilla IRA. A SEP is indeed "special," because in reality it's an employer-sponsored retirement plan. The employer might have 25 employees—or the employer, you, might have one employee: you. But because it's an "employer" plan, there are a fair number of rules and regulations on who is eligible to use it.

Over the past decade, SEPs have become popular, growing some 20% each year. You'll see why in the next chapter, which discusses Keoghs and SEP retirement plans.

Your trusty IRA is still a superb small tax shelter. Whether or not it's tax-deductible is not as important as the long-term tax-deferred buildup of earnings or gains.

CHAPTER 12

SEPs and Keoghs—Retirement Plans for the Self-Employed

In this chapter, we'll examine two of the simplest and most basic retirement plans of all—plans designed for the self-employed. We are talking about Simplified Employee Pensions (SEPs) and Keoghs. Both these retirement plans can be used by employers whether or not they are incorporated.

In truth there is no such plan as a "pure" Keogh today. Since the first pioneering Keogh plan came from Congress in 1962, through many years of changing legislation virtually all the differences in terms of pension law between the corporate employer and the self-employed employer have been blurred. The word "Keogh" today in reality is a marketing term, more than a legal definition, for small business plans. Most defined benefit or defined contribution plans for small business and the self-employed follow the same rules.

Why then, do we label this chapter on retirement plans "SEPs and Keoghs"? Our central thrust throughout this guide is how individuals can use—or participate in—a wide assortment of retirement plans. So this chapter is written primarily for the self-employed as individuals.

Just as we will not give the detailed pension rules that an employer of 100,000 must follow, we can't outline all the rules that an employer of two people must likewise follow in order to use a SEP, or a so-called Keogh plan.

What does follow is a general review of how these plans work, and as always—when you might have a choice—we'll give some pros and cons for each.

We will be explaining the difference between them in a few words, but at the outset let's talk about the similarities. You should note that both these plans can be opened only by an employer, and not by an employee. In a two-person partnership, neither person could open a Keogh or a SEP individually, but the partnership could collectively do so for both of them.

A self-employed person, who after all is really nothing more than a one-person (himself) employer, can open up a plan.

The employer doesn't have to be one person, or a mom-and-pop shop. It could be a large law or consulting firm, with perhaps 50 partners, and 150 other employees.

SEP Stands for Simple

Why was U.S. Representative Eugene James Keogh immortalized with his name on a bill, while the SEP plan, as important as it is, does not have a sponsor's surname attached?

It could be chance, or a political roll of the dice, or the fact that no one anticipated SEPs would become so popular. We bet on the latter. The legislation authorizing SEPs back in 1978 was buried so deep in a general tax and revenue bill that you needed a backhoe to unearth it.

As a result, Keogh will forever be identified with a man; SEP after a concept: "Keep it simple."

Call it truth-in-labeling. SEP is exactly the way Congress described it: "simplified."

A SEP is:

• Easy (read less costly) to administer: less record keeping; less paperwork.

• Self-directed. Each participant has his own account, so the employer does not have the responsibility of making investment decisions for his employees.

• No annual reports to the government are necessary.

The Patron Saint of the Self-Employed

Most senators and representatives leave light footprints on the sands of history. They may have been faithful in tending to their constituents' needs; they may even have risen through the ranks to be party leaders or committee chairmen. But rarely—no matter how strong their influence—will the attachment of their surnames to a bill make them household names.

It's rare, but it does happen. And as proof we offer the late U.S. Representative Keogh, from Brooklyn. We could tell you that he served faithfully in the House for 30 years, and was a powerful member of the House Ways and Means Committee, but that probably wouldn't mean a thing to you.

No, you remember him for being the patron saint of the self-employed.

One of the most popular retirement plans of all times is named for Eugene James Keogh.

We can't stress that last point too much.

In most pension plans the employer is required to report peri-odically on the status of the plan to either the Treasury or Labor Department (and sometimes to both). Some pension plans are also required to deliver, to all participants, a "Summary Plan De-scription."

Not so with SEPs. Congress said, let's make this retirement plan easier to use.

Note, we said "easier." An employer is not completely off the hook when it comes to government regulations, if he chooses to open a SEP. There are still various tests the employer has to pass, and checklists to follow.

However, a SEP clearly is the easiest way for the self-employed, sole proprietorships or partnerships (including professional corpo-rations and subchapter "S" corporations) or small businesses— be they incorporated or unincorporated—to set up a retirement plan.

In 1992 up to $30,000 per self-employed individual could be con-tributed to a SEP, and if the employer met certain eligibility tests, employees were able to defer part of their income.

In order to establish a salary-deferral SEP, the employer must have a business that has 25 or fewer *eligible* employees who were in the SEP plan during the prior tax year. (This 25-employee limit explains why large firms—which want to utilize the salary-deferral-plan feature in a SEP—don't have SEPs.)

Who is an eligible employee? Any employee who has worked for the company in three out of the last five years; is at least 21 years old, and has earned $374 or more from the employer in the year of the contribution. (This figure was the 1992 rule. It's indexed for inflation, so it changes annually.)

Also, if all the eligibility requirements are met, at least 50% of the eligible employees *must* agree that they will actively use the salary-deferral feature.

Finally there is a "nondiscrimination" test, which says, in essence, that higher-paid employees cannot defer a significantly larger percentage of their salary than lower-paid workers. (Details on that are far too complicated to go into here. Check with your accountant, or financial adviser.)

How much can employees defer? In 1992 this was no more than $8,728 of salary, or up to 15% of their income, but that 15% figure must also include the employer's contribution. This figure is indexed, and so will change in future years. So if the employer of a worker making $100,000 a year makes a $10,000 contribution to the employee's SEP, the employee would only be able to contribute another $5,000 (in terms of a deferred salary) of his own money.

This salary-deferral option works virtually the same way as an employee's 401(k) contribution.

As in a regular IRA, all SEP contributions—from both the employer and the employees—are 100% vested from the moment they're put into each person's account. The investments in a SEP can be as varied as the ones in an IRA, ranging from stocks and corporate bonds to mutual funds to certificates of deposit to unit investment trusts to government bonds.

And also, as in a regular IRA, since the SEP can be self-directed, you can change your investments as economic conditions change or as your own goals shift.

How a SEP Works

With the background out of the way, let's explain how a typical SEP would work.

Let's assume that your salary is $75,000 and your employer's contribution is 10%. Remember that the $7,500 is a business expense to your employer, and the $7,500 contribution you receive from your employer won't be taxable until you withdraw it from the SEP. (Most of the rules on withdrawals from IRAs—see Chapters 11 and 25—apply to SEP withdrawals as well.) We'll also assume that your employer's SEP plan meets the various requirements, and thus makes you eligible for salary deferral.

Given all this, you decide to take advantage of the salary-deferral option, and you're going to defer as much as you can. Since your employer has already contributed $7,500, that means you can defer $3,750. Remember, the two contributions to your retirement plan can add up to no more than 15% of salary, which is $11,250 in this example.

There's one intriguing twist to all this. If you wish, you can also add up to $2,000 to the SEP as your annual IRA contribution. *What this fact makes clear is that you can have both an IRA and a SEP, or an IRA and a Keogh. To have both an IRA and a Keogh you must have self-employment income.*

The reason why you can throw your regular IRA contribution into your SEP is that, in truth, the SEP is only an extension of an IRA. When you think about it, SEPs are nothing more than a particular kind of IRA, one geared for people who are either self-employed, have self-employment income, or who work at small companies.

However, as you'll see in a minute, you can't make your IRA

contribution into a Keogh. A Keogh is a lot closer to a corporate pension plan than it is to an IRA.

Let's say our employee decides to add his IRA contribution to his SEP. Here's what his SEP could look like at the end of year one:

Employer contribution	$7,500
Salary-deferral contribution	$3,750
IRA contribution	$2,000
Total	$13,250

If you—and your employer—simply continue to contribute this amount for the next 20 years, and you average a 10% return, you'll end up with an impressive retirement account of $923,922.

If you start early enough, and/or work long enough, that annual contribution of $13,250 increases to $2,528,704 after 30 years. (This creates a bit of a good-news, bad-news situation. The bad news of course is that you are going to be taxed eventually on most of that money. After all, neither your employer's contribution, nor your salary-deferral contributions were ever taxed. So when you withdraw the money—probably over many years—the taxes are going to be due. The good news is that although your $2,000 IRA contribution in this example was made with nondeductible dollars, at least that portion of your total contributions *won't* be taxed on withdrawal.)

Final Thoughts About SEPs

Earlier, we labeled the SEP as an "elongated IRA," but in truth there are some differences that help distinguish SEPs from a plain pipe rack IRA.

For example, you can't make new contributions to a regular IRA after you reach 70½, but with a SEP you can, if you are still working. As with a Keogh plan, you must start taking minimum distributions out of a SEP when you reach 70½, even if you're still putting money into it.

Why would you put money in with one hand, if the law requires you to take it out with the other? Because, as the example of Milton Quincy—the California TV packager—shows, you want to take full advantage of the tax benefits you receive by contributing to your retirement plan.

As in an IRA, you can neither borrow from a SEP, nor use the assets as collateral or a loan, and the IRA prohibition on holding collectibles in an IRA also applies to a SEP.

Keoghs: Almost as Simple

Now let's look at a Keogh plan. It, too, is a comparatively simple retirement program. It's not as simple as a SEP, because in a Keogh you may have to make periodic reports to the government, so your administrative costs will be higher.

Remember, labeling a plan "Keogh" is really more of an homage to the creator of the plan than it is to a fact in pension law today.

Under the many amendments that have occurred since the first, true Keogh came about, there's little distinction now between a corporate plan and a self-employed plan. Still, Keogh as a concept has aged well since it was created some 30 years ago, and you'll find, when you go looking for advice on how to set up a retirement plan, that tax accountants and lawyers can be fanatical in their loyalty to the thoughts of Keoghs for the self-employed.

That's easy to understand. The Keogh plan allowed hundreds of thousands of Americans to start saving for retirement.

Before Keoghs, the nation's self-employed—doctors, lawyers, farmers, artists, architects, and dentists—were orphans. Their corporate cousins could have full retirement packages, but anyone who was self-employed was left out in the cold.

Keoghs changed all that. Keoghs were the first step on a long legislative path (which is still being extended by Congress today) that would create more of a parity between the incorporated and the unincorporated.

Most Keogh plans today are defined contribution plans, which means that the annual contribution limit is specific (and limited). What you take out, in retirement, is based on how much you've contributed and on what your Keogh investments earn throughout the years.

Also available—but not as popular these days because of their cost to set up and administer—are defined benefit Keogh plans, whereby the contributions in a given year can vary enormously. Those contributions are based on a calculation of what your future—or "defined"—benefits will be. You'll know ahead of time exactly what your Keogh will be worth when you retire or leave the company.

As we said before, companies—from big to small—are moving away from defined benefit plans.

However, since when it comes to Keoghs you'll probably be the one to decide which road—defined benefit or defined contribution—to take, let's spend a minute talking about when a defined benefit plan would make sense.

Suppose you're self-employed, or you have a small business, and you're in your mid-50s, and are now at or approaching your highest earning years. You plan to retire in the foreseeable future, and you've had *no* pension coverage so far.

Let's also say that your employees, if you have any, are much younger—in their 20s or 30s—and are making a lot less than you.

In this case, a defined benefit Keogh may make sense. The plan will give you a chance to catch up on your retirement planning. You'll set your retirement benefit at a relatively high number. But it won't cost the company too much. (Your younger employees will be receiving the same future benefit, but since they are younger than you, the amount of money you'll have to put away for them is less. Compound interest will make up the difference.) A defined benefit Keogh is obviously more complex than a defined contribution Keogh—so go to an expert for advice if you're weighing the relative advantages of each.

The Basics

Both Keoghs and SEPs are available at most brokerage firms and banks, and at many credit unions and insurance companies.

The rules may vary slightly from one "Keogh" custodian to another, but here's what a typical defined contribution plan would require:

- All employees 21 years old or older who have worked for the employer for two years or more (a year of service is defined as 1,000 hours or more per year) are included.

- The contribution percentage is substantially the same for all eligible employees.

- If the plan is self-directed, each person picks his own investments. The investments can be as varied as they are in an IRA, but it will be the company, and not the individual, that will be determining what the investment menu will look like.

Let us stop to underscore that last point. With a Keogh plan the employer has the option of picking the investments—and the investment advisers—for the employee. But most Keogh plans these days allow self-direction by each participant. All SEPs are self-directed. In practice, most Keoghs and SEPs offer a broad range of investments.

Keogh and SEP: Growing

When Keogh plans were unveiled, $2,500 was the maximum annual contribution per person. Now it's $30,000. (SEP maximum contributions have likewise edged up—from the original $7,500 to $15,000, and now to $30,000.) Obviously, the upper limit has grown faster than inflation.

The reason? Congressional determination to create more of a parity between the contribution level in corporate plans and plans for the self-employed.

Two Variations on a Theme

Defined contribution (aka Keogh) plans basically take two forms:

1. **Money Purchase.** The employer will make a contribution based on a fixed percentage of the employee's salary. The minimum contribution allowed per year is 1%. Under certain circumstances the minimum may be raised to 3%; the maximum is 25%. In either case, the employer cannot contribute more than $30,000 per employee.

   If you're self-employed, a different formula applies. Your contribution will be based on "earned income" which, in essence, is the amount of money you earned, minus both the Keogh contribution itself and one-half of your self-employment (Social Security) tax.

2. **Profit Sharing.** The employer's contribution, which cannot exceed 15% of an employee's salary—is generally discretionary. The contribution, by formula, must be the same for all eligible employees. And like the money purchase plan, there is a $30,000-a-year maximum.

Since a money purchase plan requires the employer to make a regular contribution at a fixed percentage each year come hell or high water, then from the employer's point of view, it *is* a very fixed—and sometimes onerous—obligation. (What happens if the employer doesn't make the contribution? The IRS could assess a penalty. While it is possible to convince the IRS to let the employers change the level of contribution, the employer is better off not establishing it in the first place if there is any chance there will be trouble in meeting it.)

To avoid the fixed obligation of a money purchase plan, some employers prefer to limit their contributions to a profit-sharing plan.

You can understand the decision. Simply stated, by going solely with profit sharing, the employer can decide each year whether or not to fund the plan.

Great if you are employer, not so wonderful if you are an employee.

Perhaps to even out that inequity, what some employers will do is strike a balance between the two variations of the plan. They'll have a money purchase plan that calls for a 5% contribution, and in tandem they'll also offer a profit-sharing plan. This way, when the company has a good year, the money purchase contribution of 5% will be enhanced by a profit-sharing contribution of, say, 15%, so that a hefty total of 20% will be contributed.

In a bad year, the profit-sharing contribution can be cut to nothing, and the company will only be required to contribute 5% to the money purchase plan.

From the employer's perspective, using the profit-sharing and money purchase plans together helps control benefit costs.

From the employee's vantage, it guarantees that there will always be some kind of employer contribution—come rain or snow—and yet it gives employees a chance to share in the company's success, when it has a good year.

What Happens When You Leave the Company?

When you change jobs, or retire, you'll be able to roll your Keogh assets over into an IRA, to another qualified retirement plan, or you can take a lump sum distribution. (For the pros and cons of each choice, see Chapter 25.) If you're in a SEP, in effect you're already in an IRA, so you may want to leave all the money there, and draw it down as you need it upon retirement. What happens if you need the money sooner?

Some Keogh plans may permit you to borrow from your own account, provided that you are not a principal of the business. That means, by definition, that if you are self-employed and unincorporated, you will not be able to borrow against your account.

A Difference in Deadlines

A Keogh plan must be adopted by an employer by the last day of the tax year. This, not surprisingly, often leads to accountants scurrying around on New Year's Eve. Once the plan is adopted, opening an account and funding the actual contribution can be done up to the tax filing deadline, including extensions, for that year.

A SEP plan, however, can both be *opened and funded* up to the employer's tax filing deadline, including extensions. There are times when an employer, intending to adopt a Keogh, procrastinates too long, and blows the December 31 deadline. Often he then tries to recover gracefully by opening a SEP. There is nothing wrong with that. Over the long term, the return on either can be very satisfactory.

Yes, you can have a SEP and a Keogh, or several SEPs, provided that your total annual contributions do not exceed the limits we mentioned earlier. However, for simplicity's sake, we suggest as few accounts as possible.

We Rest Our Case

We say repeatedly in this book that you can grow rich slowly. We'll show you how either a SEP or a Keogh could deliver the bacon to you.

In this example, we won't even go to the max—which at $30,000 a year would have you on a fast track. And since this is hypothetical, we'll ignore probabilities—that in real life, you might start low in a SEP or Keogh, say $3,000 a year and you might end high, at $30,000 a year. And here's one more probability that we won't factor into this equation. Just as Congress has through the years raised SEP and Keogh limits, it's likely—but by no means guaranteed—that sometime in the years ahead Congress will increase the limits again.

But no matter—we'll just give you a simplistic, almost median, scenario.

Suppose you contribute a flat $15,000 a year to either a SEP or a Keogh starting at age 30 till you retire at age 65.

Your Total Contributions	The End Result—If You Earn:			
	6%	8%	10%	12%
$525,000	$1,771,812	$2,741,532	$4,471,901	$7,251,946

The bottom line—in terms of how investing smarter coupled with time and compounding can mean enormous differences—proves our case.

Either a Keogh or a SEP is a near-perfect retirement plan for the self-employed. Check 'em out—they run under different rules and regulations but, at best, a tax-deferred contribution of almost $30,000 can be fed into your retirement pot each year.

CHAPTER 13

Investing Efficiently: Dollar Cost Averaging—Automatic Reinvestment of Dividends

Throughout this guide we stress "invest smarter." We would now like to add two more words to that advice: "invest efficiently."

Or maybe we should say, "invest *more* efficiently." After all, if your investment horizon is long-term, you are already investing efficiently by putting your retirement money to work tax-deferred, and by letting the money you earn on those investments compound.

That's good, but you can do even better if you dollar cost average, and then automatically reinvest the dividends you receive. Both simple tactics harmonize beautifully with a long-term investment strategy.

Let's start with dollar cost averaging. This elementary device helps protect your assorted retirement portfolios from the inevitable price fluctuations in equities.

Markets Do Fluctuate

With dollar cost averaging you eliminate market-timing risks. Instead of fretting over market fluctuations, you take advantage of them by recognizing that those fluctuations offer opportunities over the long term. If you dollar cost average over a full market cycle—about five years on average—you should be able to accumulate shares at below-average prices, as we will demonstrate later. But before we get there, let's spend a minute explaining exactly how dollar cost averaging works.

With dollar cost averaging you invest a fixed amount of money at a regular interval, instead of buying a lot of shares of a stock or a mutual fund all at once. For example, instead of plunking down $20,000 tomorrow to buy a specific stock or mutual fund, you might buy $5,000 of that investment tomorrow and then another $5,000 every six months till you've bought $20,000 worth. It's highly probable that since you are making those four different purchases during a two-year period you will end up paying four different prices for the stock or fund.

By buying shares, or units, at different prices, you'll be accumulating more shares when the market is down, and fewer shares when the market is up. Thus, you're taking advantage of market downswings.

Systematic Investing: Automatic Averaging

The key to making this work is investing systematically, such as through a plan where you, or your employer, make monthly contributions to your defined contribution retirement plan, or a salary-deferral plan such as a 401(k), 403(b), SEP, or Keogh account. Dollar cost averaging even works nicely if you are "only" putting $2,000 a year into your IRA. (You can invest $500 every quarter, or $166.66 every month.)

How well does dollar cost averaging work? Very.

On the next page we'll look at three examples in three different markets—fluctuating, rising, and declining—to underscore that point.

We will assume—in this decidedly long-term scenario—that you invest $3,000 every January 2 over the next five years.

Is there any danger in using dollar cost averaging? Yes. At its most extreme, you could keep averaging down toward zero.

If the stock you are investing in steadily falls, dollar cost averaging will ease the pain a bit, but unfortunately the fact will still remain that your investment is constantly losing ground.

Dollar cost averaging does not eliminate the need to constantly monitor your investments. Failure to do so, even if you follow a dollar cost averaging program, can cost you a bundle.

Fluctuating Market

Regular Investment	Share Price	Shares Acquired
$3,000	$10	300
3,000	5	600
3,000	10	300
3,000	25	120
3,000	15	200
Average share price: **$13.00** ($65 ÷ 5). Cost using dollar cost averaging: **$9.87** ($15,000 ÷ 1,520).		
$15,000	Totals	1,520

Rising Market

$3,000	$5	600
3,000	10	300
3,000	15	200
3,000	20	150
3,000	25	120
Average share price: **$15.00** ($75 ÷ 5). Cost using dollar cost averaging: **$10.95** ($15,000 ÷ 1,370).		
$15,000	Totals	1,370

Declining Market

$3,000	$30	100
3,000	25	120
3,000	20	150
3,000	15	200
3,000	10	300
Average share price: **$20.00** ($100 ÷ 5). Cost using dollar cost averaging: **$17.24** ($15,000 ÷ 870).		
$15,000	Totals	870

Plowing Your Dividends Back

One way to keep your portfolio growing is by automatically plowing your dividends back into your investment.

The underlying principle here is exactly the same as it is with dollar cost averaging. You like what you're buying, so you keep on buying.

The only difference is that instead of writing an additional check, you instruct either the broker who holds your stock, or the mutual fund, to take the dividends it would otherwise have paid you and use them to buy more shares instead. Many self-directed retirement accounts also offer automatic reinvestment options—but again, we caution that not all securities and their dividends can be reinvested automatically.

The Case for Equities

In the markets, anything is possible and it's conceivable that you *could* indeed dollar cost average down to zero. We suggest the alarms should have gone off for you long before that happens. If you're on the *Titanic* and you see the deck chairs sliding every which way, something is up (or down).

Our case for dollar cost averaging in equity is tied to the long term. We remind you what history tells us. In the period from 1926 to 1990, equities, as measured by the Standard & Poor's 500 stock index, provided a compounded annual return of 10.1% from capital appreciation and reinvested dividends.

Over that 65-year period the total return on equities was about twice the return of long-term corporate bonds, and more than three times the compounded annual inflation rate. (See our more detailed examinations of long-term equity investing in Chapters 15 and 17.)

Virtually all mutual funds have a dividend reinvestment option.

How about stocks? It's not as widespread as mutual funds, but it's often true there too.

Some financial services firms, if they're holding your shares in safekeeping for you, are able to automatically reinvest dividends of most stocks listed on the New York Stock Exchange and the American Stock Exchange.

A few of the very biggest NYSE and AMEX companies—those with a huge base of shareholders—will even offer dividend reinvestment plans directly to shareholders who are holding the shares themselves. (We might add, if you are keeping the shares at home, that we trust you have your own way of safekeeping the certificates, and that you're not just squirreling them away in little packets under all those expired insurance policies. Replacing lost stock certificates takes time and money.)

When it comes to the over-the-counter market, the automatic reinvestment program isn't as widespread as it is with NYSE and AMEX securities, but it is becoming increasingly easier to order automatic dividend reinvestment for the most widely held OTC securities.

You'll note that automatic reinvestment programs are basically dollar cost averaging in a different guise. Just as with dollar cost averaging, if you automatically reinvest your dividends you'll be investing a fixed amount (the amount of the dividend) at a specific time (when the dividend is paid, usually quarterly or semiannually).

There are two reasons to dollar cost average and automatically reinvest dividends. First, it's efficient. It saves you time and effort. Second, and even more important, if you truly believe in the investment, and you are dollar cost averaging, in the long term you should be able to accumulate shares over a full market cycle at below-average prices.

PART III

Saving Smarter

CHAPTER 14

Setting Your Goals

Baskin-Robbins has 31 flavors. The Music Man has 76 trombones, and Disney has 101 Dalmatians.

When it comes to types of investors, the number is something approaching infinity.

As a quick walk down Main Street any day proves, everybody is different, and nowhere is that difference more apparent than when it comes to investing. Some people feel comfortable only if they are wearing a belt, suspenders, and an elastic waistband at the same time, while others—to mix images for a moment—are willing to risk everything they own on a single roll of the dice.

Asking what kind of investment is best is like asking if it's better to have $2 million in tens and twenties, or $2 million in fives and fifties. Either one is perfectly fine. It just depends on which one you are comfortable with.

And that's an important point. All the financial advice in the world—no matter how carefully reasoned, and no matter how many times the "experts" can prove that it makes sense—is wrong for you if that investment keeps you from sleeping at night. You can know on a gut level that it makes absolutely no sense to pay off your 4% mortgage if you are going to use money that's currently earning 6% to do it. But that rational knowledge does you absolutely no good if every time you think about your mortgage you envisage a dark-haired man, with a long black cape, hovering outside your door waiting to foreclose.

If that's how you feel, then for Pete's sake, pay off the mortgage, even if the rational part of you knows that you'll always have enough money to keep your house. A good night's sleep is worth whatever money you may be "losing" by paying off the mortgage. You have to follow the investment path that's right for you.

Profiling Yourself

Knowing how somebody else would handle a financial situation can serve as a guide, but it can't—unless you like tossing and turning at night—be taken as your personal gospel. *You* have to be comfortable with how *you* are investing *your* money.

But while everyone is different when it comes to deciding where to put one's own money, people still can be divided into six basic investor types. We are going to give you descriptions of each, and then use the different "types" as our point of departure for the discussion that will follow about investment strategies.

See which of our descriptions comes closest to the way you handle your money, and then look for your particular "type" in the next chapter, to determine how you might want to allocate your assets as part of your master strategy.

Before we ask you to profile yourself, step back, and once more look at *why* you're saving money, why you're fretting over your investments.

238

The immediate purpose of investing is to build assets for a future purpose—for funding college educations for your children, or for taking care of your parents (or yourself, some 30 years from now), or for building a retirement home. It's not the money that counts, it's what you want to do with it—eventually.

Who Are You? Where Are You Going?

Conservative (focused on maintaining capital). This type of investor is most concerned about conserving what he has. If your primary concern is to make sure that your investments are as safe as humanly possible, even if that safety may cost you 1%, 3%, 5%, or more in potential returns, you probably fall into this category.

Want to make sure? Here's a simple test. You frequently say such things as, "Once I know that my investment is absolutely safe, then, and only then, do I want to hear about what kind of yields it may produce."

People like this tend to have most of their money in government (and the highest-rated corporate) bonds. Just about all the rest of their money is in cash, or cash equivalents such as money market funds. They *may* own a few stocks, but you can just about guarantee that those stocks are going to be high-grade utilities—electric and gas companies, along with telephone stocks, all of which have a history of paying high dividends. When these people feel daring they'll go out and buy a blue chip.

As the nation's oldest money has proven over the last 200 years or so, there is very little wrong with this approach to investing. There's a catch to this: there's an inflation risk. In other words, this strategy works only if inflation doesn't outstrip your earnings.

239

Conservative (concentrating on current income). There is no way that you could be considered a high roller, but you are willing to absorb a modest amount of risk to your principal to obtain an ongoing *and secure* income stream.

Bonds—again high-rated corporate issues, along with government obligations—will probably make up the bulk of your portfolio. However, you, unlike your more conservative counterpart, are willing to put the majority of your remaining assets into blue chip stocks—shares of big companies (their market value is measured in billions of dollars) with a long history of paying dividends to their shareholders. Those blue chips will have the potential for growth, but not surprisingly this type of investor will first look at the dividend these stocks pay.

Searching for income and growth—today. You are looking for the best of both worlds, but you don't want to take too much risk.

Growth-oriented, conservative investors emphasize that their principal must be safe, but they're willing to accept *some* volatility, *if* that volatility leads to increased growth possibilities.

This is still a far cry from saying that these people are willing to throw caution to the wind. They are still basically conservative investors. That means the growth they are looking for could come through something as simple—and safe—as the compounding that occurs when they automatically reinvest the dividends paid by the stocks they hold. Similarly, instead of receiving a monthly check, for the interest earned on their money market funds, they could let those earnings be automatically reinvested as well.

The fixed income portion of this investor's portfolio will probably be concentrated in U.S. government securities, quality corporate and municipal bonds, and perhaps some zero coupons. Their equities? Probably blue chips.

Searching for growth and income—tomorrow. Unlike the first three types of investors—who are focused on the kind of return they are earning today—*you,* if you fall into this category, are willing to look a little further out. Your goal is to achieve above-average *capital gains* over a three-to-five-year period. If that means you have to accept some price volatility in the interim, so be it.

Given this approach, the bulk of your money—perhaps as much as three-quarters of it—is going to be in stocks, given the fact that stocks have outperformed everything else over the years. While you'll own a lot of blue chips, you'll also probably have some growth stocks and will have invested in some small capitalization companies as well. (By "small cap," we mean firms whose total market value—i.e., the worth of all their outstanding shares—is $500 million or less.)

The small cap stocks you pick will tend to soar in bull markets. Unfortunately, they can fall just as fast when the market turns bearish.

Capital appreciation. You want to move a bit faster. Not only are you trying to outperform the market, over a two-to-three-year period, but you are willing to move among asset classes—stocks, bonds, cash—on a regular basis in order to do it.

Again, because you are looking for growth, much of your assets—maybe two-thirds—will be in stocks. But you'll own a higher percentage of small cap stocks than the people who are searching for growth and income, and you may own a few speculative issues as well.

———

Aggressive. No risk, no reward, that's your motto. You want to increase your capital, and do it quickly.

When you talk about making a "long-term" investment, you're probably talking about having your money tied up from one to two years.

Why the shortening of the time horizons? Because aggressive investors want to take *immediate* advantage of the changes in the relative values of different kinds of assets. If they think, for example, that interest rates are about to drop, they'll want to quickly shift out of cash and into bonds. Or, if they think the return they'll receive from bonds and stocks looks like it will be lacking luster over the next year or so, they'll put their money in investments with far greater growth opportunities.

By definition, this approach to the market means that aggressive investors are willing to assume a large amount of risk. They, unlike the other people we've talked about, are comfortable with volatility in the value of their investments. Similarly, they don't have any problems making large, dramatic swings from one class of assets to another.

Stocks today, bonds tomorrow, it makes little difference to them.

One way of being aggressive—possibly the most dangerous way—is to commit a lot of your money to just one issue, when it comes to the equity side of your portfolio. You're going for broke. You'll pass up the relative safety that comes through diversification for the potentially high appreciation you can receive by owning a substantial number of shares of one stock. The potential reward may be high, but the potential risk is likewise high.

Also, aggressive investors are usually far more interested in growth than they are in dividends. Holding a high percentage of stocks that don't pay any dividends—since the company's management is investing the money they would have paid out to shareholders in pursuing corporate growth—doesn't bother them a lick. They figure the capital gains produced by these stocks will be greater than any dividends they might receive.

The stocks that aggressive investors own often come complete with a decidedly speculative tinge. They're high risk. That warning we gave you earlier about small cap stocks—first to rise, first to fall—definitely applies here as well. Money invested in this kind of equity is most certainly at risk.

On the fixed income side, the aggressive investor may opt for long-term zero coupon bonds, or for high-yield corporates, including "junk" bonds. Again, those investments carry more risk, but they also could produce more reward.

How do you know if you're an aggressive investor?

Well, for one thing, you're willing to take advantage of major market moves. When investment professionals make changes in their asset allocation models you pay attention.

Swings in the professionals' recommendations are of much greater significance to someone like you who considers herself a

---

An Early Look at Asset Allocation

An asset allocation model, something that we will be discussing fully in the next chapter, is a theoretical investment portfolio that professional money managers use to help them decide where to invest.

It is typically made up of three components: stocks, bonds, and cash. A certain percentage of assets is placed in each category, with the allocation changing from time to time, depending on what is going on in the market, and in the world.

bit of a gambler. You're trying to make volatility work in your favor. That makes sense. You can afford to anticipate more, and react swiftly, since, by definition, you are not adverse to risk.

Aggressive investors seldom hedge their bets. They're willing to put all their eggs in one basket (and then they—or their money managers—watch that basket very carefully).

This approach to investing, obviously, requires a lot more time than if you opted to take a "conservative–maintaining capital" approach. But that is only a minor, potential flaw to this investment strategy.

The real problem can be summed up in three words: risk, risk, risk.

However, the possible rewards can also be described in three words: gain, gain, gain.

There *is* a difference between being an aggressive investor and being a *market timer,* someone who is constantly moving in and out of the market. The market timer is a trader.

Even if your asset allocation strategy calls for you to be aggressive in some of your investments, you are still likely to have a time frame of six months to a year for your investments. You have a strategy. A strategy of being aggressive, but a strategy nonetheless.

Market timing—that is, moving in and out of the market based on what you think the market is going to do in the next week, day, or hour—is a tactic. It's not a strategy.

Of the six investor types, where do you fit?

Profile yourself. If you need help, ask your financial adviser or consultant to put you through even more of a wringer. They'll have more ways—including some sophisticated attitudinal probes—of profiling you.

Out of your profile will emerge your investment goals. And in the next chapter, we'll give you guidance on how assets can be allocated—again, as a part of a long-term strategy—to achieve those goals.

Everyone—in his or her investment temperament—is different. Profile yourself. Establish your investment comfort zone. Estimate your tolerance for investment risk. Then you'll be ready to set a long-term strategy for both conserving and building assets.

CHAPTER 15

Allocating Your Assets

When it comes to investing, the old saw says, there are no sure things. But with all deference to conventional wisdom, we've found one certainty: change.

Financial markets change. They shift. They were volatile last year; they're volatile now; they'll be volatile tomorrow.

How do you deal with these gyrations? You could quit your job and spend 24 hours a day—and that's what it would take, since worldwide financial markets are now so closely linked—responding to every move in the markets. Or you can do something that's a bit easier. You could follow a simple, two-step approach to investing.

Step 1. You make your investment decisions based on your *long-term* financial goals. (We talked about how to establish those goals in the previous chapter.)

Step 2. Next, you divide your assets in such a way that you'll be able to achieve your goals. This second step is known as *asset allocation.*

Let's step back—for a moment—and examine the differences between "tactical" investing and "strategic" investing.

Strategic investors, as we've seen, typically take the "long view." Their investment horizons usually run three to five years. And it is not unusual for strategic investors to think 10, 20, or even 30 years out.

For tactical investors, 30 days can be an eternity. Their maximum time frame is six months, and usually they act far more quickly— often moving in and out of a stock in the same day.

How you can be successful taking the tactical approach is something that is best left for another book. A short-term approach to the market is not for the faint of heart. Plus, tactical investing can lead to extreme portfolio turnover, something that can be quite expensive, since you have to pay a brokerage commission on every trade.

However, tactical investing can be extremely rewarding. Merely making an eighth of a point on an investment that you were in for just a few hours can lead to a phenomenal annualized return.

There certainly is a place for tactical trading in the vast spectrum of investing, but it's not something we'll be examining in a retirement planning book called *Grow Rich Slowly.*

Our focus is on setting a long-term strategy, and then allocating your resources accordingly. If you do this, the time and effort you devote to your investments will be held to a minimum.

The key to making all this work is building on what you've already done. Previously, we asked you to determine your goals, now we're going to ask you to set a strategy for your various investment portfolios based on those goals.

We use the word "various" advisedly—because you'll need different strategies to achieve different goals. For example, your strategy for putting your kids through college may be markedly different from your plan for building a retirement nest egg. This makes sense. You may have just six or eight years before the first tuition check is due, while retirement might be 25 years away.

However, while your time horizons may be different, the fundamentals remain the same. In each case how you decide to allocate assets to your portfolio should be based on three things:

- **An analysis of your overall finances.**

- **Your own personal tolerance for risk.**

- **The time you have to accomplish your goals.**

Once you have a strategy in place, your investments will be picked, and your assets—that is, your initial investments, plus the gains they've achieved—will be allocated accordingly.

You've already analyzed your finances, and by this point you have a pretty good idea of the type of investor you are and what your portfolio objectives are (aggressive, conservative focused on maintaining capital, whatever). Let's now spend a minute talking about the third leg that makes up the asset allocation triangle: time.

The time frame you establish to achieve your goals will depend upon your age, and when and how you plan to use your assets.

We stress this for a reason. Most people say they are saving for some "long-term" objective. But "long term" means one thing to a 40-year-old, who is beginning to plan for a retirement that is 25 years away. It means quite another to someone who is 60 and is only now starting to think seriously about his investments.

When we use "long term" in the following discussion, we will be talking about a time frame that *at the very least* will last between three and five years.

Think Long Term—and We Mean It!

But let us tip our hand, and tell you what's coming up: no matter how long "long term" is for you, determine your investment and asset allocation strategy and stick to it. Consistency is the key to a winning strategy. That means you have to ride out the extremes. This is what strategic investing is all about.

Okay, with the background out of the way, let's explain how asset allocation works in practice.

Someone following an asset allocation model will distribute her assets among stocks, bonds, and cash. The money is spread across these three categories in order to reduce portfolio risk, preserve profits, and improve total return.

Institutions and money mangers use this investment approach to achieve high total returns, while reducing overall price volatility in their portfolios.

Now when you read magazine profiles on these money managers, frequently you'll see them mention that they rely on sophisticated economic models that employ dozens of data bases, and a roomful of computers that crunch millions of bits of disparate financial data every second in order to determine the absolute best way they should be investing—and allocating—their money.

Well, bully for them. But to be honest, the underlying concepts governing asset allocation are not that tough. With some forethought, and reasonable diligence, you can use it as a way of building, and protecting, your assets over the long term.

After all, what you are trying to do is pretty simple. You're trying to create a portfolio that exploits major economic trends.

Exploiting Economic Trends

Those trends will change, so your allocation will eventually change. But the fact that you are looking three to five years out means you don't have to make panic moves, or react to every financial twitch worldwide.

Remember, you're not a day trader. You're not trying to time the markets. Since you have a longer perspective, you're reasonably well insulated from the daily news events that cause the peaks—and valleys—in financial markets.

News events affecting the market can be scary: presidential illnesses, military coups, corporate bankruptcies. Wars begin. Wars end. The Fed primes the pump. The economy falters; it heats up again. Throughout it all, your guiding philosophy is to maintain a long-term perspective. Don't react with haste. As we said, you will change the allocation of your assets, as market conditions—and your own personal needs—change. But even those changes should be consistent with your long-term strategy.

Okay, you have to start somewhere, so where do you begin? Our suggestion would be to begin by listening to the pros—be they money managers, pension fund managers, financial services firms. Where do they say you should be putting your money, and in what amounts?

They'll be quite explicit. From time to time, they'll offer "benchmarks," suggested percentages, for each type of investment. Increase your cash position, they'll say. We're buying more stocks, they'll tell you. We've become quite bullish (or bearish) on bonds, because we think interest rates are in for a slow—but steady—drop (or climb).

Now clearly these professionals are making their recommendations every day to large corporate pension accounts, and to huge multinational clients. While these investment experts may not be used to talking to the little guy, they do spend their professional lives trying to figure out where markets are going. So listen to what they have to say, and then adjust their suggestions to fit your own needs. Hitch your wagon to their star. Why shouldn't their recommendations—scaled back, perhaps—apply to you?

Let us underscore that point. We're all different. We all have different needs and different financial objectives. There is no one, single mix appropriate for all investors. The right allocation, or mix, *for you* depends on your age, your family's needs, your employment status, in short—your objectives.

With that in mind, let's show how asset allocation would work in practice. Say the portfolio model the experts are suggesting calls for you to have 55% of your assets in stocks, 40% in bonds, and 5% in cash.

That's our starting point. Then, as we said, you have to do three things: Complete an analysis of your overall finances; double-check your own tolerance for risk, and, finally, figure out how much time you have to accomplish your goals.

To make this concept absolutely clear, let's see how this would play out in practice.

The Triple Squeeze—Three Plans Needed

We'll deal with a couple unlucky enough to be facing the triple squeeze—planning for their children's college funds; investing for their own retirement needs; and helping to fund their parents' health needs.

If you're in this situation it turns out you don't need one asset allocation strategy. You need three. One to govern your college funding plans, a second that will cover your own retirement needs, and a third to deal with the cost of your parents' health care.

Let's begin with the question of how you are going to put your 11-year-old daughter—your only child—through college.

The approach here calls for you to be conservative. You have to remember that the first tuition bill will be arriving in just six years, and that you will be spending all the money you have earmarked for college within a decade from today. (See Chapter 5, "Paying [Saving] for Your Children's College Educations.")

Sure, over the long haul, stocks outperform every other investment—a point we will be explaining in detail in a minute—but that's *long term*. Short term, if you invest in equities there can be fluctuations that affect principal, and fluctuations are something you can do without in trying to figure out how you are going to pay for school. You need to know that when your daughter is ready to go to school, the money is waiting. You don't have a lot of room for risk.

However, you can afford to be more aggressive for another goal: retirement. When it comes to your 401(k)—let's say—this is truly long range. After all, suppose you're pretty certain that you are going to put in another 15 years at your company. Given that, you don't want to be too conservative when it comes to investing your retirement money. Fixed income investments—such as guaranteed investment contracts (GICs)—just don't make sense, since you should be worried about inflation, and rightfully so.

You don't want inflation to outstrip, or erode, your savings. The best way to preserve your retirement assets is to ensure, as best you can, that those assets grow.

If you accept this premise, you'll be willing to take modest risks with your 401(k) money. That means a good portion of that money—maybe even a higher percentage than what is called for in the benchmark asset allocation model—will go into equities.

Even with college taken care of, and a general approach to retirement decided upon, you still have one more decision to make: How are you going to handle parenting your parents?

Parenting Your Parents

In general, with the funds you're allocating for your parents' care, you'll take a conservative approach. You'll want income, of course, but you'll be conservative in seeking that income.

Why?

There are a couple of reasons.

First, you'll probably be using some of your parents' money, as well as your own, to help pay for their needs, and as a rule older people tend to be extremely conservative with their money. They are not going to be comfortable if you put some or all of their funds into South African gold stocks or the latest high-tech venture to pay for their future. In fact, things that you believe are appropriate and safe—such as investing in a growth and income mutual fund—may strike them as too risky.

From an economic point of view, their position probably doesn't make sense. But, as we said, no matter how good an investment might be, it is not appropriate if you (or your parents) are just not comfortable with it.

Second, you'll want to be conservative because, quite frankly, you don't know what you are up against. A parent who is in excellent health today may need long-term care starting tomorrow.

When you are facing this kind of uncertainty, it's best to have your money—or at least a good portion of it—readily accessible. If you have to call on your assets quickly, you don't want them tied up in anything whose values might fluctuate substantially over the short term.

But even if you take a conservative approach, there is still a bit of room for innovation when it comes to paying for your parents' health care.

We don't recommend that you dip into your IRA to help your parents—but if you are forced to tap it, that decision should automatically force you to reevaluate your own retirement-planning strategy.

Odds are that your original retirement plan had called for you to live in comfort thanks to retirement income that would be coming in from several sources: Social Security, your employer pension plan, your 401(k), your IRA, and your other investments.

Obviously, if you use your IRA money to help your parents, the amount of money that will be available to you upon retirement will have decreased.

Running Out of Time? Be Conservative

As we have seen, you can have three different investment objectives, with each one of them calling for a different allocation strategy.

Okay, by this point you're willing to concede that every person's financial situation is different, and that each person will have his own particular approach to asset allocation, ranging from extremely conservative to aggressive.

Does that mean there are no hard-and-fast rules?

No. There are two.

One constant: The less time you have to accomplish your investment objective, the more conservative you should be.

If you are going to need the money in the immediate future—your daughter is starting college in a few years, for example—you don't want to do anything that is going to jeopardize her education.

The *second constant* is something that we have stressed all along. You must be comfortable with the investment decisions you make.

All the rules, investment books, counsel you receive from your financial advisers are worthless unless you can sleep with your investment decisions at night. In other words, if you are a conservative investor at heart, then by all means take a conservative approach, regardless of what the investment model may say is "right."

Let's go back to our theoretical benchmark model to see what may actually happen in reality.

Let's suppose that this is what the model says is the right asset allocation formula for today's circumstances:

	Stocks	Bonds	Cash
Benchmark	55%	40%	5%

If you got that advice, and you were running your company's $100 million investment portfolio, what you would do would be pretty straightforward. You'd put $55 million in stocks, $40 million in bonds, and have $5 million in cash, or cash equivalents, such as a money market fund.

But how would different types of investors react to the news?

We have already talked about how one family would react. Now let's suppose we have three people, all women age 45, who are wondering where they should be putting the $50,000 they have saved for their retirement. The money is currently sitting in a passbook savings account and they are trying to figure out what to do with it.

Since all the women are in the same financial situation, and have exactly the same goal (to retire in 20 years) the only thing that will be different about how they choose to allocate their assets will be their approach to investments. Recalling our discussion that began on page 239, where we talked about investor profiles, we'll assume that one is *conservative,* and concentrating on current income. Let's say the second woman is looking for capital appreciation; she's looking for growth and income. For terms of this discussion let's call her a *moderate* in her approach to markets. And finally, our third woman is likely to throw caution to the winds. She's our *aggressive* investor.

Each will use the model as her benchmark, and then invest according to her nature. On the next page you'll see how those different investment portfolios would look.

What fairly jumps off the page is the disparity in how much money is invested in stocks. The conservative investor is significantly "underfunding" her equity investment according to the recommendations called for by the benchmark model, while the aggressive investor is significantly "overinvested." However, this shouldn't have come as any great surprise. After all, there's a reason why these women got their "conservative" and "aggressive" labels.

By the way, being "aggressive" does not necessarily mean your whole focus is on equities. It really means that you are aggressive in exploiting trends, in taking quick advantage of change, real or

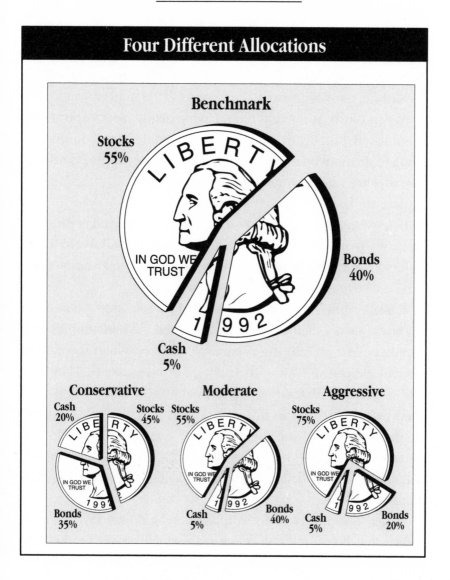

anticipated. There are times, for example, when being "aggressive" could call for you to make a major switch in assets from cash and equities to bonds—in order to aggressively take advantage of a developing and attractive bonds situation.

History Points the Way

In these models, even the most conservative of investors still has 45% of her assets in stocks.

At first blush, you might think having nearly half of your retirement assets tied up in equities is not a particularly conservative thing to do. So why does—and indeed, why *should*—a conservative investor have so much money in stocks?

Because history shows it's the right thing to do.

Being conservative doesn't mean burying your head in the sand. You always have to be vigilant, and consider the real world. That's a lesson, unfortunately, that many investors—especially those who are saving for retirement—never learn.

Consider the findings of Merrill Lynch's latest retirement-planning survey. Some 88% of retirees identified inflation as their number-one concern. But a paradox surfaced when those same retirees were asked about their choice of investments. They said, not surprisingly, that safety of principal was the thing they considered most in picking an investment.

After safety of principal, these investors listed the following factors as important: being assured of a lifetime income, earning regular income and dividends, and having easy access to their funds.

If their response was not surprising, why do we say there was a paradox? Because if you choose investments *solely* on the basis of safety, the best you are going to do is stay even with inflation. And the odds say that the purchasing power of your money will actually fall over time, if you put your money in things that absolutely guarantee the safety of your principal.

To preserve capital, you need a strategy that will build wealth and increase income. Why? Because you need a way to combat inflation.

Protecting your assets—let alone trying to grow them—is keyed to protecting your purchasing power. To look at it another way, you must counter the erosion caused by inflation if you want your investments to give you an enjoyable retirement. Stocks historically have been the best bet against inflation. That's true, even if you begin your analysis back in the 1920s, and include how stocks performed during the Depression.

However, since few of us were active investors in the late 1920s, and into the 1930s, let's just take a look at what has happened over the 40 years beginning in 1951.

As the chart on the next page shows, since 1951 equities have outperformed both cash and bonds by more than 100%. Similarly, they have outperformed just about any combination of stocks, bonds, and cash that you could have devised.

And for people who are tempted to say that real estate and/or other investments had to outperform the market in the go-go 1980s, we offer another comparison, on page 296.

We rest our case. If you're investing long term, stocks are the way to go.

So Why Have Any Money in Cash?

If stocks have performed this well, why have any money in cash (or cash equivalents) at all? Why not be fully invested in stocks and/or bonds at all times?

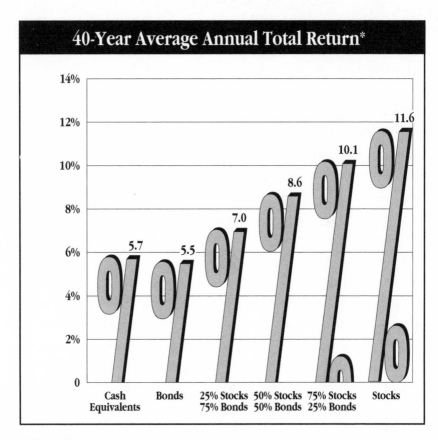

40-Year Average Annual Total Return*

*1951 to 1990

There are three reasons.

You want to have at least part of your assets in cash:

1. **In case of emergencies.**

2. **To take immediate advantage of opportunities.** (Having some cash on hand will allow you to switch into another investment almost immediately.)

3. **To pay for the taxes that will be due,** once you start drawing down the money that is in your retirement accounts.

Let's take them one at a time, starting with emergency use.

To paraphrase a bumper sticker, problems happen. When they do, you'll need an emergency source of funds. Sure, you can always sell your stocks, bonds, real estate, or your baseball card collection, for that matter, if you need to raise money. But converting those assets into cash will take time. And in addition to taking time, it could prove costly. Depending on when the emergency occurred, you might find yourself trying to sell stocks while the market is extremely bearish, or trying to unload your real estate holdings when the market is glutted with properties. A cash horde, be it under your mattress or in an all-purpose banking or central assets account, is your security blanket.

Some people, such as Martha Skylar, our advertising executive from Atlanta, treat the money they've put away in their 401(k)s, or IRAs, as their emergency fund. While innovative, this idea could prove costly for two reasons.

First, if you spend your retirement money on a current emergency, it means that money won't be there once you retire. Your mother was right. You can't eat your cake and have it too.

Second, withdrawing the money early from your retirement account could have severe tax consequences. You could find that money being added to your ordinary income, for tax purposes, *and* you could also be forced to pay a 10% penalty on the early withdrawal as well—see Chapter 11. By the way, the law prohibits you from borrowing from your IRA, but the law does permit you—if your employer agrees—to borrow from your 401(k) or your 403(b).

Another reason for keeping a ready supply of cash on hand is, ironically, because there could come a time when you would want to be 100% invested in stocks or bonds. For example, due to a sudden change in the market, an ultra-aggressive benchmark calls for putting as much money into equities as you possibly can.

Or you may be offered an opportunity—maybe far outside of the markets—that is simply too good to pass up. (You get a chance to buy a vacation home at 60% of its true value; you have an absolutely sure thing in the fifth at Aqueduct.)

When opportunity knocks, you want to be able to open the door with cash in hand. People don't always want to wait around while you liquidate your other assets.

Finally, a good reason for having part of your holdings in cash is that it may be wise because at certain times the law gives you little choice. For example, once you've reached 70½, you probably will have to start to withdraw money that you have put away in tax-advantaged retirement accounts, such as IRAs, SEPS, and Keoghs. There is an extremely limited exception to these minimum distribution requirements. Consult your accountant or tax adviser to see if you completed the forms necessary to be eligible to make this special election.

Uncle Sam Is Looking at You!

Why does the government insist that you withdraw your money?

Well, it would be nice to think that Uncle Sam is only interested in your welfare. We'd love to picture a benevolent bearded uncle (played by Jimmy Stewart) sitting in Washington saying, "You know, these people have saved all their lives. They're truly good Americans. Before it's too late, let's suggest to them, spend some now, and buy that little red coupe they've always dreamed about."

It would be nice. Unfortunately, it just isn't so.

Here's what is really going on behind the mandatory withdrawals.

The underlying philosophy that led Congress to create IRAs, Keoghs, and all those other lovely tax-deferred accounts went like this: the government is willing to let you defer paying taxes on your retirement assets for years—maybe even for decades—in exchange for knowing that at some point *you will have to pay the taxes you have put off.*

After some Congressional debate, it was decided that the absolute latest point you would be able to defer those taxes would be age 70½.

Once you turn three score 10 (and a half), you'll most likely have to *start* withdrawing your retirement assets. And, of course, once you withdraw the money, the taxes are due.

How much you have to withdraw is governed by your life expectancy. The government figures out how long it is that you are likely to live, once you turn 70½. It divides the assets that you have put away tax-deferred by the years it thinks you have left, and says this is the absolute minimum that you must withdraw each year. The macabre idea is that you will have withdrawn all of your tax-deferred money in the moment just before you die. (If you want to withdraw more than the minimum, it's perfectly all right. In fact, you'll probably make the IRS happier. The more you withdraw, the more you'll obviously have to pay in taxes.)

Given all this, keeping a cash reserve on hand is wise. This way you'll have enough money on hand to pay the taxes due, instead of being forced to sell other assets when the timing may not be right.

A final comment on your cash allocation. One of the joys of an

IRA is that once you've passed age 59½, you can stop worrying about early withdrawal penalties. Starting when you are six months shy of 60, you have access to your money anytime you want, and that remains true for the next 11 years. After age 70½, as we've said, you'll probably have to start withdrawing the money on a planned basis. But between ages 59½ and 70½, you can take out as little or as much as you wish.

An example. Suppose you're retired, and at long last you decide to add the deck onto your house, a decision that is going to cost you $25,000. If in looking over your investments, you decide it makes the most sense to withdraw the money from your IRA, then do it. You can always adjust your allocation formulas later.

Note: While there is no early withdrawal penalty for taking money out of your IRA, once you turn 59½—how could there be, you aren't withdrawing it early?—there is still another major factor to consider: taxes.

Remember, the money in your IRA account has been accumulating tax-deferred. Some of that money—and all the interest it has earned—will be taxed as soon as you withdraw it. This also includes gains. By "some," we mean the money will be taxed on withdrawal if it had been contributed on a deductible basis—that is, it was contributed before taxes. If the contributions were nondeductible—made after taxes—the money will not be taxed on withdrawal. But all earnings and gains—on either before-tax money or after-tax money—are always taxable. For more explanation of deductible and nondeductible contributions in IRAs, see Chapter 11, and for information on IRA withdrawals, see Chapter 31. You should note that if you made nondeductible contributions to your IRA, the percentage of each withdrawal that will be taxable will be determined according to a formula. More information regarding this formula is available in IRS Publication 590.

If you are still working when you take the money out, your withdrawal will be added to current income, possibly causing you to pay a huge tax bill.

This is why it is usually better to wait until retirement—even if you have already turned 59½—before you withdraw tax-deferred retirement money.

A Final Thought—A Kick or a Pat

One of the great appeals of the asset allocation strategy is that you don't have to spend an inordinate amount of time managing your assets, important as those assets are. The strategy helps you determine where you should put the money, and in what amounts.

But, as we said at the very beginning, this does not mean that you make one investment decision today ("let's see—60% stocks, 30% bonds, 10% cash") and then you are done forever.

In the case of an aggressive investor, you will be reviewing your allocation decisions *at least* once a month. In other cases, you might be reviewing your portfolio quarterly. But in *every* case you should be going over everything at least once a year *at the absolute minimum.*

The review is a natural enough idea. Having gone through the vitally important process of figuring out your own profile as an investor, picking time horizons, establishing objectives, determining your asset allocation, and then investing accordingly, you still have to ask—periodically—"How am I doing?"

The answer may lead you to pat yourself on the back, or kick yourself in the backside. But you'll never know for sure, unless you review.

Allocating assets means that you structure your personal investment portfolio to best match your long-term objectives. Few things are static in investments. Your portfolio—your allocation of assets—should change as the world changes. In the best of all worlds, your portfolio will exploit market and economic trends.

CHAPTER 16

Tax-Free Investments

A key component of our 4-S system of retirement saving is "saving tax-advantaged." Elsewhere, we have talked about the advantages that come from investing with pretax dollars (usually in retirement plans), and how you can make money if you are allowed to defer paying the income tax that is due on your earnings or gains. Here, we'd like to talk about the third way you can save tax-advantaged, and that is by saving tax-free.

If you are in a relatively high income tax bracket, earning tax-free income can be an integral part of your savings strategy. Municipal bonds (popularly called *munis*) are one of the few remaining sources of tax-free income, and they will be our focus in this chapter.

The Basics

Municipal bonds are securities issued by state and local governments, and their agencies. The bond issuers borrow the money they need by selling bonds, which are, in effect, IOUs. The borrower agrees to repay the loan in a fixed period of time, say, 30 years. In exchange for the use of the money, the issuer usually makes fixed-interest payments semiannually to bondholders over the life of the loan. As a bondholder, you are a creditor. This is in contrast to equities where by buying stock you become a part owner of the company.

Why would you buy a muni or equivalent? There are five reasons:

- **Tax-exempt income.** Municipal bonds issued by government units within a particular state are exempt from federal, and in most cases state and local taxes, to residents of that state. So, in most cases, if you are a New York State resident, and you buy a New York City municipal bond, you will not have to pay any federal, state, or local taxes. Bonds issued by U.S. territories (the Commonwealth of Puerto Rico, the U.S. Virgin Islands, and Guam) are also free of federal, state, and local taxes.

Tax-Free Income: A Matter of Tradition

The interest earned on most municipals is exempt from federal income taxes. This exemption reflects the long-standing American political-philosophical tradition that it's much to the public good to finance certain local projects, and so the nation can afford to give special tax incentives to investors in these projects. Often, interest is also exempt from state and local taxes. The Supreme Court, in fact, has recently reaffirmed that Congress has given state legislatures and local governments this right to issue tax-free bonds, which in effect, lowers the various governments' net interest costs. We will talk, in detail, about how this works a bit later in the chapter.

- **Safety.** The bonds are backed by promises from a government authority that they will be paid. As we note later, there is a distinction between the types of promises government entities make about repayment. While there have been defaults, it doesn't happen often. (The default rate is less than .003% of all bonds issued.) Of course, while the issuer promises to pay you the full amount when the bond "matures," or comes due, there may be fluctuations in a bond's market price in the interim. More on that later in this chapter.

- **Flexibility.** Maturity dates on municipal securities can range from several months to 30 years or more. You can decide when you want your principal back, and choose your bond's maturity accordingly.

- **Diversity.** There is a wide range of types of bonds available, ranging from general obligation bonds—secured by the full faith and credit of a state or local government—to bonds backed by revenues from a particular project, such as a toll road or bridge. There are insured municipals for the extremely safety conscious, and zero coupon municipals that offer investors an assured way to compound their money tax-free, provided the bonds are held to maturity.

- **Marketability.** There is an active trading market for most municipals, so selling your holdings before maturity should not be a problem, although the price you receive will depend on market conditions at the time you sell.

How to Increase Spendable Income

Interest payments on tax-exempt municipals are generally lower than on taxable investments—including corporate bonds—that have the same quality and maturity. But because the federal government doesn't tax the interest you earn, you may get more after-tax spendable income from a tax-exempt bond than from a taxable bond or some other taxable investment.

By the way—should you buy munis in a tax-deferred retirement account—such as an IRA, or a SEP? The short answer: no.

It's redundant to put something tax-exempt into a tax-deferred account. And besides—it just doesn't work to your advantage.

When Tax-Free Doesn't Mean Everything Is Tax-Free

If you expect to drop into a lower tax bracket when you retire, time your municipals to expire after retirement day. We will be talking about maturity dates a bit later on in this chapter.

Although the tax-free income is indeed tax-free, it can affect your other taxes. Once you are retired, and drawing Social Security, those Social Security benefits are not taxed unless your adjusted gross income (AGI) exceeds $25,000. The government's definition of AGI includes *all tax-free income, and half of your Social Security benefits.* Thus, the taxable amount would be half the excess over $25,000 but no more than half of your Social Security income.

If this is a confusing wrinkle to you, don't hesitate to go to the experts: your accountant or your financial adviser. Our advice also is to not hesitate to go to the ultimate source: the Social Security Administration itself. In both the national headquarters and the branches we checked, we have been impressed with the people we've talked with. They *are* helpful. They—in any local branch in the country—will do their best to explain the Social Security R and R: Rules and Regulations. Try them.

Whatever earnings—from any source whatsoever—you eventually take out of a tax-deferred retirement plan *will be taxed.* No game-playing allowed—so just don't do it.

Now let's get back to how you can increase your spendable income with munis. For example, if you are in the 31% federal tax bracket, you would have to earn 7.97% from a taxable investment to match the take-home yield of a tax-exempt municipal paying 5.5%.

The following table shows how this works:

Tax Equivalent Yield

Federal Tax Bracket	Tax-Exempt Yield						
	3.50%	4.00%	4.50%	5.00%	5.50%	6.00%	6.50%
	Taxable Equivalent Yield						
15%	4.12%	4.71%	5.29%	5.88%	6.47%	7.05%	7.64%
28%	4.86%	5.56%	6.25%	6.94%	7.64%	8.33%	9.02%
31%	5.07%	5.80%	6.52%	7.25%	7.97%	8.70%	9.42%

Consider the effect of state and local income taxes in making the comparison between taxable and tax-exempt securities. (The advantage of municipals can be even greater if you live in a state with high taxes, and buy bonds that are exempt from state and local taxes.)

There is a relatively simple way to compare which investment— taxable or tax-free—would leave you with more at the end of the year.

Here's what you do:

Deduct your tax bracket from 100, and find the remainder. Then divide the tax-free yield being offered by the remainder. The result tells you how much you would have to earn from a taxable investment to equal the tax-free yield being offered.

Let's use an example from our table to show how this works.

Say you are in the 31% tax bracket and are thinking about buying a municipal bond paying 5%.

You'd subtract your tax bracket (31) from 100, and get a remainder of 69. You'd then divide the 5% yield by the remainder (69) and discover that you would have to earn 7.246% in taxable income to equal a 5% tax-free investment.

Two Kinds of Markets

There are two markets for municipal bonds: the primary market and the secondary market.

The primary market is for new bonds just sold by a municipality and offered for the first time to the public by a municipal securities dealer or syndicate of dealers.

The secondary market is the trading market in which previously issued bonds are bought and sold.

How to Buy Smarter

As an investor in municipal bonds, you are a creditor. Naturally, before you lend your money, you'll want to know who the borrower is, how secure your loan will be, what return you'll earn, and when you'll get your money back. Here are some of the things you should look for.

Par value. This is the amount of money that will be paid back to you at maturity. Most municipal bonds are issued and sold in denominations of $5,000 par value. However, terminology in the municipal market assumes a par value of $1,000. So, 25 bonds represent $25,000 in par value.

Coupon rate. This is the stated interest rate that the borrower promises to pay. This rate, which is usually fixed for the life of the bond, is expressed as an annual percentage of the bond's par value, and is generally paid in two equal parts every six months.

For example, 10 bonds (that is, bonds with $10,000 par value) with a 6% coupon will pay $600 in interest annually, in two interest payments of $300 each.

Book-entry registration. Bonds used to be issued with interest coupons physically attached. Every six months, the bondholder would clip a coupon and present it for payment of interest.

However, since 1983, municipal bonds have been issued in registered form. The owner's name is carried on the books of the issuer, and interest is paid by check to the registered owner on the appropriate date.

Registered municipals are issued either in certificate form or book-entry form.

When a bond is registered in certificate form, the owner's name is actually printed on a physical certificate. If the bond is sold, the certificate must be reregistered in the new owner's name.

The trend in the municipal industry is to use book-entry registration. In other words, the owner receives no certificate.

With book-entry registration, ownership and transfer of ownership are recorded through computer entries at a central clearing house. Your transaction confirmations, and periodic account statements provide proof that you own book-entry bonds.

Bond prices. Bond prices are stated as a percentage of par value, the value of the bond at maturity.

If a bond is quoted at 100, it is trading at 100% of par value. Since, as we said, the bond market—for trading purposes—assumes a par value of $1,000, a bond quoted at 97 would have a value of $970. A bond trading at 103 would have a value of $1,030.

Bonds trading below 100 are said to be trading at a discount. Bonds trading above 100 are trading at a premium.

Yields. Municipal bonds are often quoted in terms of yield, rather than price, since there are so many issuers and maturity dates.

A bond's yield and its coupon interest rate are not the same thing. Yield generally refers to the return you will earn on your investment, and it can be calculated in several different ways:

Current yield. This shows the relationship of a bond's coupon rate to its current price. In this relationship, the numerator is the coupon rate. The denominator is the current price.

For example, if "five" bonds ($5,000 par value) have a 6% coupon rate and are priced at 100 (they cost $5,000), their current yield is 6% (6/100). If those same bonds are priced at 120 (cost $6,000), the current yield drops to 5% (6/120).

Yield to maturity. This is the yield that is used to value bonds when they are bought and sold in the secondary, or

274

trading, market, because it provides a consistent way to compare values of securities. It represents the projected return you will earn from all principal and interest payments received over the life of the bond.

Yield to maturity also takes into account that a bond purchased at a discount (to par) will ultimately be redeemed at a higher price, which could result in a capital gain for you. A bond purchased at a premium to par will ultimately mature at its lower par value, without any recognizable tax loss.

Yield to call. Municipal bonds are often issued with optional call provisions that allow the issuer to call, or redeem, the bonds prior to their maturity.

Why would issuers choose to call in their debt?

One possible reason is that interest rates may have declined since the bonds were issued. Calling the bonds would give the issuer the chance to pay off its debt with new bonds that would carry a lower interest rate.

Call dates and prices are generally specified, although some bonds are noncallable. If the bonds you are considering buying have a call provision you should know when and at what price the bonds may be called. (As a protection for investors, bonds usually can't be called for a certain number of years—generally at least 5, and often 10—after issue, and the call price is often above the bond's par value.)

Yield to call is equivalent to yield to maturity, except that it is calculated based on a particular optional call date and call price. You should look at the lower of yield to maturity and yield to call in projecting your potential return.

Why Do Bond Prices Fluctuate?

If you buy a bond when it's issued, and hold it to maturity, there is little to worry about. Odds are overwhelmingly good that you will get back all the money you loaned the issuer, plus the interest you were promised.

However, after municipal bonds have been issued, and before they are called or mature, their prices will fluctuate to meet changes in the general level of interest rates and rating changes.

Whenever interest rates rise, prices on outstanding municipal bonds normally fall.

Whenever interest rates decline, prices on outstanding fixed income securities, including tax-free municipals, usually rise. It is easy to understand why.

For example, assume "Big City" issues new noncallable municipals, that promise to pay 6%, or $60, for each $1,000 of par value. If you buy five bonds ($5,000 par value) for $5,000 and receive $300 in interest each year, your bonds have a current yield of 6%.

So far, so good.

Now assume that a year later interest rates in general have risen and new bonds from "Little City," comparable to the Big City ones you bought, come out and are paying 7%, or $70 in interest for each $1,000 of par value, and that the maturity is similar. Because $5,000 will now produce $350 in interest, instead of the $300 you are receiving, your "Big City" bonds are clearly worth less.

If you want to sell your Big City bonds in the secondary market, you'll find the price will have dropped from the $5,000 you paid to around $4,300. Why? Because at $4,300 the $300 in annual interest that the bonds pay produces about a 7% yield.

Now, let's look at the example another way. Suppose interest rates fall instead of rise.

If the newly issued Little City bonds comparable to your Big City bonds are only offering 5% in interest, then your old 6% bonds are worth more than the new ones coming out. In this case, you'll be able to sell your bonds for around $6,000 because they will only have to offer a current yield of 5% to be competitive.

Again, if you hold municipal bonds until they mature, as many investors do, you will get back your full par value—$5,000 in our example. But if you sell the bonds during their life, you may do so at a profit or a loss depending on yield levels in the market at the time you sell. The transaction will be taxed accordingly.

There are two other factors that can influence a bond's price and yield: quality (or creditworthiness) and maturity.

Let's deal with them one at a time.

Quality. The issue here is simple. How certain are you that the issuer will pay you back with interest as scheduled?

A high-quality bond typically yields less than a low-quality bond because there is considered to be relatively little risk that an issuer with a good credit rating will fail to make interest and principal payments.

Generally, if the creditworthiness of a bond weakens after you buy it, the bond's price will drop and its yield will rise to reflect the greater risk. Conversely, if the bond's credit quality improves, its value will increase and its yield will decline.

How do you determine a bond's credit quality?

Most investors use the quality ratings assigned to municipal bond issues by three recognized independent advisory services: Moody's, Standard & Poor's, and Fitch. These services analyze and grade bonds according to their investment qualities, and their ability to pay principal and interest. Some states—and their local governmental entities—are on a much sounder financial footing than others. The ratings reflect that standing.

The services rate the bonds on a scale, with three "a's" being the best:

Moody's:	Aaa	Aa	A	Baa
S&P:	AAA	AA	A	BBB
Fitch:	AAA	AA	A	BBB

It is important to keep in mind that most municipal bonds are regarded as second in quality only to U.S. Treasuries. To bond professionals, the comparisons of quality among the more highly rated bonds are matters of degree, rather than judgments of whether one bond is safe and another unsafe.

The quality ratings for all three services do continue below Baa or BBB. Issues rated lower than that are sometimes referred to as "junk bonds." That is not technically accurate. The bonds do have some worth. But the low rating is the advisory service's way of telling you that the bond is issued by a municipality with questionable financial backing. It isn't often that a municipal bond receives a junk rating, but it does happen.

Why is a "junk bond" appellation put to municipal issues? True, the vast, vast majority of high-yield bonds that can be labeled "junk" are indeed corporate bonds. (And in corporate issues, as we will discuss in Chapter 17, page 297, there is "good junk" and there is "bad junk.") But the theory of "junk"—higher than normal yield coupled with higher than normal risk—certainly can apply to a *few* municipal issues.

Issues rated below Baa or BBB are generally suitable only for more sophisticated investors who are willing to understand the increased risks, and perform the research, involved in their purchase. The interest rate on junk bonds will look attractive. But always remember that the reason the bond is paying so much is because of the risk involved.

Maturity. When the bonds mature is the second thing that influences a bond's price and yield.

Municipals with longer maturities typically yield more than those with shorter maturities because you have to wait longer to receive all your interest and principal. That means greater risk, since something could go wrong in the meantime. To compensate you for that risk, you receive a higher yield.

Longer maturities also fluctuate more in price than shorter maturities, which gives them greater potential for price appreciation and price depreciation.

Kinds of Municipal Bonds

Municipal bonds can be classified according to their payment source—where payments of principal and interest will come from—and according to their tax status.

According to Payment Source

General obligation (GO) bonds. Payments of principal and interest on GO bonds are secured by the full faith and credit of an issuer such as a state or local government that has taxing power. In effect, the issuing body promises to use every means possible to help assure that interest and principal will be repaid to investors when due.

279

GO bonds issued by local governments are typically secured by their unlimited taxing power. Bonds issued by states are often direct debt obligations of the state. In the event of default, bond-holders have the right to compel a tax levy, or legislative appropriations, to get their money back.

Revenue bonds. Revenue bonds are payable from a specific source of money—usually the charges, tolls, or rents from the facility being built. Examples would include highways, bridges, airports, hospitals, and water and sewerage treatment plants.

Because the full faith and credit of an issuer with taxing power is not pledged to secure revenue bonds—the money to repay the bonds comes from the revenue earned by the facility—they may be considered somewhat riskier than GO bonds and may offer higher yields.

Notes. Municipal notes are short-term issues, usually with maturities of less than a year. They include bond anticipation notes (BANs), revenue anticipation notes (RANs), tax anticipation notes (TANs), and tax and revenue anticipation notes (TRANs).

Notes are usually issued to provide temporary funds and repaid when anticipated revenues or taxes are collected, or when proceeds are received from a long-term bond issue.

According to Tax Status

Interest income on all municipal bonds issued before August 8, 1986, remains tax-exempt for the life of the bonds. If you buy these bonds in the secondary market, the interest you receive will be tax-exempt, as it was for the previous owner.

Bonds issued after August 7, 1986, fall into two classifications:

Essential purpose municipals. Usually issued by a municipality as a general obligation debt, they can be issued to build roads, bridges or tunnels, hospitals or schools or colleges. Sometimes they will be issued to pay for some public power projects and water and sewer systems.

Interest is fully exempt from federal income tax, and bonds from in-state issuers are also exempt from state and local income tax in most cases.

Nonessential purpose municipals. These bonds are usually issued for student loans, housing projects, some solid waste systems, some industrial development projects, and some port and airport authorities. Typically, more than 10% of the issue is used for private activities.

For tax purposes, these bonds are broken down into two categories:

Alternative minimum tax bonds. Interest is treated as a preference item for individuals subjected to the alternative minimum tax (AMT). Interest is fully exempt from federal tax for individuals not subject to the AMT.

In many cases, AMT municipals offer investors higher tax-free yields than they would receive from regular municipals. Since the tax on this type of bond is a preference item, that is, it is added back into income for people subject to the AMT, the issuer has to pay a high yield to attract higher-income investors.

However, if you are not subject to the AMT, and most individuals are not, the result of buying these bonds is that you receive a very attractive yield.

Taxable municipals. Interest is subject to federal income tax, but bonds from in-state issuers are exempt from state and local income taxes in most cases.

Zero Coupon Municipals

Zero coupon investments—which we will discuss in detail on pages 295–97—offer attractive, predictable growth. They are fixed income securities that do not pay periodic or semiannual interest. Instead, you purchase zero coupon securities at deep discounts to their par value, and collect your principal, plus all your interest, at maturity. Your total return is the difference between the price you paid to purchase the security and the security's par value at maturity.

The interest you earn on zero coupon municipals is exempt from federal income tax. That can be a big advantage over taxable zero coupon instruments which require you to pay taxes on the interest in the year in which it is earned, even though you don't actually receive that interest until maturity.

Zero coupon municipals can be an excellent way to build assets for specific long-term goals, such as a child's college education, or your own retirement, because they give you the comfort of knowing exactly how much a specific sum of money will grow to in a given number of years. And with a wide selection of maturity dates available, you can select the maturity that matches the time you'll need the money.

Insured Municipals

Even though municipal bonds are extremely safe investments, they are not safe enough for some. Enter municipal bond insurance.

Municipal bond insurance represents the promise of an insurance company to pay debt service—typically including both principal and interest payments—when it comes due, if the issuer defaults and fails to make the payments. Generally, the insurance is for the life of the bond.

Over 20% of all new issues coming to market in the last five years have carried municipal bond insurance. In addition, many municipal bonds have been insured in the secondary market.

Bonds insured by the major municipal bond insurance companies usually receive the highest credit rating from the rating agencies. While insured municipal bonds typically yield less than uninsured bonds—the difference goes to pay for the insurance—the difference is often quite small.

Treasuries: Partially Tax-Exempt

The other main source of tax-free income is U.S. Treasury securities, but they are only partially tax-exempt.

All Treasuries, which are direct obligations of the U.S. government, are subject to federal income tax, but they are exempted from state and local taxes. That makes Treasuries particularly attractive to residents of high-tax states such as New York, California, and Massachusetts.

Because they are backed by the full faith and credit of the U.S. government, Treasuries are considered to be the safest investment around. They come in three forms: Treasury bills, which mature in one year or less; Treasury notes, which mature in one to 10 years; and Treasury bonds, which mature in 10 to 30 years.

Two Alternative Ways of Investing in Municipals

You can also obtain the benefits of municipals by investing in either a municipal bond mutual bond fund or a unit investment trust.

Unit trusts and mutual funds are suitable for smaller investors because the initial investment requirement is usually fairly small. While bonds are traditionally sold in $5,000 units, you can generally invest as little as $1,000 in a unit trust or mutual fund.

And in some brokerage accounts—central asset accounts—it's even possible to put your "spare" cash into a tax-exempt money market mutual fund that invests in short-term tax-free state and local securities—and fund dividends are free from federal income taxes.

However, unit trusts and mutual funds can also be attractive to large investors because they offer the benefits of wide diversification and professional securities selection through a single investment.

Both mutual funds and unit trusts offer tax-exempt income, usually paid monthly, and you may be able to reinvest the income automatically.

Some mutual funds and unit trusts invest in just one segment of the market: insured bonds, or bonds with short maturities, or even bonds of one state with high income taxes, to name just three examples. This variety allows you to choose a mutual fund, or unit trust, to meet your specific needs, should you choose to go this route.

As part of your total investment strategy, consider municipal bonds—individual bonds or mutual funds or unit investment trusts invested in municipals—as a proven way to produce tax-free income. If you are in a high tax bracket, and you also live in a state with high income taxes, then tax-free interest might easily surpass interest from higher yield but taxable investments.

CHAPTER 17

Investments—Both Sheltered and Nonsheltered

Once you have an investment blueprint you follow it—but your obedience can't be slavish. In real life your goals will bend to market changes—there will always be something new on the horizon—and changes in your own life. If your goals are relatively stable, the appropriate asset allocation for you may not shift often, but it will change from time to time.

To make sure you can respond appropriately, you have to know what kind of investments are out there. That's the purpose of this chapter. We want to talk a little bit about the catalog of investments available to you—concentrating on some that you wouldn't normally use in retirement accounts.

After all, while preparing for your retirement is important, it's only one part of your financial planning. There are still kids to put through school, an elderly parent to take care of, or a new home to buy. If one area of your financial planning suffers, invariably they all do. To make sure that doesn't happen, you should know a little bit about all the financial tools at your disposal.

In Chapter 16 we reviewed how tax-free income could be a part of your investment and/or cash flow strategy, and in the next chapter we'll tell you about annuities. Here, we'll spend most of our time reviewing other investments and tactics that you might use, focusing primarily on investments that will work best in your nonsheltered, that is, taxable, investment accounts.

As in so much of your financial life, when you are thinking about investments outside your retirement account, much of your time will be spent worrying about taxation.

In long-term retirement accounts, taxes are not much of a factor. Generally, when you withdraw money from a retirement account you'll be taxed at whatever current tax bracket you're in.

But in a nonsheltered account, timing can be everything, when it comes time to determine how the earnings or gains on your investments will be taxed.

Here's what you have to keep in mind: Any gain is short-term *unless* you own the investment for at least one year and a day. Hold it for a shorter period, and it will be taxed as ordinary income, which means the tax rate can be as high as 31%. The maximum rate on any long-term gain is 28%. In addition, in a nonretirement account, your current dividends or earnings will be taxed each year. In a self-directed retirement account, you have no current taxes to worry about. What counts is total return. If your investment is earning 6% in dividends a year, and is gaining 5% in value annually, then your total return—none of it being currently taxed—is 11%.

Borrowing Money to Make Money

In a selected few retirement accounts—such as a 401(k) and certain other types of profit-sharing plans—it may be possible to borrow money from the account, and use it elsewhere. We don't suggest that you do this casually—but you should be aware that this option may be available in some accounts. (In many plans—such as in IRAs or SEPs—you are not allowed to borrow from the account, or pledge the assets as collateral otherwise.)

But in a nonretirement account, you may be able to borrow against your investment assets, and in effect, increase the purchasing power of your account. Margin accounts are the clearest example of this.

Here's how a margin account works. You pledge your securities

---

Donating Securities to Charity

The distinction between long term and short term is particularly important if you are planning to donate securities to charity. Only assets held long term will qualify for a charitable deduction equal to the fair market value. Deductions for short-term holdings given to a charity are limited to the original cost of the security.

The moral: Check the calendar carefully. It could mean a considerable difference in deductions.

By the way, if the securities you're planning on giving to charity carry an unrealized capital loss, our advice is: *Don't donate them. Give the cash instead.*

Here's why. You can't take a capital loss unless you actually sell a security for less than you paid. So don't donate the loser. Sell it. That obviously establishes the loss for tax purposes. Then give the charity whatever cash you receive for the stock.

You get a charitable contribution deduction, plus a deductible capital loss.

as collateral, and the financial services firm at which you have the securities will lend you money at rates that typically range from one to two points over prime.

How much the financial services firm will lend you will depend on the kind of securities you pledge as collateral. You can borrow up to half the value of eligible stocks, mutual funds, unit investment trusts and convertible bonds, and between 70% to 90% of the value of nonconvertible bonds, Ginnie Mae's, and most government issues. There are even some firms that will allow you to borrow up to 95% of the value of the Treasury securities you pledge as collateral.

The advantage of borrowing against your securities is clear: you can diversify your portfolio without liquidating your investments. (That also means you can diversify without giving up any of the yield your investments are producing.)

Before we go into this in detail, let us first give you a warning: *Leverage works both ways.* If the investment you make with a margin loan increases, you can make a lot of money. If it heads south, you stand to lose a lot. At the extreme, your loss could increase your debt to the point where you would be asked to bring in cash or additional marginable securities to reduce your loan. This is called a maintenance or margin call. If you're unable to bring in additional assets your financial services firm would be forced to sell some of the securities you pledged as collateral in order to cover the debt.

How do you manage the risks associated with this kind of borrowing? With intelligence. By being judicious, instead of shooting for the moon.

Specifically:

Borrow against a stable portfolio. The more stable the assets you have pledged as collateral, the less likely it is that they will suddenly nose-dive.

Buy less-volatile investments. Following this advice, you won't make as much. (No risk, no reward.) But then you won't be risking as much, either.

Use stop-loss orders. When you buy, determine the point at which you'll sell, should your investment fall.

Let's say you are buying 1,000 shares of a stock at $40 a share with the full expectation that it will climb to $50. Recognizing that the price may fall, you enter a stop loss at $35. If your shares drop to $35, the stock is automatically sold at the market price.

That price may be $35, or a little more, or a little less.

When the stock hits $35 a share, it will automatically trigger an order to sell. If the stock continues to fall, you may end up getting $34.50. If it bounces up, after hitting $35, you might get $35.25.

By entering a stop-loss order, you are protecting the downside. You know ahead of time how much money you stand to lose.

In this example—where you bought 1,000 shares at $40 a share and ended up selling at $35—your loss would be $5,000, before transaction fees. That's a lot, but at least that's all it is. If the stock hits $35 a share, and continues to drop, it is no longer your problem. Your loss was capped back with the stop-loss order.

Borrow conservatively. If you borrow 20% of the purchase price of a stock, the stock would have to decrease by 70% before it triggered a maintenance call. That's what we mean by borrowing conservatively. If you borrowed up to the maximum allowed, 50% of your stock's value, then only a 29% decline would cause a maintenance call.

The following chart tells the story:

100 Shares of XYZ (purchased at $60 per share)		
% of market value borrowed	**Maintenance call when price goes below**	**% Decline that triggers maintenance call**
50%	$42⅞	29%
40%	34¼	43%
30%	25¾	57%
20%	17⅛	71%
10%	9	85%

Hedge by writing a covered call. This is a conservative strategy that calls for you to sell an option on securities you own. A covered call limits your upside gain, but it also provides some downside protection against loss.

Okay, we've preached conservatism, and warned you what the bad news can be, now let's show you how borrowing money can make you money. (In this example, we're *not* taking into account commissions or interest charges on the money you borrowed that would have lessened your profits. Your interest costs, naturally, will vary—depending on how long you pay interest before you sell. Conversely, we are also not including possible dividends from the stock that would have increased your return.)

First, the cost of borrowing through a margin account is relatively reasonable. These rates will change—constantly—but in the chart below is a typical (as of mid-1992) comparison of various interest rates. (Of course, a margin credit line is a secured loan, while the other two are unsecured.)

Now for the really good news. Let's spend a minute explaining how a credit line strategy can pay off:

Suppose you have $20,000 in cash to invest. You buy 500 shares of a stock at $40, and sell at $50. Your net gain is $5,000, which is a 25% return on your investment. That's good.

But suppose that to start with, you decide to borrow money, and add it to the cash you have to invest. Look what happens.

Instead of 500 shares, we'll say you buy 1,000 shares at $40, using your $20,000 in cash, and another $20,000 you have borrowed from your financial services firm. When you sell at $50, your profit (after you've repaid the loan) is $10,000, which is a 50% return on your initial cash investment of $20,000.

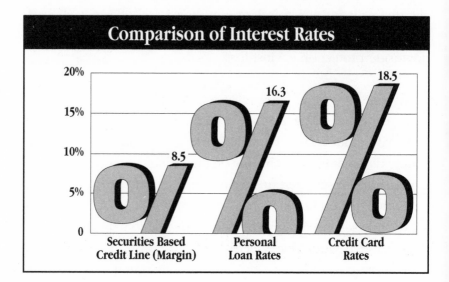

Other Ideas

In these few pages, all we can do is give you a cursory look at the investment choices available. If any one idea catches your eye, and you want to learn more, visit your neighborhood bookstore or library. For example, in just two complex areas—the futures markets and options strategies—you'll find dozens of books or guides.

If you want to do your research the quick way, ask your financial consultant for help. She'll be glad to talk to you about whatever interests you, and chances are she'll have brochures, leaflets, or fact sheets available.

Obviously, not all investments will be suitable for you—but you should be aware of the basic characteristics of each. The more you know, the easier it is to reject what doesn't fit you.

We think of the investment choices out there as forming a pyramid. At the base are investments that are liquid, and virtually risk-free. Included here are things such as money market funds and U.S. Treasury notes and bonds. Then as you climb you encounter different kinds of investments designed to meet your different goals. The illustration on the next page captures what we mean.

Comparing the enormous range of investment possibilities to a pyramid, or a mountain, leads to an obvious parallel. How many of us can—should—climb to the top?

Everyone will have some assets in the *low-risk/safety-prone* base of the mountain. Everyone who's looking long term to retirement will have considerable assets, if not most, in the middle two tiers, or investment zones labeled: *Conservative Growth Income* and *Growth.*

Different Investments to Meet Your Different Goals

High Risk/ Speculative

Raw land, commodities, options and futures, precious metals, speculative common stocks, high-yield corporate and municipal bonds.

Growth

Direct investment, investment real estate, high-quality corporate bonds, high-quality municipal bonds, investment grade and growth common stocks and certain growth mutual funds, REIT's.

Conservative Growth/ Income

Investment grade common and preferred stocks, selected utility common stocks, selected growth and income mutual funds, investment grade municipal bonds and corporate bonds, single premium life insurance, variable annuities, U.S. Government agencies.

Liquidity, Low Risk or Safety: Base

Money market funds, passbook savings, certificates of deposit, U.S. Treasury notes and bonds, U.S. Treasury bills, cash value of life insurance, fixed rate annuities.

Very few investors who are saving for retirement should climb to the top: *High-Risk, Speculative.* There is a difference between mountain watching and mountain climbing.

Over the year hundreds of thousands of people in the Seattle-Tacoma area will catch a glimpse of Mount Rainier's peak—at some 14,000 feet—but few will climb it. Similarly, we'll guess that of those many Anchorage citizens who've seen Mount McKinley, or who have flown over it, only a handful have climbed the 20,320 feet that make up America's highest peak.

That's the way we feel about the peak of the investment pyramid. Look at it, marvel at it, but be very careful in climbing it.

As to the middle portion of the mountain, or the pyramid, your investments—as we have said all along—should be diversified.

Not just in your various retirement accounts, but in your non-retirement accounts as well.

Why? Because it reduces volatility.

Let's compare the 10-year average (1981–1990) performance of stocks, bonds, real estate, and money market investments and compare it to a diversified portfolio split equally among those four groups.

As this chart on the next page shows graphically, while stocks gave you the best average performance for the decade, the diversified portfolio provided what we believe is the best combination of stability and return.

With that by way of background, let's discuss the investment choices you have.

Among them are:

Common stock. There is hardly a chapter in this book where we haven't talked about how important equities—be they individual stocks or in mutual funds, unit investment trusts, or managed portfolios—are to your long-term picture.

Why?

Because history has consistently proven that equities are the best way to counter the effects of inflation. In Chapter 15, "Allocating Your Assets," you'll find a fairly complete discussion of equities' place in the sun.

Zero coupons. Zeros, in their many forms, are like those old

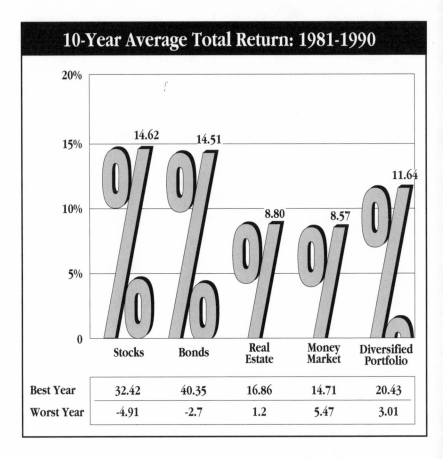

10-Year Average Total Return: 1981-1990

	Stocks	Bonds	Real Estate	Money Market	Diversified Portfolio
Best Year	32.42	40.35	16.86	14.71	20.43
Worst Year	-4.91	-2.7	1.2	5.47	3.01

war bonds or savings bonds you or your parents bought years ago. Remember? You—or more likely in the case of a savings bond, a relative—paid $18.75 for each bond. You got them as a present, held them for a while, and received $25, or more, back when you cashed them in.

With a zero you pay $600 today, for example, for something that will be worth $1,000 at maturity. Zeros can be an excellent way to save for retirement, because you'll know ahead of time exactly what you'll be getting.

If you invest in a zero, you collect all your principal, and all the interest that principal earned, at maturity. However, the law insists that the interest be calculated, or "imputed," each year. In other words, even though you didn't actually receive any interest from the zero which is maturing 10 years from now, the IRS wants you to report one-tenth the interest that you will eventually receive on this year's Form 1040.

A lot of people find this psychologically damaging. The way to avoid the problem, of course, is to put zeros into a retirement account, such as an IRA. If you do, no taxes will be due until you withdraw the money.

Zero coupon investments have been structured from corporate and municipal bonds, CDs, and U.S. Treasuries. Whatever the investment is in, zeros are always sold at substantial discounts to their face value. The longer the maturity the greater the discount.

Junk bonds. These are bonds that have a high yield, but earn a low grade from a rating service, such as Standard & Poor's or Moody's. In the 1980s the investment world was jammed with junk bonds, mostly corporate, but some municipal. There are fewer now, and all we can say is that there are good junk bonds and there are bad ones. Check the ratings, do your homework, and decide whether junk bonds are for you, whether the high yield is important. You have to consider carefully the risk-reward trade-off here. If you're thinking of this as a retirement investment, the risk might be too high for the reward. If you do decide to seek high yields, you could diversify by buying high-yield mutual funds or unit investment trusts.

Futures. We have nothing against "futures," in all their varia-tions. In fact, watching the dynamics of the futures markets is fascinating.

On one side you have the hedgers, business people who regu-larly use a commodity and are trying to protect themselves from sudden increases (or decreases) in the price of oil, wheat, gold, or whatever.

On the other side are the speculators, who take a position in the hope that the price will go up (or maybe down) to their benefit. The two jockey back and forth constantly.

And futures markets—which not too long ago were limited to raw materials—now have broadened enormously to encompass the world of financial instruments as well. You can be a seller (or a buyer) of Eurodollars, Japanese yen, or British pounds futures, or you can bet that bond, stock, or Treasury prices will rise or fall.

It's clear that there is a lot of money to be made, or lost, in futures. It's also clear that there's a lot of professional guidance available to you.

As a rule, investing in futures is not a good way to ensure a successful retirement. The markets are too volatile. The only exception? There are professionals—either through managed funds or partnerships—who could manage these investments for you. But again, you need to be able to sleep nights.

Convertible bonds. Some people will tell you it's like buying the best of stocks and bonds all in one.

You're buying a bond (so you're buying a steady rate of return), but you're also buying the right, at a specific time down the road, to convert that bond into common stock of the issuing company.

Companies like this device, because if you do convert to stock, you are in effect swapping the money they owe you—remember bonds are nothing more than IOUs—for equity.

You like convertibles because you're not going to make the conversion unless it means a nice gain for you. This is a conservative way to play the future.

Real estate. Can you make a lot of money in real estate? You bet. Have we figured out how to do it? Nope.

If you became a real estate investor in commercial properties on the East Coast in the early to mid-1980s, you might have made more money than you knew what to do with. (And each region of the rest of the country has had its cycles.) If you invested in the commercial market five years later, you may have lost your shirt.

It's not that we want to give short shrift to the direct ownership of real estate as an investment, it's just that it is beyond our province. So while you certainly can invest in raw land or income-producing property, they are usually beyond the realm of most security accounts.

That said, we will comment a bit further on what is probably the best single real estate investment for you: your home. (It's so important, we've devoted a whole chapter, Chapter 23, to how you can access that investment at the proper time.)

While you're thinking about *all* of the potential investments in the world, remember what a rare investment your home is. You can use it (that is, live in it) while paying down the mortgage, which helps increase your equity. (And if your home appreciates in value during this time, so much the better.)

Cash. This is so simple. Why even think about it as an investment? The short answer: cash can earn money for you, while you are figuring out where to invest it. Plus, you also want to have a certain part of your assets—say between three and six months' salary—readily available to handle emergencies. When there is a problem, you want to have cash on hand.

When we say cash, we are also including "cash equivalents," such as short-term Treasury bills and CDs. You could go out and buy these individually, but the smart way is to acquire them through a money market mutual fund, a pool of investments with maturities of one year or less.

The chief characteristics of money market funds are safety

and liquidity. They also generally earn a rate of return equal to inflation.

Fixed income securities. Specifically, we are talking about corporate and government bonds. Municipal bonds, of course, are fixed income securities, but tax-exempt.

Fixed income securities are IOUs. The borrower—be it a corporation or government entity—agrees to repay the loan in a fixed period of time, say, 30 years. In exchange for the use of your money, the issuer usually makes fixed-interest payments, semiannually during the life of the loan.

If you buy a high-quality bond when it's issued, and hold it to maturity, there is little to worry about. Odds are overwhelmingly good that you will get back all the money you loaned the issuer, plus all the interest you were promised.

However, after the bonds have been issued, and before they are called or mature, their prices will fluctuate to meet changes in the general level of interest rates. That is, whenever interest rates rise, prices on most outstanding bonds will fall. Whenever interest rates decline, prices on outstanding fixed income securities, such as bonds, rise. But there is always the obligation to repay you fully at maturity.

We covered, in detail, which fixed income securities might be tax-free in Chapter 16, but here's a quick synopsis:

Corporate bonds: Fully taxable.

Government (U.S.) bonds: Subject to federal tax, but free of state and local taxes.

State and municipal bonds: Generally free of all taxes. (Even if you are subject to the alternative minimum taxes [AMT], there are still some municipal bonds you may want to invest in. See Chapter 16.)

Certificates of deposit have interest rates that are typically tied closely to the Federal Reserve discount rate. These investments can be short term—one to three months—but they typically range from three to five years. They are usually federally insured up to $100,000 per taxpayer.

Collateralized mortgage obligations (CMOs): These could be part of your fixed income portfolio, although they do carry a higher degree of risk than CDs. They are fully secured mortgage-backed securities. Sold as $1,000 bonds, these are interests in a pool of specific mortgages.

Generally, you'll receive a monthly check, although some CMOs pay quarterly, and that check will represent interest on your money, plus a partial return of capital.

You can buy short-term, medium-term, or long-term CMOs. As with corporate or government bonds, CMOs with longer maturities generally will yield more than bonds with shorter maturities. The yield is usually higher than U.S. Treasuries or corporate bonds with comparable maturities, but there is always a chance of early repayment, especially if interest rates decline. If that happens, you face the risk of having to reinvest the proceeds when interest rates are lower.

Both return of principal and interest is guaranteed—either by the U.S. government, in the case of Ginnie Maes, or by quasi-government corporations (Freddie Macs and Fannie Maes).

Mutual funds and unit investment trusts: Just about all the investments we talked about in this laundry list can be purchased through mutual funds or unit investment trusts (UITs). Through either, you are letting a professional either select, or select and manage, your investments. And by investing in a mutual fund, or a trust, you are automatically diversifying.

The objective of the mutual fund or trust is clearly stated, so you can pick the ones that best match your objectives.

Mutual funds and UITs are so integral a part of a long-term investment strategy—in either a taxable or nontaxable account—that we've devoted two chapters (19 and 20) to them.

Option notes: Relatively new on the investment scene, these are equity securities, limited to a particular company, which seek to deliver a predictable return. These investments combine, in effect, equities with a zero coupon instrument. These are convertible securities, which means you're allowed to convert your investment into a specific number of shares of the underlying common stock. Because of the conversion feature, or option, you may be able to share in the upside movement of the underlying common stock, whether or not you actually convert from notes to stock, because the value of the notes should rise as the price of the underlying stock rises.

Three points to remember:

1. *If your investments are non-sheltered, that is, they're not in a retirement account—how they are taxed is important.*

2. *Borrowing against these securities to buy additional securities—if done judiciously—can be a useful tool.*

3. *Market changes and shifting of your personal objectives means your investment mix will also change. But, no matter what, stay diversified.*

CHAPTER 18

Annuities

Let's begin with a simple question: Do you want your money to grow tax-deferred and then provide you with a guaranteed income?

If you answered yes, you might want to look into annuities as a way of funding your financial future.

An annuity is a contract between you and an insurance company. (Please note: an annuity is not really life insurance. While the money you invest, plus net gains, less any withdrawals, will be paid to your beneficiaries when you die, there is not a tax-free death benefit as there is with life insurance—more details in a few pages.)

The way it works is simple: You pay a premium to the insurance company—either in one lump sum or periodically, depending on the type of annuity—and in exchange the insurance company guarantees to pay you income in the future. That income could be for the rest of your life, or a set number of years, or some combination of the two. It's your choice. You can decide to take the income immediately or you can defer your payments until some future date, say, somewhere near your retirement.

Why do I need to put more money toward my retirement, you might ask. I already have an IRA, 401(k), and a company pension plan. Who needs more?

All those retirement plans are good, and you can if you want take a quick bow for being so farsighted, but annuities offer a big advantage—a whole new dimension to retirement assets—that you should consider, no matter how much money you have already put away otherwise for your retirement. *Annuities have no annual contribution limits.*

While there are tax laws that control how much you can put each year into your 401(k), IRA, and almost every other retirement plan, you can put as much into an annuity as you like.

Let's compare the tax-deferral features of an annuity to tax deferral in other plans. Money that you put into your 401(k) is salary deferred—so taxes are deferred (as we discussed in Chapter 8). Your IRA contribution—depending on your eligibility—may also be tax-deductible and *all* the earnings or gains *are* tax-deferred.

If you are buying an annuity *outside* of a retirement plan, the basic investment is after taxes, but the earnings or gains in the annuity *are* tax-deferred.

The money that you put in an annuity earns interest that accumulates tax-deferred until you begin to make withdrawals (details a little later) or begin to receive your regularly scheduled payments.

In addition to having your money growing tax-deferred, there is another benefit as well. Annuity payments are composed of two parts: the interest on the money you invested, plus a return of the money you invested originally.

The portion of the check you receive that is the return of principal is not taxed.

As in any investment that is tax-deferred your investment grows rapidly for three reasons: (1) Your original investment earns interest, (2) that interest earns interest, since it is automatically compounded; and (3) the money you would ordinarily pay out for taxes remains invested—earning interest.

Here's How They Work

There are two types of annuities—immediate and deferred—and two ways that your investment can earn money, by earning a fixed rate or a variable one.

Let's walk through each type.

An immediate annuity is just what the name implies. You put in a fixed sum of money, and the annuity begins paying you income immediately. (In this case, "immediately" means no later than 12 months after you bought the annuity.)

People who buy immediate annuities are usually trying to supplement their retirement income, and have found the income being paid by the annuity appealing because it can be used primarily as a systematic liquidation of principal and interest over their lifetimes, no matter how long they live.

Deferred annuities, not surprisingly, accumulate their earnings tax-deferred.

Let's answer the question that probably just leaped into your head: "Suppose I buy a deferred annuity *today,* and then suddenly find I need that money *tomorrow!*"

Should you need that money to take care of an emergency—or for any other reason—you can get it, but it might cost you a little. Most deferred annuities allow you once a year to withdraw—free of a company charge—up to 10% of the total value of your annuity. For amounts over 10% withdrawn in a single year, the insurance company may impose a charge.

Note that when you take the money out, the tax laws require that you first withdraw the earnings, which are taxable, and the excess in your withdrawal would be a return of your investment, and so would not be taxed. However, on top of that there may be a 10% federal tax penalty imposed for early withdrawals if you're under age 59½.

Given all this, you shouldn't think of your annuity as a checking account. Instead, think of it as a long-term accumulation tool for retirement.

Deferred annuities come in three flavors: "fixed," "variable," and "modified guarantee." Those terms refer to the kinds of rates they pay, and how much knowledge you'll have up front about what your annuity will be worth, when it comes time for you to start drawing out your money.

With a **fixed annuity** you will know the "floor" (the minimum you'll earn) for the life of the contract. But for a certain period—this could be one, three, or five years—you'll be guaranteed a fixed rate of interest, which may be more than the floor.

The major advantage of a fixed annuity is security. You have a contract that guarantees what you'll earn.

If you buy a fixed annuity, which offers a fixed rate of interest for a specified period of time, the contract value won't be subject to market fluctuations. The value of your annuity will increase every day. Even if you make a withdrawal from time to time, the balance remaining in your annuity will continue to earn the fixed rate that you were guaranteed. And at some point in the future you can formally "annuitize"—that is, start to receive a set or guaranteed amount.

Variable annuities appeal to folks who want the opportunity for the higher returns that may come from assuming higher risks.

If you picture a variable annuity working much like your 401(k) account, you'll have a pretty good idea of what happens to your money.

In a variable annuity, the insurance company offers as investment options a diversified portfolio of securities—for example, stocks, bonds, or other securities.

Just as with your 401(k) investments, *you* select how the money is allocated among the choices available. (Generally, you'll have the freedom to switch investments, say, between stock, money market, and bond portfolios, without charge or tax liability.)

The value of your annuity? It will depend on the performance of the portfolio you've selected. If you're in a stock portfolio, and stocks go up, your annuity is worth more. If the stocks go down during the life of your annuity, its value is less. Some variable annuities also offer you choices of putting a portion of your money in a fixed account that offers a fixed rate of return, just like a fixed annuity. And, as we said, it usually is easy to switch your investments back and forth among all the choices you're offered, but there may be some restrictions on the ability to transfer out of the fixed account.

A **modified guarantee annuity** is similar to a fixed annuity with one major exception.

Typically, if funds are left to the end of each guarantee period you choose, the principal and interest are guaranteed. However, if funds are withdrawn prior to the end of the guarantee period, a market value adjustment may happen. If prevailing interest rates have increased since the commencement of the guarantee period, the adjustment will be negative. Conversely, if the rates have gone down, the adjustment will be positive. This kind of annuity generally offers more guarantee period interest rate choices (one to ten years) and thus a set of varying interest rates, both short and long term. Because of this "market value adjustment" feature, interest rates will generally be somewhat higher than in a conventional fixed annuity.

Payout Options

Just as you can set the maturity date of your annuities, and decide what they are to be invested in, you also can determine how you want your income and principal paid back to you.

Let's take your options one at a time.

Life only. Life annuities might as well be called "insurance against living too long." Once lifetime payments begin, they do not stop—even if you live to be 187.

The only potential problem with this type of policy—from the point of view of your heirs—is that if you die immediately after picking this option, your heirs do not receive a refund of any of the money you paid into the policy. To be macabre, you're gambling that you'll live for (almost) forever, or, to be more realistic, *longer than average.* The insurance company is betting that you won't beat the averages.

Their bet is based on the actuarial "experience" of thousands (if not hundreds of thousands) of people.

Your bet, however, can be based on your family's life lines. If your grandparents are reasonably agile in their 80s or 90s, are frolicking around the world, odds are on your side. So if you're in great health and long life seems to be running in your blood, you may want to consider taking the bet.

Life, term certain. This offers some protection against an early death.

The first part of this annuity works exactly like the "life only" option. You are guaranteed to receive a payout for as long as you live.

However, if you die before a set period of time (for example, 5, 10, 20 years after annuity payments began), the income payments you would have received will continue to be paid to the named beneficiary until the end of the fixed period. Because of this feature, each payment will be less than that of a pure "life only" policy.

Joint and survivor annuity. The payout continues during the lifetime of two people, usually husband and wife. Upon the death of the surviving annuitant, the payments stop.

The joint and survivor annuity may also have a time protection component, and may also offer a value protection feature that we will talk about next.

Life, refund annuity. This offers some protection against an early death. This type of annuity continues to pay you for as long as you live, and also guarantees that your beneficiary will get a cash refund, or an installment refund upon your death. Usually the refund is for the amount of your original principal less the total of payments already received.

As with "life, term certain" payouts, "joint and survivor," and "life, refund" annuities provide for lower payouts than a pure "life only" annuity.

That takes care of annuities whose payments are contingent on how long you live. There are two kinds of payouts that have nothing to do with when you die.

Term certain payouts. The annuity payments continue for a set period of time, for example, 10 years, 20 years, whatever. Usually the minimum is 5 years. At the end of the predetermined period, the payments cease. If you die before the time period is up, the payments will continue to your beneficiary. These are particularly useful for funding scheduled premiums for life insurance or for long-term care insurance.

Amount certain payments. Here the payments last as long as the money does.

You pay in a set amount, determine when you want to start receiving your payments, and also determine how big you want them to be. You'll continue to receive a check, until the balance (what you paid in, plus interest) has been liquidated. If you die before the money runs out, your beneficiary receives the remainder.

So This Is the Greatest Thing Since Sliced Bread, Right?

Well, no. Not quite.

If you invest in an annuity for the right reasons, yes. As wonderful as annuities are, there are a couple of things we should under-score.

If you plan on using annuities as your emergency fund, find another investment. The money you put in to buy an annuity is not readily accessible, and, as we said, there may be penalties and tax consequences for early withdrawals.

Second, annuities are not the way to go if you are trying to figure out ways of paying for *pre-retirement* needs such as putting your kids through college. While the annuity accumulates earnings or gains tax-deferred, all distributions of earnings are taxed at ordinary income rates, rates that may be higher if you are still working. And remember, interest paid prior to the owner turning 59½ may also be subject to a 10% federal tax for early withdrawals.

This brief review of annuities is admittedly cursory; there are enough varieties of annuities these days to fill a book (or several books). But we do feel that annuities are an important part of good, comprehensive financial planning. Since the features of annuities can be complex, ask your financial consultant for a more detailed explanation. Let him or her help you through the mazes.

Be sure to check out an insurance company's safety. How safe are they? Evaluations from insurance rating companies—such as A.M. Best, Standard & Poor's, and Moody's—are available, and financial magazines periodically will give you the ratings of top companies.

Remember, a guarantee is only as good as the guarantor.

In addition to ratings, a sound insurance company should maintain an investment portfolio that is broadly diversified among industries and issuers. If you're buying a variable annuity, the historical performance of the investment manager for the account is important. Unlike brokers and dealers in the securities markets—which are regulated on the federal level by the Securities and Exchange Commission, the stock exchanges, and the National Association of Securities Dealers, as well as the states—the regulation of insurance companies is pretty much a state affair, and some states take their regulatory duties more seriously than others. Insurance company separate accounts, which form the basis for variable insurance products, are, however, regulated by the SEC in a manner similar to the regulation of mutual funds.

In an annuity, your investments can grow tax-deferred. There are no annual contribution limits. A drawback: you can't tap annuities easily for emergency use. Used judiciously as a part of your long-term strategy, annuities can be an important part of comprehensive financial planning.

CHAPTER 19

Mutual Funds: Leave the Flying to Someone Else

Back at the turn of the century, long before the age of instant celebritydom, the most famous person in America wasn't an athlete. (We didn't have "Monday Night Football" back then.) He wasn't a rock star. (Since television wasn't around, we didn't have MTV.) He wasn't even a politician. He was a poet: Oliver Wendell Holmes (and father of the great Supreme Court justice, who became, in his own right, almost as famous as old dad).

Everyone knew his bearded visage. Well, almost everyone. The story has it that Holmes was on a train, and the conductor, who didn't recognize him, roused Holmes from a nap.

"I need to see your ticket," the conductor sternly demanded.

Holmes couldn't find it, and while still half-asleep began fumbling through his pockets.

The conductor watched his befuddled passenger turn his jacket inside out, and finally the railroad man figured out who was aboard his train.

"No need to find the ticket, sir," the conductor said. "Sorry to have bothered you."

By this point, Holmes was fully awake and furious. He kept patting his pockets, and searching all about his seat for the missing ticket.

The conductor started to get nervous. After all, you never know what can happen if you upset the most famous man in America. The conductor figured the safest thing to do was apologize again.

"Please don't look anymore, Mr. Holmes. I don't need your ticket. Be our guest."

Holmes frowned, and then shouted: "I'm not looking for you, young man. I'm looking for me. I'm trying to find out where I'm going."

You Know Where You're Going

Having penetrated this far through the financial planning thicket, you—unlike the famous Mr. Holmes—know exactly where you are going. In fact, you probably have several destinations in mind: covering college costs, building a retirement nest egg, parenting your parents, taking care of your long-term health care, designing trusts for your children.

You've developed an investment philosophy, focused on specific objectives, and have allocated your assets. The question now is: How do you manage it all?

When it comes to managing investments, we certainly believe there is a growing trend toward self-direction. And over and over again we have talked about ways you could manage your own IRA, or SEP, or 401(k), or 403(b). Our reasoning is simple. Who is going to watch your money more carefully than you?

But there is an alternative to consider. You take on a professional. You could lay out the itinerary, select which roads to take, and off you go. Or, you could let someone else do the driving. Better yet, since we're now in the 1990s, let someone else do the flying. You pick the destination, then turn your travel over to a professional pilot who schedules the trip, checks the weather patterns, reviews the maintenance logs, visually inspects the plane, monitors the fuel, and files the flight plan.

If you and other passengers choose this form of travel, all you do is hop on, give a thumbs-up to the pilot and say, "Let's go." The pilot gets the tower clearance, and you're aloft.

Let's further define this way of traveling. You pick the destination, and how to get there (there are private jets and then there are Concordes). You decide how much to spend (or invest). Your professional—the pilot—then makes the decision as to market timing and the specific investments.

If you substitute "fund manager" for pilot, you have a pretty good idea of what these professionals do.

Hiring managers to do the work for you is what this chapter, and the next two, are all about. We are going to suggest three different ways of letting someone else do the driving (or piloting) to help you obtain your goals. You can:

1. Invest in mutual funds.

2. Invest in unit investment trusts.

3. Hire someone to manage your entire portfolio.

4. Invest in closed-end funds.

Let's start with mutual funds.

Mutual Funds

While the first mutual fund in the U.S. was created back in 1924 (and mutual funds existed in Scotland some years before that), it really wasn't until the 1970s that the concept took off—and then exploded throughout the 1980s and early 1990s—as the chart on the next page shows.

By mid-year 1992, there were more than $1.5 *trillion* dollars invested in mutual funds. In fact, mutual funds are so popular that they are owned by one out of every four American households. That's an awful lot of people who are willing to let someone else do the driving, or flying, for them.

In response to this demand for professional money management, there are now more than 3,500 mutual funds. They cover many different objectives. In a minute, we will give you ideas on how to winnow the 3,500 funds down to a manageable list of a dozen or so—so you can really figure which one (or two) best fit each of your investment needs. But first let's look at what a typical fund is, and how it works.

A mutual fund is nothing more than a pooled investment program. The fund makes investments on behalf of individuals—and institutions—who share common financial goals.

An investor, that is, you, selects a fund that has an investment objective and risk tolerance that are similar to your own. That's important, since each mutual fund is different. Your goal, and the goal of your neighbor may be different. You may want long-term capital growth, while your neighbor is interested in current income. Mutual funds could be the right investment for both of you—but they are going to be two different mutual funds with two different objectives.

To help the fund achieve its objectives, the fund's manager

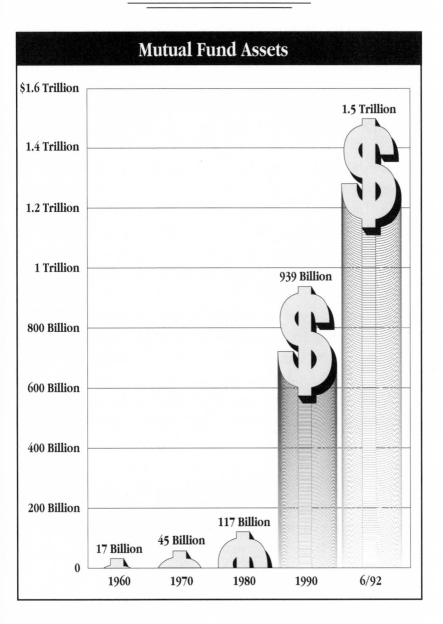

Mutual Fund Assets

will pool your money with that of other shareholders who have similar objectives. Then she'll buy investments that may include stocks, bonds, and/or money market instruments that she feels will help the fund's investors meet their goals. The securities that the money manager buys form the underlying portfolio of the fund.

Since this idea of diversification is so important to your grand investment strategy, let's spend some time on it. A mutual fund is a pool of securities that you buy into—thus, you're spreading your investment risk through diversification. Since you are participating in a diversified pool, the risk of loss to your total investment from a loss in any one security in the fund is, to put it mildly, considerably reduced.

The fund may end up owning dozens, or even hundreds of securities, even if it is a sector fund, let's say a mutual fund that specializes in one particular industry, such as health care. And it's true, even if the fund only buys companies of a certain size. (An example? A "small cap" growth fund is likely to invest only in emerging growth companies with capitalization under $100 million.)

Okay, enough of the background. Let's get to the good part. How do you make money investing in mutual funds? You receive dividends, and the price of your shares could include capital gains. These shares could rise because the value of the holdings may rise. Of course, the value of the shares can also decline.

Remember, the mutual fund buys a bushel of stocks, or bonds, or money market instruments, and the like. When the fund earns money on its holdings—one of the stocks it owns pays a dividend, for example—it distributes these earnings, net after expenses, to its investors.

You get those earnings either through the fund passing along the dividends and interest it has earned on its investments, or should the fund sell the securities at a profit, you receive those net earnings as a capital gain.

By the way, you don't have to take those distributions in cash. In fact, unless you truly need the money we suggest you don't. Rather we think you should reinvest any interest, dividends, and capital gains you receive in the purchase of additional shares of the fund. In many funds you can do this automatically, if you wish, with no fuss and bother, and without paying a sales charge on the reinvested shares.

Let us underscore what exactly is going on, if you invest in a mutual fund. You are buying shares of an investment company. The manager hired by the company, and not you, decides what stocks, bonds, or other financial instruments it should buy to accomplish its goal—to provide long-term growth, or whatever—a goal that you share, otherwise you wouldn't have bought shares of the fund in the first place.

Each share that you buy represents your slice of the pooled holdings. Dividends, interest, and capital gains received by the fund—after deduction of fund expenses—are paid out to you in proportion to the number of shares owned. So, even if you own just one share you'll be getting the exact same investment return *per share* as those who bought thousands of shares at the same price. (But the *total* return obviously won't be as large.)

Renting Someone Else's Mind

Why would you want to buy a mutual fund, as part of your retirement planning? Because:

1. It saves time.

2. It diversifies your holdings, and thereby reduces risk.

3. You're employing someone else's expertise.

4. It's easy to find funds that match your specific asset and risk allocation strategy.

5. The initial minimum investment may be as low as $250.

There is a very pragmatic reason why you might choose to invest in a foreign market through a mutual fund. For some markets that may be the *only* practical way for you to do it.

Governments need to get comfortable with the idea—with the reality—of liberalized markets. These markets tend initially to be downright restrictive as they go through sea changes, and in some newly opened markets foreign investments can be made *only* through mutual funds. For example, until 1991 Taiwan's stock market was restricted in this fashion.

Let's look at a specific example to show how all this works in practice.

Suppose you're struck by the economic future of Latin America. Many Latin American countries have been moving toward market economies and capitalism. In some of these countries entre-preneurial urges are bursting free, and you may have heard about the growing stock markets of Argentina and Mexico. And there is talk of exchanges in other countries opening or expanding. You figure that opportunities will abound in emerging markets in coming years, and you may want to seek profits from this new era of capitalism.

You're thinking long term; you don't necessarily believe you'll find an overnight success, so you're prepared to dig in, invest, and try for the potential big gain. Of course, this particular investment strategy—we remind you—should account for only a portion of your total strategy.

Theoretically you could jet to Buenos Aires or Mexico City, do a lot of investigating—talk to company officials, tour the plants, visit with employees and people in the industries—guess about future demand for goods, and then invest in what you think are the best of the Argentine or Mexican companies being spun off by government or being started up. (In this case, you're not restricted to mutual funds. You could—if you wish—buy individual stocks.)

Or you could do it the easy way, the practical way. You search among the 3,500 mutual funds for ones that invest in Latin America. Find a handful that have the same broad objectives you do, winnow the list down to the one or two that look best (details on how to do that in a few pages) and invest.

In other words, you'd hire the driver and then you sit back and enjoy the ride. The road—or flight—may be bumpy here or there, but the money manager of the XYZ Latin American Growth Fund would do all the work, all the driving, all the piloting.

And there *is* a lot of work that the manager has to do, not only in finding the stocks that best fit the fund's objectives, but in also making sure the fund is not overly dependent on just one stock. That's the diversification advantage that we talked about before.

Now doing all this requires a good deal of expertise, in addition to time and effort. And that's the third big advantage of investing in mutual funds. You get to employ a professional to help you accomplish your goals. You're renting her expertise.

Memo to Your Managers: Have a Good Night's Worry

By buying into a mutual fund, you've hired a manager whose job it is not only to monitor the investment performance of the fund assets day by day, hour by hour, and even minute by minute, but also to review constantly the direction of the long-term strategy of the fund. Depending on your location, they work—or worry—perhaps even while you're sleeping.

Let's go back to that fictional manager we created just a few words back: the guardian angel of the XYZ Latin American Growth Fund. He's not just fretting over the emergence of markets and which companies to invest in. He's also sweating out global problems. How will currency devaluations hit his creation? Is the strong (or weak) dollar hurting or helping? There's always something subsurface out there that can play havoc with—or be astonishingly bountiful to—the well-planned strategy. Better he should worry than you.

If the fund you've picked is a large equity one —at least a billion in assets—a manager (or managers) will spend every minute they are at work deciding what to do next with the money in their care.

A smaller fund, say, one with "just" $100 million in assets, might be managed by one person who has several different funds under her wing.

But in either case, the fund manager buys securities that fit the fund's objectives, monitors the performance of both the securities and the economy, and when either changes, adjusts the fund's holdings accordingly.

Why, you might ask? Why should there be any adjustments at all? After all, we have stressed from the very beginning that you should be a *long-term* investor. We've told you to set a strategy and stick to it. That's what Chapter 14, "Setting Your Goals," and Chapter 15, "Allocating Your Assets," are all about.

If the goal of your investing—whether it be by picking your own stocks, or hiring a professional—is to invest long term, why would you want your fund manager to make constant adjustments to the stocks in your fund's portfolio? Isn't all that buying and selling at odds with being a long-term investor?

No. In fact, the portfolio manager may be constantly buying or selling the portfolio's assets so that you can achieve the fund's objectives, in light of ever-changing market conditions.

Tacking a Winning Way to the Finish Line

All the trimming and tacking—as every good sailor knows—the professional fund manager does is designed to keep you on course and allow you to reach your goals. As long as the investment—that is, the specific funds you've picked—is doing what it's supposed to do for you and is meeting its objectives, you really shouldn't care whether the individual components that make up the whole of the investments are held for one day or for two decades. Your goal, in its simplest form, is always focused on a numerical performance. For example, you may want first to preserve assets, then you may want to increase the assets.

As to how much money you want to make—that depends on

your risk tolerance. But the overriding purpose of preserving assets and increasing assets is to eventually *do something* with your savings. Your goal in making money is not to make money per se but rather, it is first to make the money, and then—eventually—to use the money to put your kids through college, have a comfortable retirement, take care of your aging parents, or whatever.

To accomplish the fund's objectives, the fund managers have bought dozens, maybe scores, maybe hundreds of securities that are all consistent with the fund's objective. Periodically selling some of those holdings in no way detracts from the objective. In fact, it does quite the opposite. It may help the fund achieve its goal that much sooner.

A Marriage—Five Minutes or Five Years

Good fund managers know that marriages to investments are temporal. The unions may be made in heaven, but they seldom will hit a golden anniversary. There *will* be a time when the security has to be sold. It is no longer performing in such a way that will help the fund achieve its objective. This could come a month after purchase, a year, or hopefully longer. Or it may be that the security performance has more than met the fund manager's goal, and the time has come to reap the profits. Investments are bought to be sold. The "investment game" is clearly performance against expectation, and a constant examination of the world—that is, the state of the economy and the markets—in general.

Keeping Score

If this is a game (and we *don't* take money lightly) it's a deadly serious one. How serious? With a fund, the score is posted at the end of each trading day. You'll know the next day exactly how well your fund did.

Those results are always stated in terms of the fund's net asset value, or NAV. Net asset value is a quantification of precisely what the fund is worth. It is determined by taking the market value of the fund's holdings, subtracting its expenses (such as transaction costs, overhead, etc.), and dividing that figure by the number of shares in the fund.

Figuring out what your part of the fund is worth is simple: you multiply the number of shares you own by the fund's net asset value. Although you can figure out the value of your holdings daily, our suggestion is that you don't race to the tables in your daily paper while you're still having your first coffee. Remember, you *are* thinking long term. So be casual daily, but make sure you figure out your gains or losses on a quarterly, or certainly no less than a semiannual, basis. We repeat—with a fund, think long term.

You do want to check periodically—to make sure that the fund is still meeting your expectations.

Unhitching the Wagon

We don't say your eyes have to be constantly beady, but they do have to alight, from time to time, on your investments. Your mutual fund investments have to be accountable to your goals. If something isn't working, a change may be in order. If you've hitched your wagon to a mutual fund star that is no longer rising, find a new one.

Don't make a change on overnight drops, and don't be hasty. Before you make the change, find out—ask your financial consultant—why your fund isn't meeting your goals. If comparable funds are suffering likewise, you may want to ride it out. But—if you're not able to justify the fund's performance—don't be afraid to make the change.

You don't have to make decisions alone. Ask for help. You shouldn't be shy in asking your financial consultant to do the work of narrowing down the many funds to a handful crafted for you. You are paying for counsel. The reverse is true. Remind your financial consultant that you also welcome guidance on when to sell the funds. (Chapter 22 explores fully the review process you should apply to your investments.)

It's a Big Candy Store

But before you can figure out how well your fund is doing, you have to own one—or more—of the 3,500 funds out there.

How do you decide which fund(s) is right for you?

You have two choices. You can have your financial consultant narrow down the field for you. Or you can do it yourself.

The advantage of relying on someone else is obvious—and, in fact, it mirrors the reason you decided to invest in mutual funds in the first place: you save time, and you get a chance to draw on someone else's expertise. You don't have to try to determine which is the best growth and income fund for you. They'll already know.

However, if you decide to go it alone, you'll find deciding which fund to pick is more time-consuming than it is difficult.

In fact, part of the work has already been done for you.

At least once a year (and in some cases, quarterly), *Business Week, Forbes, Money,* and *The Wall Street Journal,* among other financial journals, segment mutual funds in the country by objective: income fund, growth and income fund, bond funds, health care, high tech. (You name it, a fund exists, and probably more than one.)

Then, having divided the funds by category, the publications rank each fund based on how well they performed over the last 12 months.

So picking a fund is a piece of cake, right? You just go to the category you are most interested in, such as growth and income funds, find out which was ranked number one, and plunk down your money, right?

Who's Running the Store?

Would that life were that simple.

First off, as you always hear in investment ads: "Past performance is no guarantee of future success." So, just because last year was great doesn't mean that this year will be.

Second, one year does not a fund's performance make. You want to know how well a fund does in bull markets, bear markets, and every market in between. After all, you are in for the long haul. Those tables we mentioned earlier may also give you total return for 3, 5, and even 10 years.

Then there is a question of who is managing the fund. Were

those stellar returns—which, let's say, got XYZ, our hypothetical fund, to the top of *Money*'s list—produced by a fund manager who has just decided that Elm Street in Walla Walla is a whole lot nicer than Wall Street in Manhattan, and has just up and quit? Raising rhubarb is less stressful than picking stocks. Who's going to manage the store now?

And what about the question of expenses? Operating philosophy? The list of potential questions goes on and on. And unfortunately, they can't be fully answered by looking at a list compiled by a business magazine.

While you should use your financial consultant to winnow that list of 3,500 to a handful, you still must make the ultimate decision yourself. That decision will involve answering the questions we rattled off above, coupled with whatever others you can think of.

Fortunately, the answers can be found. After you and your consultant have pared down your list ask for a free prospectus for each fund. (Or, you could always call up the funds you are interested in—you'd be hard pressed to find one that does not have a toll-free number—and ask for a free prospectus.)

Reading the Fine Print

By law, each fund must make available to you a prospectus, which is a detailed summary of what the fund is, and what it invests in. The prospectus will explain the fund's underlying investment philosophy, and will highlight its primary and secondary objectives. In addition, the prospectus will point out the risks of investing in this particular fund. There are *always risks* of one sort or another.

The information will be quite detailed. For example, funds, by regulation, are not allowed to invest more than 25% of their assets in any one corporation. But many funds, in order to meet their own diversification goals, may have more stringent restrictions. The fund management might say that the fund will never buy more than 5% of the shares of a given company. The fund may have limits on types of investments it will make in any industry sector. (No more than 10% in bank stocks, for example.) The fund may also spell out the maximum percentages to be invested in equities, bonds, or money market funds. The fund's internal guidelines can be quite precise. A money market fund, for example, might be precluded from investing in Eurodollar or Yankee dollar obligations. Or there could be a balanced fund that would promise that at least 25%, say, of the assets would be invested in bonds and the remainder in stocks.

There could be a natural resources fund that will specify what percentage of its assets will be in companies in the energy business, or in mining. You get the idea. The prospectus will spell out investment objectives of the fund, and will also tell you what risks the fund may face.

Let's look again at a money market fund: the guiding investment here might be that the primary objective of the fund is low credit risk, and the secondary goal is yield.

But even after you know the broad parameters of the fund, plow on to the fine print. For example, will the fund be selling securities short or lending securities? And exactly what fees will you be charged?

The prospectus will give you a detailed listing of transaction expenses—what it will cost you to buy or redeem shares of the fund—an explanation of how the fund's operating expenses are calculated, and how much they have been in recent years. Let's deal with them one at a time.

There may be fees imposed in your fund for things like the

buying or redeeming (selling) of your shares, such as there might be a sales charge, or "load" imposed when you buy your shares. Typically, there will be a load if you buy your mutual fund through a registered sales agent, such as a financial consultant or financial planner. In essence, you might think of the charge as a way to pay for your financial adviser's advice.

How much will this sales charge cost you? By law, a "front end" sales charge cannot be more than 8.5% of your total purchase price. (The load of course, could be far less: 3%, or perhaps 5%.) Generally, once you've paid your initial fee, there will be no additional fees when you sell the fund.

Often you're given an option on how to pay the sales charge. A fund might have two classes: Class A (front-end sales charge) and Class B (back-end sales charge) shares. Let's say that for a Class A share you might pay a 6.5% upfront charge, and there would be no sales charge of any kind when you sell. For a Class B share, for the same fund, you would not be charged an initial fee, but your annual fee, under a 12b-1 plan (named after an SEC rule), could be

---

Reading Prospectuses

In *Reading the Mutual Fund Prospectus,* put out by the Investment Company Institute, the mutual funds industry trade group, there is a brief explanation of why prospectuses are not all that readable:

A prospectus is a legal document that carries stiff penalties for any misstatements or omissions. Thus, it must contain information that may appear overly technical to some investors. Although the U.S. Securities and Exchange Commission, the federal agency that regulates mutual funds, has simplified prospectus requirements in recent years, what remains is still relatively technical compared to, say, your daily newspaper.

1% of assets, plus you would face a 4% exit fee if you were to move out of the fund over the next two years. For every year thereafter, the exit fee would drop 1%. After five years, there would be no exit fee—it disappears.

Suppose you invest in a given fund that's a member of a family of funds. You may get another break. Say there are 10 or more, or even 20 funds, all under one umbrella. Once you've made the initial investment, if your goals change or the world changes, and you want to try a new tack—well, it's often possible to shift from one family member to another within the same fee structure, with no additional sales charge.

Some mutual funds have no load at all, hence the designation no-load.

But note: No-load does not mean no cost. Every mutual fund is going to charge you something—expenses and fees—for managing your money. (This holds true for load-funds as well. The load is just the sales charge. There will be a management fee, as well.)

And then there are annual operating expenses. These charges reflect the fund's cost of doing business—of transaction costs, custodial services, and the like. You don't pay for these costs directly. Instead they are paid by the fund—and your proportional share of the expenses is deducted from the earnings of the mutual fund's assets. That's why you'll see the expenses expressed as a percentage of the assets in the prospectus.

Everyone counsels: *"Read the prospectus carefully."* Indeed, the SEC mandates that every mutual fund should tell you that in its sales literature. We agree. Even if you are going to let someone else do the driving, or flying, you want to be sure they are taking you exactly where you want to go. This is not a mystery trip you're taking.

Investing money long term isn't exactly an eight-minute drive to the nearest convenience store. Every major trip has its delays: an unexpected stop here, a major detour there, a roadblock that forces an itinerary change. But a mutual fund investment leading to retirement is a long-term commitment. So the bottom line question still is this: Is your driver, or pilot, taking you—with reasonable speed, in safety and comfort, and in a fairly direct line—where you want to go?

Butterfly Straddles and Mutual Funds

A final note, this one to the sophisticated investor, the kind of person who says, "Yes, yes. I know all that. Mutual funds are wonderful. That's how I got started when I began investing years ago. But now I'm into things like butterfly straddles. I handle my own options strategy. Mutual funds, for me, are, well, passé."

What you are really saying is that you can run your own portfolio, and we have no doubts that you can. In fact, you are living proof that self-direction works, and works quite well. You have certainly passed Investments 101 with flying colors. Maybe you're even in the masters program now.

Even so, you might want to consider returning to mutual funds. After all, all professionals, from time to time, call on other professionals for help. Why would you need help? For the same reason a grizzled world-class skipper will accept help in a new harbor. Everyone can use a bit of assistance in unfamiliar waters. Don't go it alone.

Go back to our scenario of investing in Latin America. As experienced an investor as you are, these are still probably uncharted waters for you. Given this kind of investment opportunity, relying on an investment professional—one who knows Latin America and can fit it profitably into the global puzzle—makes sense, even for the most savvy individual investor.

Maybe it won't be as much fun as picking your own stocks, but it may be far less risky.

If you want to go one step beyond self-direction, you can invest in mutual funds. You find a fund (or funds) that matches your objectives, including your risk tolerance—and then you hire the fund manager to do the flying for you. In a fund, you're also automatically investing in diversification.

CHAPTER 20

Unit Investment Trusts and Closed-End Funds: Less Is More

One of this country's great architects, Mies van der Rohe, built a long, distinguished career based on one simple dictum: "Less is more."

The same can be said about unit investment trusts and closed-end funds.

Unit Investment Trusts

Unit investment trusts pool your money with other investors' and use the combined funds to buy a portfolio of securities.

It sounds like a mutual fund, and in fact there are a lot of similarities.

- You don't buy individual stocks or bonds; rather you buy units in the trust, and, as in a mutual fund, your unit represents a percentage of the underlying assets in the trust. That means you receive a proportional share of the distributions and earnings.

- The trusts are created with a particular goal in mind. There are, for example, municipal investment trusts that deliver tax-advantaged income, and corporate bond trusts that seek to provide a relatively high, taxable income. The trusts can be even more specialized, focusing on the stocks of electric utilities, or companies in the food, energy, and health care industries, to name just a few.

- There is a professional supervisor of the securities in the trust.

- As in most mutual funds, there may be a sales charge.

Buy and Hold

There are, however, some major differences between mutual funds and unit investment trusts (UITs).

First, in a UIT the overall strategy is to "buy and hold."

In a mutual fund, a manager utilizes market timing to buy and sell securities in the portfolio. Size of investment, type, and, in particular, the choice of securities, will change with regularity in response to market conditions. In a mutual fund, you'll remember, the fund manager is constantly buying and selling stocks, searching for the right combination that will allow the fund to achieve its goals.

In a unit investment trust, the approach is quite different. The trusts are *not* actively managed. Oh, sure, under limited circumstances a security could be sold or replaced, especially where holding it would be detrimental to unit holders. But active management is clearly not the intent. The trust is put together in such a way that the return on your investment will be anticipated in advance. The only way to achieve that predictability is: *(a)* know ahead of time what securities will make up the trust, and *(b)* keep the portfolio intact.

Obviously, if the trust is not constantly buying and selling securities, the trust's expenses will be less. That's another way the trust is better able to try to predict its return in advance.

Aiming for a Short Life

The second difference between mutual funds and UITs is that the life of the trust is known ahead of time.

A mutual fund, in theory, could exist in perpetuity. In the case of the XYZ Emerging Growth Company Fund, for example, the mutual fund manager could spend the rest of his working life looking for stocks that fit the fund's objectives. Securities are bought and sold. The management is constant. Upon retirement, the fund manager would turn the reins over to someone else, then she'd retire, and a third generation of money managers would set off looking for growth stocks, and on it would go, presumably forever.

However, UITs are defined not only as to what is in their portfolio but also in terms of how long they will last—usually anywhere between three and thirty years. Over that defined time, the trust pays you interest or earnings—and may return some principal as well. At the end of the trust's predetermined life, its remaining assets are sold, and the proceeds are distributed to investors.

If you don't immediately need the money you'll be receiving from the trust, you have two choices:

You can simply let the cash flow into a money market fund. Let the money accumulate—always earning daily money market rates—and from time to time, you switch it out of the fund, and make a more permanent investment.

Or, assuming you're investing long term in a retirement account you may want to keep on doing what you have been doing. It's often possible to automatically reinvest the money from a UIT at no sales charge into units of the same trust or into a separate trust. Reinvesting helps to compound your income.

One other thing to note about the payout. The check you receive from the trust will normally be an income distribution, but occasionally it will also be a partial return of your initial investment, as securities mature or are called, redeemed, or sold. (The trust will let you know before tax time how much of each you received.) As we have pointed out before, you don't have to pay taxes on a return of principal.

Being Nimble by Being Small

Finally, there's another marked difference: unit investment trusts may be more nimble in taking advantage of special, one-time investment concepts. And because they are finite trusts they can afford to contain a much smaller pool of money. Let's contrast that with mutual funds, which naturally think long term. In a large asset management company, there may be a dozen or even several dozen different mutual funds. Their total assets could mount into the tens of billions.

But within a unit investment trust group, over a decade or two, there may have been as many as 500 different trusts, each with a defined one-time investment strategy and each with a defined time of existence and a mandatory termination date. All were created to serve specific investment situations and objectives. As opposed to a typical mutual fund, which may start life with a value of $25 million or $50 million or even more, and which hopes to grow in size, a unit investment trust can be created, and can function efficiently, with a value as low as $10 or $20 million. And its future isn't predicated on expansion.

Since the kinds of UITs that can be created are almost limitless, we won't attempt to catalog all of them—but two of the consistently most popular concepts have been fixed income trusts in either corporate bonds or municipal bonds. We will point out two other concepts that seem particularly applicable to retirement accounts.

Utility stock trusts. If you like the regular income that comes from dividends, plus the opportunity of sharing in the potential for dividend increases and capital gains that can come from the stocks in the trust's underlying portfolio, then this trust is the right one for you. Total return—earnings plus gains—is what you're after here.

Market index trusts. This type of trust is structured to simulate the performance of a broad-based market index, such as the Standard & Poor's 500 stock price index. This kind of trust is designed to enable you to participate in broad market trends. The value of your investment rises, or falls, as the market does, and as you'll remember, over long periods of time the stock market has historically outperformed all other investments.

Closed-End Funds

There's one more way you can have a portfolio of securities managed by a professional. You can buy into a closed-end fund. It's sort of a hybrid between a mutual fund and a unit investment trust.

In a closed-end fund you'll know in advance of the offering exactly what management's objectives, goals, and potential strategy are.

But while the fund is made up of many securities—much like a mutual fund—there is, once again, a huge difference. Once the initial public offering, or IPO, is completed, it's completed. It's a one-time creation. From then on, the shares of the closed-end fund will be traded in a secondary market (usually on a stock exchange), just like common shares of companies, and you pay a commission to buy or sell. However, a "regular," or open-ended, mutual fund will probably issue shares forever, if the demand is there. That doesn't happen in a closed-end fund.

Never say never, right? What does happen from time to time is that some closed-end funds, after getting shareholder approval, convert to open end, that is, regular mutual funds. When that happens, of course, the fund will keep issuing shares to meet demand.

In a closed-end fund the number of shares is finite. But although the number of shares is set, that doesn't mean the fund is just sitting there. It's continuously managed. That is, the portfolio manager is constantly selling or buying securities in order to improve the portfolio. So in that sense, the active management of a closed-end fund is more like that of a mutual fund than that of a less-active unit investment trust.

A closed-end fund is listed among the stock tables, and not in the mutual fund section of your newspaper. The difference stems from how the two funds are valued.

Supply and Demand—Discounts and Premiums

Remember how we calculated the value of an open-ended mutual fund? It required nothing more than taking the fund's net assets—stocks, bonds, money market investments—subtracting liabilities, and dividing by the number of shares outstanding. You're able to figure a regular mutual fund's net asset value (or NAV) at the end of every business day. (Rather than "you" doing it—we really mean that the calculations are done for you, and you'll see the NAV in the next day's mutual funds tables in your newspaper.)

However, with a closed-end fund, supply and demand—not arithmetic—determines the value of the fund's shares.

The reason for that is simple. Since the fund is not issuing any more shares, if you want in, you have to buy out someone who is already a shareholder. If there are more buyers than sellers, the share price rises; if the demand is slight, prices may drop below the NAV.

If you really want to become a shareholder, you'll be willing to pay the seller more than the net asset value of the fund, for his share. You're buying at a premium.

If there is less demand—if the market is not valuing the share at its book value, let alone at a premium—the fund may trade at a discount to its NAV, which is determined in exactly the same way it is for an open-end fund. There's a special table—it appears only once a week in *The Wall Street Journal*—called "Publicly Traded

Funds," which will give you a unique calculation, the percentage difference between each closed-end fund's net asset value and the last market price.

If indeed, whatever the reason, the shares do trade at a discount, say, of 10% or 20%, you may well decide the shares are a bargain. And you may want to buy more. Just as you may want to take advantage of the discount, not too surprisingly the fund managers may also decide to buy back their own shares, bylaws permitting. A good price—for either individuals or for money managers—is a good price.

Unit investment trusts, based on a buy and hold strategy, are put together by professionals, and have a definite strategy and a definite life. Closed-end funds are also one-time creations, but are more actively managed, and usually have an indefinite life. Either one lets you buy into a broad portfolio of securities.

CHAPTER 21

Hiring Your Own Portfolio Manager

If you invest in a unit investment trust, someone else will be selecting your investments. But as we've seen, they won't be overly active.

A mutual fund manager will buy and sell assets to make sure the fund's holdings are consistent with its goals. So, the manager will be taking a reasonably active role in managing your money.

However, if you want the most personalized management of your money, hire a professional portfolio manager. If you do, you'll delegate to this professional the complete day-to-day care and feeding of your portfolio.

It's a premium service, and the minimum that you must invest, and the fees that you'll pay, will reflect that.

If you are buying into a mutual fund, the minimum investment will rarely be more than $5,000, and often it's $1,000 or less, especially if you are using your mutual fund as an IRA, or as a 401(k) investment. (If you're participating in an employer-sponsored

401(k) or 403(b), your biweekly contributions could be as low as $10 or $20.)

Unit investment trust minimums tend to be about the same as mutual funds, so they, too, are well within the reach of most people.

The same cannot be said about professional portfolio managers. Very few will talk to you, unless you have at least $100,000 to invest. Minimums of $500,000 are common, and there are a significant number of portfolio managers who will require you to put $1 million or more in their care.

If you have that kind of money—and you'd be comfortable in letting a professional have total control over how it is invested once you've established the guidelines—then a portfolio manager is for you.

How do you find one? What do they do? And what will it cost? Three good questions, and we'll take them one at a time.

Selecting a Personal Portfolio Manager

Finding one takes some effort. Go to your financial consultant and spend a lot of time talking to him, or her.

Be specific about your goals, how comfortable you are with risk, whether you prefer bonds to equities, and talk about what your time horizons are. (Work out the asset allocations that we suggest to you in Chapter 15.)

Also, tell your financial consultant what you are looking for from your investments. Do you want growth? growth and income? or is preservation of capital the most important thing?

In this discussion, it would not be out of line to specify a minimum return you expect to achieve on your money. After all, it's your money.

The more specific you can be with your answers, the better.

If you are not specific, your financial consultant should try to pin you down. You should be profiled. You can expect to answer (at the very least) the following half-dozen questions:

1. Do you foresee any special circumstances that will require you to have immediate access to your money? For example, do you think you'll have to liquidate 30% of your portfolio to put your kids (or grandkids) through school?

2. Are there any special constraints you want to put on your investments? Speak up if you don't want to be invested in certain stocks or industries (tobacco?) or even in certain parts of the world.

   The reason doesn't have to be political, or moral. You may not want your manager to buy shares of XYZ Corporation because you already own a lot of it through your 401(k), employee stock ownership plan, IRA accounts, or other accounts.

3. Are there any legal restrictions? For example, if this is your own pension account, there may be limits on the type of investments you can buy. (A pension plan may limit you, or even prohibit you, from participating in options strategies, for example.)

4. Do you have a geographic preference, when it comes to picking a portfolio manager? Do you want him or her to

live nearby—a backyard presence—so you can meet conveniently? Maybe you couldn't care less, saying that results are all that matter, and you'll call, write, or fax if you want to communicate.

5. What kind of track record do you want your portfolio manager to have? You may say you don't even want to talk to anyone who hasn't been in business at least 10 years. Similarly, you may want them to have at least $50 million (or more) under management.

6. How do you feel about fixed or tax-free income? Not all investment advisers include munis in their portfolios. Some portfolio managers specialize in equity, some in fixed income.

Only after you have answered all these questions can your adviser provide you with a short list of professionals who are right for you. This matching process is not done casually, and ultimately it is not done by your financial consultant.

He'll give you a roster of names, winnowed, of course. It is up to you to select one.

What Do They Do?

Your portfolio manager will do basically everything you would, if you could devote all your time to managing your investments. You will set the objectives, but he will carry out your strategy—*without consulting you on a day-to-day basis.*

Yes, you will get periodic reports—probably quarterly—telling you how well the portfolio manager is doing with your money, but the decisions about how that money (your money!) will be invested will be the portfolio manager's alone. He will be buying and selling stocks that are held in your name; deciding which bond is right for you; and what percentage of your portfolio should be in cash.

If you think about it, this is just a more extreme version—a very personalized exercise—of what a mutual fund manager does. However, if you are uncomfortable with this arrangement, then don't enter into it. It's that simple.

If you like the arrangement, the next question is how—and how much—will the portfolio manager get paid.

What Will All This Cost?

Having a portfolio manager may be both a necessity and a luxury, and the bill you get for her time will reflect that.

When you hire a portfolio manager you usually will pay an annual fee which will be a percentage of the assets being managed. If you have a $500,000 portfolio, and the portfolio manager charges a 2% annual fee, you will be levied an annual fee totaling $10,000. Typically, fees run between 1% and 3% of the money being managed. You may get a bit more of a break, if your portfolio is invested solely in fixed income securities. It's not that the portfolio manager is being altruistic, rather she is just trying to reflect reality. It takes less work to find, buy, and hold fixed income investments than it does to find, buy, and then actively trade equity investments.

This may not be the end of the fees, however. They may go up, and interestingly enough, they may go down.

When your assets under management exceed a certain level—say $500,000—the percentage you are charged may drop. Instead of 2%, everything above $500,000 may be assessed with just a 1.5% fee, and that fee may drop even further as your account crosses higher thresholds such as $1,000,000 or $5,000,000.

That's the good news. The bad news is that if your original base fee is low—say 1% of assets—you will typically pay extra for transaction costs including brokerage commissions, and reporting and administrative charges. Total fees can quickly escalate from 3% to 5% of assets. An alternative is to agree to an all-inclusive fee arrangement—which includes all costs and fees. The charge typically could be a flat 3% of assets. These types of accounts are known as *wrap accounts,* because all the charges are wrapped together and included in the fee. A portion of these fees may be deductible. (As part of this premium service, you may receive a special report that will evaluate your portfolio's performance.)

How Do You Know How Well They're Doing with Your Money?

Okay, you're comfortable with having a professional portfolio manager making investment decisions for you, and fees strike you as worthwhile. Fine. But even so, you don't want to give your investment adviser carte blanche forever. Your needs may change; the investment adviser you decide upon may be holding certain securities that have recently gone out of favor; to your mind their hand may have gone cold. Periodically, you want to see how well your portfolio manager is doing with your money.

How will you be able to figure out how well your portfolio manager is doing? As we said above, you may be getting a special report card on their performance. This report is *not* prepared by your portfolio manager, rather it will be done by your financial consultant's firm, or an outside auditor. In either case, the special report which comes to you as a part of the premium, or wrap service, will be independent, objective and will key on three areas:

1. **Return.** Is your manager meeting the target you set for her? Your report should compare your portfolio's performance to benchmarks such as how well the S&P 500 did over the same period. Your report may even compare your manager's performance to the results turned in by other professionals who have similar financial objectives.

2. **Risk.** How much risk was taken with your portfolio, compared to the risk associated with other investment choices, such as putting your money in a bond fund, or a fund that mirrors the performance of the Dow Jones Industrial Average?

3. **Responsibility.** Who gets the credit (or blame) for how well your portfolio performed? Was it your manager's decisions, or market conditions, or your own choice of an asset allocation mix that caused the value of your investments to increase (or decrease)?

   The report should be self-explanatory, but if it isn't, ask for help. That's what your financial consultant is there for.

Then, once you understand the information, evaluate it in partnership with your consultant. Are you happy with the results?

As we have preached all along, think long term. One bad quarter does not necessarily a bad portfolio manager make. However, if it becomes clear—over many quarters, or perhaps several years—that your manager is not meeting your objectives, especially compared with the performance of other managers with similar goals, it is up to you to let her go. You hired. You may have to fire.

You then have to decide if you want to try again with a new manager, or manage your investments yourself.

And What Will You Do for an Encore?

We just asked you to review the bidding if you're unhappy. What to do with the opposite results? We'll close the chapter by suggesting what you should do in the face of a roaring success. Let's say that your portfolio manager's performance far surpasses the target you've agreed on. You're pleased as punch. What next? What do you tell your manager?

Our advice: take a beat from the late Otto Klemperer. This famous German conductor—renowned by the public for his brilliant interpretation of the Beethoven symphonies—was also known, and privately respected, among his musicians as a demanding taskmaster. He was sparse with praise.

But after one absolutely brilliant performance in rehearsal, he relented, cracked a slight smile, and simply said, "Good."

His musicians—stunned at the rare display of acclaim—burst into spontaneous applause. Then the maestro's smile vanished, and he said, "Not *that* good."

In music there's always another performance; in the markets, there's always another day, another year, another performance.

If you want the ultimate long-term management of your portfolio—hire a portfolio manager. A portfolio manager will mold your portfolio to fit your specific goals, your risk tolerance. It's a premium service—but it's the most personalized service you can buy. The manager takes care of the day-to-day care and feeding of your portfolio, and you may receive special report cards on the results of your strategy.

CHAPTER 22

Reviewing Results: Weathering a Shower

If you're truly thinking long term—if you're trying to grow rich s-l-o-w-l-y—there may come a time, during decades of patiently trying both to build assets and to preserve them, when a passing shower will happen.

We earnestly hope this won't happen too often, but it *can* rain on your investment parade. Most times it will be brief. But even if it rains harder, our advice? Weather it. The sun will come out, if not tomorrow then the day after, and the value of your assets will continue to rise. No matter how heavy the rainfall, odds are you won't need an ark.

But you may need an umbrella to deal with the decline in the value of your assets, to keep yourself from getting too wet, however brief the shower.

Our advice throughout this guide has been to diversify. So, if you wake up one morning and find your investments are shrinking, chances are that they are all not shrinking equally. Some will be performing less well than others, and getting rid of those laggards is the place you want to start.

True, we have told you to be patient, but that doesn't mean you have to let cobwebs grow on your assets. By the way, the time when you are putting individual investments under the microscope is also the obvious time to step back, and look at the whole picture—that is, reassess your total allocation of assets. Has there been any change in the base or benchmark recommendation?

When you first picked your allocations—ranging from conservative to aggressive—you were given a recommended mix based on that point in time. But the mix was not etched in stone. The mix will change. It *should* change from time to time. So a reassessment of your assets should be both small and big. As economic conditions change, or your goals change, or the assets values change, you may want to adjust your asset allocation. Ask for help from your financial consultant in the review of how your assets are allocated, and how they are performing.

Review the Bidding

That said, let us underscore something that is probably obvious. Before you make any drastic changes, take another step back and review the bidding.

You—perhaps in consultation with your investment consultant or adviser—had some time back picked a number. A goal. Or maybe several goals. You knew exactly how well you wanted your assets to perform in the coming years. Before you established your goal(s) you had looked at a large spectrum of investments. You winnowed the options down, as you clarified your objectives, and that list got even smaller once you factored your risk tolerance into the mix.

Only after you did all that research did you allocate your assets in an attempt to achieve the goal that seemed quite attainable at the time.

All this is another way of saying you spent an awful lot of time before you decided to put your money into the investment you are now thinking of selling.

Before you do anything, check with your financial consultant to get the complete background of what exactly is going on.

Has a sudden swing in the economy been particularly tough on this investment?

Is this investment a laggard compared to similar ones, or is it the entire sector that is having problems?

Is the problem cyclical, or an indication that things are bound to get worse?

Cut Your Losses

Get the facts. Don't be trigger happy. But once you're armed with the information, decide. No matter how you are controlling your assets—totally, through self-direction, by investing in mutual funds, or relying on a portfolio manager—always remember one of the oldest adages on Wall Street: Run with your gains, *but cut your losses.*

If you do decide to cut your losses, don't panic. Don't take your remaining assets and try to gain everything back overnight. Remember, time is on your side. Some of your remaining assets may continue to grow, thanks to the wonder of compounded interest, and—depending on what the investments are—thanks to total return. Simply sell your bad performers and move the proceeds to more-promising investments. Don't dwell on the past.

However, if the losses are more consistent than you would like, regroup. Try a new tack. Give someone—something else, perhaps a new funds manager—a shot at your goal of obtaining growth and income.

How often do you do this reassessing of your assets? At least

---

The Courage of Your Convictions

Let's suppose a stock has dropped considerably, but you are convinced that intrinsic value remains hidden in this particular investment. You *know* that the downturn is unwarranted. Then by all means don't sell. In fact, you may want to show the courage of your convictions and *double up* on your investment. Or, you may not want to double up, but you do want to buy *some* more shares.

You are not going to do this with abandon, of course. But if you are truly convinced that the investment is a good one, its drop in price gives you an excellent opportunity to buy more.

This is virtually the same as dollar cost averaging, but instead of investing in a systematic way (buying the same dollar amount of a stock or fund every month for a year, or for years, for example) you buy more one time only. Either way, you end up lowering the average cost of each share.

Let's say that originally you bought 1,000 shares of this investment at $35 a share, and the stock has since fallen to $26. If you buy another 1,000 shares now, you'll reduce your average cost of all 2,000 shares to $30.50.

Let us repeat what we said above. *Don't throw good money after bad.* But if you're convinced—after doing additional research—of the long-term prospects of your investments, buying more may be an excellent move.

---

annually. (Remember, you are thinking long term.) If that seems like an eternity, try quarterly, or even monthly.

Do Your Winners Offset the Sinners?

A final thought: as opposed to the occasional time when you confess to a slight shrinkage, we earnestly hope there will be far more times during the course of your long-term investment strategy when you'll be able to crow—softly, of course—"Look at this! Not too shabby." Your aim is always to offset the occasional sinner with a steady bundle of winners.

If this never-ending effort to build and preserve assets is a family quest—make sure your spouse hears the good news. Don't wait till you tote up net worth, once a year. As success surfaces, speak up—take a bow. Give yourself a verbal pat on the back.

Long-term investing means you weather the storms. If you have a weak performer, the prudent course may be to sell, and move on to a more promising investment. Just be sure you always keep your long-term goals in mind when reviewing individual performance. But remember that economic conditions do change; your own goals may shift.

PART IV

Harvesting Your Savings

CHAPTER 23

When It Comes to Retirement, There's No Place Like Home

House rich, cash poor.

Those four words are probably uttered most often when people are asked to describe their economic status. That's especially true as you begin thinking about retirement.

Having a lot of money tied up in your house is a problem, of course, but as problems go, it's a very nice one to have. Think about what the saying "house rich, cash poor," actually means.

It's not that you don't have any money. You do. (Think back to the net worth statement you did. The equity in your house was probably your largest asset.) It's just that all that equity—the difference between what you could net once you sold your house and what you currently owe on it—is locked within your four walls.

How can you get that equity out? That's what this chapter is all about.

But before we begin discussing financial strategies, a slight departure. We promised at the outset that *Grow Rich Slowly* would deal with the money side of retirement planning. We weren't going to get into a discussion about the personal side, like where to live, when to retire, and how much you should leave to your favorite nephew Harold in your will. And that's still true. We don't feel comfortable about advising you on personal choices—with an exception or two that you'll find in this chapter.

Perhaps more than any other retirement issue the question of where you're going to live once you've retired is an extremely personal one. While it might make the most *economic* sense to sell the house and move to a different part of the country, or even a different part of the world where housing prices (and the other costs of living) are less, it may not make *personal* sense at all.

You may like your house and the memories it contains. Your roots may be so deep, and your friendships so strong, that even *thinking* about moving is painful.

If that's the case, don't move. We are not about to suggest you sell your house strictly for financial gain.

So here's our starting point. It's your house; it's your money; and it's your life. If you like the old place, and the fact that it's paid for (or soon will be), if you love the idea that kids and grandkids will always have the same place to come back to, then do nothing.

We're Moving—Next Door

For what it's worth, most people these days don't take off for warmer climes once they retire. Only about one in four people sell their homes and head elsewhere once they stop working. Of those who do move, about three-quarters move no more than 30 miles from where they presently live. They're generally going through their own kind of downsizing, trading away the acre lawn and the extra bedrooms for a smaller, easier-to-maintain town house or condo, perhaps in a senior citizens' community.

Continue living where you are content in knowing that your spouse or heirs are going to inherit a nice place to live. If there is a mortgage, and you have no plans of moving, you may want to think about refinancing, and/or prepaying the mortgage to make the homestead a bit more affordable.

Keeping the house may not make the most financial sense, but the decision could be priceless, when it comes to your peace of mind.

If you really do plan to pass on your cherished homestead to your children, or even grandchildren, talk it over with them first. If you're to the point of joint maturity when you can be frank about big money matters with one another (some parent-children relationships never, never reach this point, even when the parents are in their 70s, say, and the "kids" are in their 50s), make sure they're brimming with bright expectations over the future gift.

If they presently live down the road, the future move back to the big house may be the answer to their dreams. But if they're some distance away—100 or 500 or 2,500 miles down the road—the reality may be they *won't* be moving back, and so when the time comes, what they'll really be doing is dealing long distance with a real estate broker. And finally, how do you leave one house to a son *and* a daughter, or to even more people?

You do have other options, even if you want to stay put. The most intriguing is selling your house, and then leasing it back.

There are three major variations of sale-leasebacks, ranging from the basic to the fairly complex. Let's take them one at a time.

1. **All in the family.** You sell your house to your children, and then rent it back from them for the rest of your life. If you're over 55 you may not have to pay any federal tax on up to $125,000 of any profit generated from the sale. (We'll talk about how that works in a minute.) Plus, as the buyer, your children will get all the

benefits that come from owning rental property: deductions for interest expense, property taxes, depreciation and maintenance costs.

Please note: If your children's adjusted gross income exceeds $100,000, the IRS restricts their ability to deduct these items, if they result in a loss.

Here's how that restriction works:

On actively managed real estate there is a $25,000 limit on the amount of losses that can offset regular income. That limit exists for everyone.

However, the cap is reduced by 50 cents for each dollar that exceeds $100,000 on adjusted gross income. That means, of course, that it does not exist if your adjusted gross income is $150,000 or more.

If your children fall within the $100,000-plus category, they may be better off treating the purchase of your house as their second home, instead of a rental. That way they can benefit more from the mortgage interest, and property tax deductions, which would be disallowed because of their income.

Now all this brings up a fairly obvious point. Even though sale-leasebacks can be a family affair, they are not simple to arrange, or account for. Our advice is to check with a lawyer who has experience with real estate sales and rentals, and mortgage and annuities, and make sure your financial adviser is comfortable accounting for these types of transactions.

This can be a good deal all the way around, but it is not perfect. First, the rent you pay your children is taxable income for them. Second, to qualify for the tax deductions we talked about a minute ago, the kids must charge you a rent that is roughly comparable to other rentals in the area. The government does give a slight break for having reared your own landlord. The tax courts have ruled that your children can charge you as much as 20% less than the going market rate, because they are eliminating the risk of renting to strangers.

That, in turn, raises the question of whether you *want* your kids to be your landlord. You love your kids dearly; they totally reciprocate, but as you *both* move into adulthood, the question is who's parenting whom. After all the years of telling them to clean up their rooms, your kids might start to return the favor and begin commenting on how you are maintaining what is now *their* property.

If the thought makes you uncomfortable, you may prefer:

2. Sale-leasebacks, or life tenancy arrangements, with a nonfamily member.

This is another way of eating your cake (selling your house) and having it too. (You don't have to move.)

You sell the house to an investor, but reserve the right to live in the house, as a renter, for life. However, because you have reserved a life tenancy, you may not get as much for your house as you probably would through an outright sale. (Note, though, that unlike your children, the outside investor has no familial reason to charge you less than market rent.)

3. **Giving it all away.** This approach works just like the first two, except that you don't sell your house. You give it to charity, through a charitable remainder trust. (Chapter 29 explains this device much more fully.)

As part of your gift, you retain a life tenancy that would allow you, and your spouse, to remain in your home for your combined lifetimes, or a set number of years, depending on how you structure the gift. (You may be planning to move to the desert spa of Tombstone, Arizona, in seven years, once you hit 65. The terms of the gift would reflect that.)

While you're generally responsible for all the upkeep, real estate taxes, and insurance while you live in the house, you get the tax deduction for your gift *immediately*. The amount of the deduction is based on an IRS life expectancy table.

How Mortgage Financing Can Affect Your Retirement Options

As you near retirement, you can consider how mortgage financing can affect, and even make possible, some of your retirement options.

If you plan to remain in your home and have a mortgage, make certain it is financially favorable. If it is a very low rate mortgage, by all means, keep it. On the other hand, if the rate is higher than prevailing rates, consider refinancing as long as the cost of refinancing will be offset by interest rate savings.

If you *are* building a retirement home, a home equity line of credit on your existing residence can be an excellent way to temporarily finance the start of the construction or the down payment of the purchase. Then when you sell your existing home, the credit line will be paid off from the proceeds of the sale of your former residence. A home equity line can be more convenient and often less costly than traditional construction loans.

During your pre-retirement, it is more important than ever to use credit wisely. Traditional consumer credit is expensive and a home equity line or other alternative to consumer credit can mean significant savings. Interest on home equity lines is generally tax-deductible on balances up to $100,000.

Reverse Mortgages

Wouldn't it be nice if—after all these years of writing a monthly mortgage check—your bank, S&L, or mortgage company turned around and returned the favor and started writing you a monthly check? It certainly would make staying in your home easier.

Well, this financing vehicle does exist—it's called a reverse mortgage. But while you have probably heard about this concept for a while, the idea is not as widespread, or as wonderful, as you might think.

But before we tell you what it's not (that is, not wonderful), let us first tell you what it is.

A reverse mortgage allows a homeowner who has paid off, or nearly paid off, his house to tap into his home equity in one of several ways. You can receive one lump sum, a monthly check, a line of credit, or some combination of all three.

Unlike the sale-leaseback arrangement, taking out a reverse mortgage does not mean you are selling your house. You are *borrowing* against it, much like you do with a home equity loan. The difference is that you don't have to pay back the loan, or any of the interest on it, until you and your spouse either move, or die. Then the loan, plus the interest, is due in full.

How much can you borrow? It depends on a lot of things: how old you and your spouse are (the younger you are, the smaller the loan), how much equity you have in your home (obviously the more equity you have, the more you can borrow), and who is doing the lending.

Loans backed by the Federal Housing Administration, a federally sponsored agency that insures mortgages, tend to have higher costs and lower lending limits than reverse mortgages offered by private lenders. For example, no matter how much equity you have in your home, the maximum amount you can borrow under an FHA-backed loan is $124,875.

There is an advantage to taking out an FHA-backed loan. If the government guarantees the loans, you'll continue to get your reverse mortgage checks even if the bank that wrote your reverse mortgage fails.

Two other things to underscore about reverse mortgages. First, the good news. While you'll will be receiving a check, or checks, that money is neither income, nor a taxable gain. Remember, you aren't selling your house, just borrowing against it. So the money you receive through a reverse mortgage neither affects your tax rate, nor your Social Security benefits.

Now, the bad news. That money isn't sent from heaven. You are reducing the equity in the house. That means you are going to have less money later, if you decide to move, or if you need that home equity money for some other purpose. And there's even the chance that you will outlive your reverse mortgage and you may be forced to sell your home to satisfy the outstanding loan.

Borrower beware.

Moving?

You like living where you are, but since the kids are gone, the house is now too big and too much to take care of.

Or, you sure would like to take out some of the equity in your home, but you really like the area. What to do? Well, you could sell, and buy a smaller place nearby.

You also could sell, and rent nearby.

Or, after contemplating options one and two, you say, "Oh, the heck with it. Let's just trundle off to Tahiti."

But, then you start worrying about how you will pay for those grass skirts you are going to buy, or whether you really can pay for that perpetual luau for the rest of your life, so you decide to be prudent, sell the house, but hold the mortgage for the buyer, so you're assured of *receiving* a monthly check for the term of the mortgage.

The choices are yours. But each one raises a different financing question.

Your Uncle Wants You to Move: The $125,000 Exclusion

We've never quite figured this out—maybe Uncle Sam's secret desire is to run a moving company, instead of an entire country—but the government has given you a pretty good reason for moving. Some 125,000 of them to be exact.

People nearing retirement age receive a once-in-a-lifetime exclusion—up to $125,000—on the capital gain they'd otherwise have to report when they sell their house. (Actually, you will report the capital gain on your taxes, only it won't be subject to tax.)

There are a couple of things about this to keep in mind, but the exemption is pretty straightforward.

To qualify for the exemption, either you or your spouse has to be over 55. (For purposes of this exemption, you are no longer husband and wife, but husband/wife: one unit.)

But what the IRS giveth, the IRS also taketh away. So if *either* of you has ever used the exclusion before (say, for example, you and ex-spouse did, during a previous marriage), you can't use it again, even if your new partner has never applied for the exemption.

Finally, the place you are selling must be: *(a)* your principal residence (no vacation homes, please) and *(b)* must be the place where you've lived for three out of the last five years.

If you meet all the guidelines, you get that $125,000 exemption. This can be an awfully nice gift. It's a big tax advantage when you sell, but where are you going to move to? A new house? A rental apartment? And if you sell, should you hold a mortgage from the buyer?

Buy or Rent?

It's up to you. If you own your home free and clear, it's unlikely that you're going to find a cheaper place to live. However, that still leaves you with the "problem" of having all that equity tied up in your house.

One solution is to sell your house, invest the proceeds, and rent. If that makes emotional sense, make sure it makes financial sense as well. To find out, create a chart, such as the one on page 371, to make sure. Here are some hints that will help:

1. **Figure out what your current home costs you each month.** Add the mortgage, if there is one, to the monthly property tax, insurance, maintenance costs. Then add in utility costs that you *would not* have to pay if you rented. For example, few apartment rentals charge you for water, access to sewers, garbage pickup, and heat, all things you are paying for now.

2. **Determine all the tax deductions you're currently receiving for things like your mortgage interest (if any) and property taxes.** Divide those deductions by 12.

3. **If you have a mortgage, determine how much of your monthly check is going to reduce principal.** (Paying the mortgage, as we've seen, is another form of forced savings.)

4. **Subtract 3 and 2 from 1.** This gives you a pretty good idea of what your monthly housing cost is.

Once you know what your house is costing you each month, you can go ahead and figure out if renting would make more sense.

First, determine what your *net* profit would be if you sold your home. To do that, take the selling price and subtract real estate commissions (if any), closing costs, and the like, plus the outstanding mortgage(s) if any. That will give a gross dollar amount.

Then subtract your basis (the true cost of your house) from the gross payment. The remainder is your gross profit.

If you are over 55, and haven't yet taken the $125,000 exclusion, do so now (at least for the purpose of this exercise). So, subtract $125,000 from your gross profit and then multiply the balance times 28%, the capital gains rate. Next, subtract that amount from your gross profit. The remainder will tell you how much you'd net from the sale of your house.

That's good. But it's not enough. You now have to figure out how much you'll get in after-tax income on a monthly basis. (You want to determine *after-tax* income to make sure you are doing an apples-to-apples comparison. Remember that when we figured out your present housing costs—that is, in your current house—it was on an *after-tax basis.*)

Once you have calculated at a fairly accurate yield, you'll be left with two numbers: the cost of your monthly housing as a home-owner, and the monthly income the equity now in your house could generate if you sold. There are two ways of looking at those numbers. You simply can say that if the return on the sale of your house is greater than what your house currently costs you, it makes sense to sell and rent.

Here's a second option. Find out what a rental that you *absolutely love* would cost per month. Multiply by 12 and deduct the total rent from the amount of income your home equity would generate annually. If the balance is positive, it makes *economic* sense to move.

The Pleasures of Staying Put

But a couple of cautionary notes, some personal, others financial.

Personal first. There is an awful lot of emotional security that comes from knowing that the roof over your head is yours. We doubt that when you retire you'll want to make any major additions to your home. But over the retirement years ahead you can do a lot of pleasurable fine-tuning, at a leisurely pace, room by room, or in the garden. This can be immensely satisfying to you as an owner, but it's not quite the same to you as a tenant. And, to give you a more fiscal reason for staying put, odds are that your local tax rate won't climb as fast as rent increases.

This having been said, if the numbers make sense, and you have never particularly found emotional fulfillment painting the outside of your house (and writing insurance checks), enjoy your new (rented) home.

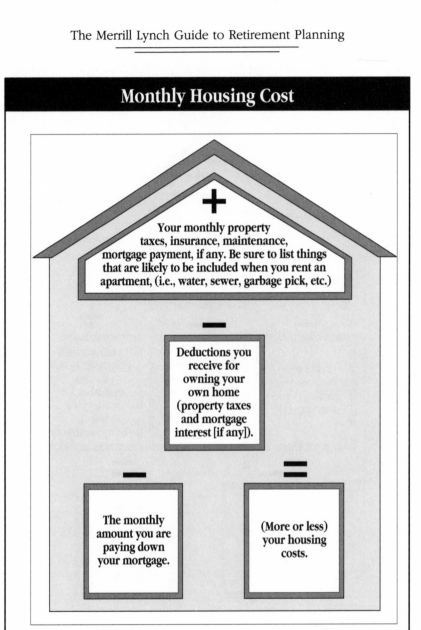

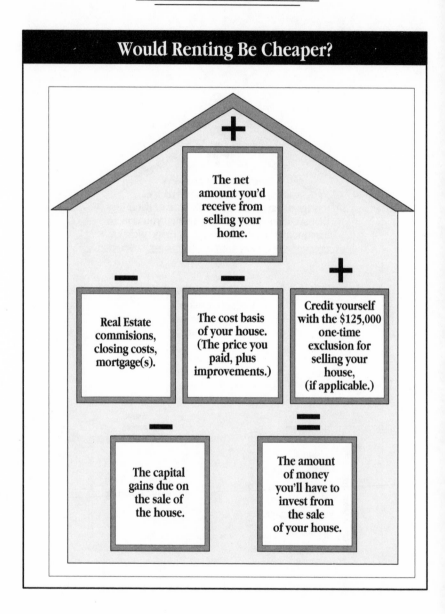

Would Renting Be Cheaper?

+

The net amount you'd receive from selling your home.

−

−

+

Real Estate commisions, closing costs, mortgage(s).

The cost basis of your house. (The price you paid, plus improvements.)

Credit yourself with the $125,000 one-time exclusion for selling your house, (if applicable.)

−

=

The capital gains due on the sale of the house.

The amount of money you'll have to invest from the sale of your house.

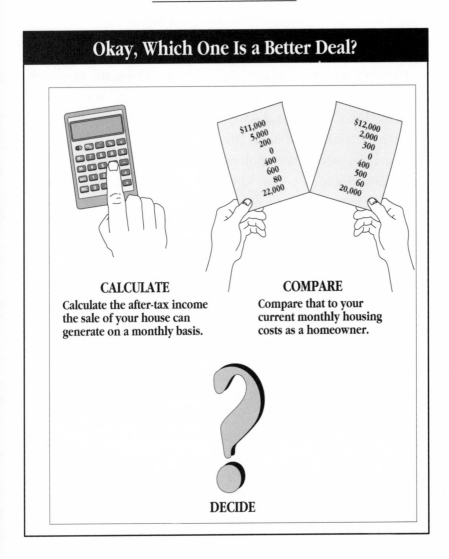

Okay, Which One Is a Better Deal?

CALCULATE

Calculate the after-tax income the sale of your house can generate on a monthly basis.

COMPARE

Compare that to your current monthly housing costs as a homeowner.

DECIDE

If You Do Plan to Sell . . .

Whether you plan to sell and move to an apartment, or sell and move to a new home down the street, or sell and then move halfway round the world, there is still one more question to address. How, exactly, are you going to sell your house?

There is something appealing about turning over the keys to the new owner and walking away with a large check. But if interest rates are high, or the banks are swamped with mortgage applications, it may take a while to close.

You have two other choices. Become a bank—albeit a tiny one—or a landlord, whose lordship consists of exactly one property: your former home.

If You Do Plan to Rent . . .

Instead of selling your house, you can rent it out. There are several strong arguments for doing just that. First, suppose the housing market is soft, but you're convinced it will rebound in relatively short order. Wait it out, and earn rental income in the interim. If you're not content with the prospects of a rebound in the short term, just stand pat with a longer-term rental. and be assured of a steady, monthly rent check. (Think of it as earning a return on your home equity.)

The third advantage is even more appealing. *You still own the house.* At any time, you can decide you've had enough of being a landlord, sell the old homestead, and walk away with your money. Let someone else take on the landlord burden. (Before renting your home you should review with your tax adviser how this will affect your taxes when you go to sell the house.)

And being a landlord—especially an absentee landlord—may quickly tempt you to do just that. There could be troubles leasing the place; your tenant may not always pay the rent on time; what happens if he wrecks the place; you'll still be responsible for the major repairs (which always seem to be more of a task for a landlord than for a resident owner). The list, as any landlord can tell you, is endless.

Still, most tenants are perfectly wonderful, and you can always hire a management company to rent the house for you. As you know by now—since we've been sounding this refrain in chapter after chapter—we *do* believe in professional management. After all, you may be hiring a manager (or maybe several) to manage your money assets, why not hire a professional manager to run your real estate assets? An asset is an asset. Your rental manager will even arrange to take care of all the maintenance that needs to be done. All you have to do, assuming everything goes well, is cash the rent check.

You Hold the Mortgage

If renting doesn't have any appeal, how about holding the mortgage for the buyer?

Here's how it could work. Let's say your house is worth $300,000. You require the buyer to put down—that is, pay to you immediately—$60,000, or 20% of the purchase price. You then give the buyer a mortgage of $240,000.

Couldn't you take your whole $300,000 and go off and invest it somewhere? Sure. You could take the $300,000 and consider buying a trio of jumbo CDs that would be federally insured. Or you could buy some annuities. Or better yet, you could now take this $300,000 and consider how you can prudently invest it to get both maximum yield *and* safety.

You're retired now—but you can still aim for an above-average return on the money.

But suppose you sell, and you take the mortgage, and bad things happen: the buyer fails to pay. This is a headache, particularly if the market is down when you eventually foreclose and sell the house all over again.

We've talked about several ways to tap the equity in your house. But what they all boil down to is this: When it comes to financing your retirement, there's no place like home.

CHAPTER 24

When to Retire

When should you retire?

In a lot of ways, it is a personal question. Is your health okay? What would you do if you did stop working? Do you know where you want to live?

We promised we wouldn't give advice on retirement life-styles. There are a host of very fine books available to help you over those hurdles. But since where you'll live once you stop working is a key to determining how you'll spend a substantial portion of your retirement income—housing is a lot cheaper in the Southeast and the Southwest, for example, than it is around New York and Los Angeles—let us make three quick points.

Things to Consider: Climate, Medicine, Taxes

First, if you are planning on moving once you retire, *always, always, always* test out the area before you move. Try the place of your dreams in all seasons.

A warm climate might be unbelievably serene in winter months, but not that pleasant in August. And the opposite can be true. A northern vacation home could be dandy in summer but deadly in the winter. (For this very reason, and because land is still relatively cheap, the middle states—from the Carolinas to Arkansas to Colorado—have been growing as popular retirement destinations in recent years.)

There are two other factors to keep in mind. Will your retirement home in the middle of nowhere separate you from the medical help you might need sometime in the future? Of the dozens of renowned medical centers across the country, we'll just single out three: Tucson, Raleigh-Durham, and Salt Lake City. These three, admittedly, are in large metropolitan areas, but you don't have to live literally within shouting distance of the university medical center. You can live in another, more placid world: 20 miles away in the country (or mountains, or desert).

And finally, before you move, check out the tax situation. Will your *tax* liability—state, city, and estate taxes—be less or more in your new domicile?

Important as all those things are, there is a more practical question to ask.

Can you afford to retire?

You are part of the new longevity. You may indeed live as long in retirement as you were in the work force. Will your resources carry you through these extra years?

The only way to know for sure is by doing the math. Working the projections. Do it now—not just a month or so before you plan to stop work, but several years (at least five) before you are ready to retire.

What Are Your "Retirement Assets"?

Each year, when you develop your new net worth statement, you update the column marked "retirement assets." As you approach the time when you think you are going to retire, take an extra long, hard look at your assets in that column.

When we say "your" assets, we obviously mean the retirement assets of each spouse. In calculating the family's net worth most assets will be jointly held. But retirement assets are not in joint accounts.

Regardless of who the named beneficiary is for the accounts or plans, they are individual assets. This is important for two reasons. First, it's highly unlikely both working spouses will retire at exactly the same moment. (Sure, you might both retire in the same year. Or it might be that one will retire this year, and the other work for another year or so.) Secondly—regardless of the timing of your retirements—you'll both have different arrays of retirement accounts, or plans.

One of you, for example, may work for a not-for-profit employer, and so you may have a 403(b) supplemental retirement plan; the other may work for a corporation, and have a 401(k) or a profit-sharing plan, in addition to an employer pension plan.

And while both of you may have regular IRAs, the number of rollover IRAs you may have will depend on how many times each of you has changed jobs and/or has worked for an employer who has closed down a retirement plan.

What will the payout from these plans be? When must you take out the money? These are the questions you want to ask now.

One of the canons in advance planning is to project ahead in order to see if your post-retirement income will be up to expectations. If the opposite happens—and you have an embarrassment of riches—here's a bit of bad news for you. You can be penalized. You may face a 15% penalty tax if the annual aggregate distribution (that is, the total of all distributions from all of your retirement accounts: pension, 403(b), 401(k), IRAs, and the like) exceeds $150,000 in any one year, or you may be penalized if any one lump sum, *which is not rolled over to an IRA* or a qualified plan, exceeds $750,000.

This excise tax could also be assessed on post-death excess distributions. A surviving spouse—under certain rules—may be able to avoid this penalty if the surviving spouse is the sole beneficiary of these assets.

Obviously, for assets this large, do see a tax or financial adviser. If you do have significant retirement assets (and other assets) and are facing this excess distribution tax on your annual takeouts and you're not yet 70½, your problem may be that you *haven't been taking enough* in distribution between 59½ and 70½. Otherwise, when you reach 70½, and are forced by law to take out the "minimum amount" from one or more accounts, you may exceed the $150,000, and so the 15% tax hits you. The solution may be to start drawing upon your retirement assets much earlier—between 59½ and 70½ (and in certain cases, as early as age 55). Again, this may take considerable planning, so do sit down with your advisers.

Part of the financial equation will also involve putting your other assets to the test: how much income will they provide in retirement? A major piece of that revolves around your home. If you do downsize in selling your present home, how will you put the net gains, after taxes, to work for you?

After you get the answers, project ahead. Will there be enough money to live the way you want to once you retire?

If the answer is no, or even if it's maybe, now is the time to do something about it. You may have been planning to stop working at age 65, but if the money isn't there, don't quit.

Although Social Security is still based on a "normal" retirement age (65 for most people, 66 or 67 for most baby boomers and people born thereafter, as we will explain in Chapter 26), the fact is that age discrimination laws have virtually excised the traditional "normal" retirement age in corporations.

In reality, of course, 65 is the standard, but the fact is that with very few exceptions you can't be forced to retire. There may be financial inducements to do so, but legally you probably won't be forced out the door before you want to leave. (In a few pages we'll discuss a fact of corporate life: "downsizing." Your company may offer a voluntary retirement program. And, of course, there are times when a company will simply shutter a plant, a division, your department, or your job.)

Not Yet—Not Yet

So if you don't want to retire, or you need to save more money to ensure a comfortable retirement, keep on working. However, keep in mind that part-time earnings will probably reduce your Social Security benefits. (See Chapter 26.) Of course, if you cease part-time work your full benefits will resume.

So you may be best off not applying for Social Security until you have retired completely from any and all paying jobs. If you do keep on working, you'll be giving your retirement investments more time to grow, plus the longer you delay taking your Social Security benefits, the larger they will be. And the longer you have earned income the longer you can keep pumping contributions into your regular IRA and perhaps your 401(k).

Not only will those additional years in the work force do you some financial good, they may do you some psychological good as well.

Psychologists, in sifting through the stress that often accompanies retirement issues, tell us that one of the greatest problems people face in retirement is replacing the self-esteem they had when they were working. Once you're retired, you may feel that you're not as important anymore. This is particularly true with professionals. As a doctor, a lawyer, a professor, you were looked up to. Now you are merely one of millions of retired people, who are all former somethings.

One solution, which has the added advantage of supplementing your retirement income, is not to retire completely. If possible, retire in stages. Change lanes—from the fast track to a slower lane. If you're a professional, you may be able to work two days out of five, or one week out of four, or maybe three months out of the year.

Your experience may not just be tolerated, it may be venerated. You can become an elder statesman(woman). You keep your high esteem, but lessen your workload.

If money is not a problem, but self-esteem is, consider volunteer

---

Early Retirement—Why 62?

Let us take a moment here to underscore a point we made earlier about *early* retirement.

Many people considering early retirement pick the age 62. Why? Principally because that's the earliest that your Social Security benefits will kick in.

---

work. If you are an accountant, help senior citizens do their tax returns or fill out medical forms; if you're a doctor, you can volunteer in a community health or drug program. A professor can lecture on her favorite subject to community groups rather than college students, and executives can donate their time to companies that are just starting out.

Your income from a volunteer effort is psychological, not tangible. But it can be just as rewarding.

You might *need* to do something in retirement. Golf and tennis may not be enough.

"But Not for Lunch"

There is one more obvious point to make about all this. Your advance planning must certainly take into account two careers. You may want to retire, but your husband doesn't. Or vice versa. That may be fine, but it certainly throws a wrench into the planned big move from home town to new town.

This point is brought home by a great story that has probably been attributed to just about everyone who has ever retired, but we like the Stengel family version best.

Casey Stengel, a baseball manager extraordinaire well into his 70s, finally retired and promptly drove his wife nuts by being constantly underfoot. Edna's edict: "I married you for better or worse, but not for lunch." With that, she gave him the heave-ho as adroitly as umpires used to.

Casey promptly went back to work, this time for a local banking firm. Peace reigned once again in the Stengel household.

Casey told everyone who'd listen, that he loved going to work a few hours every day. And Edna loved having him gone.

When to Get Serious

If, while you are young, it looks like you are on course for a financially secure retirement, great. Five years away from your projected retirement date you should really start getting serious about what needs to be done.

Maybe all you'll have to do is a bit of tweaking to your budget. Merely postponing those expensive annual vacations that you take, putting the money in a retirement account instead, may be enough to put you over the top.

You might need to do a bit more. For example, you might want to tighten your belt a notch, to make sure that you are funding your voluntary retirement programs—such as your IRAs and 401(k)s—to the maximum.

Also about five years out is the time you'll want to double-check on your vested rights in a former employer's retirement plan. You're probably getting periodic reports on the value of your former plan, but don't hesitate to call your former employer's human resources department if you have other questions. For example, if you are planning on taking early retirement from your present job, can you take "early retirement" from your former one as well? It will undoubtedly mean you'll receive less, but your former employer may give you your reduced benefits in advance of their normal retirement age.

And, of course, this is the time you want to check on exactly what benefits you will be receiving from your current employer. One of the things you may have to decide is how you want to receive those pension benefits.

Typically, you'll be offered one of two types of annuities.

Single life annuity: The income you receive is for your lifetime only. When you die, the benefits stop.

Joint and survivor life annuity: The payout will be less—typically between 10% and 25% less—but it will continue for the lifetimes of you and your spouse.

Also, the law now says that if you are married, your pension plan *must* offer this joint payout. You don't necessarily have to take the joint (reduced) payout, but you will have to look carefully at the options, and the law also requires that your spouse sign a form, which must be notarized, agreeing to whichever option you've picked (if the benefits are $3,500 or greater).

What Happens If You Get an Offer You Can't Refuse?

Unfortunately, you may not have the final choice of when to retire. In their rush toward "economic downsizing," your company may make you an early retirement offer that is too good to refuse.

Typically, your company in calculating pension benefits will add a set number of years to your age (five, let's say) and a set number of years of service (five) to the time you have already served, as an inducement to get you out the door.

If you leave now, they tell a 55-year-old who has been with the firm for 18 years, we will calculate your retirement benefits as if you were 60 years old, with 23 years of service.

As a part of a special severance inducement often given in "early out" packages, your employer might up the ante even more. A typical severance deal might be one week of pay for each year of employment. If the package is really sweetened, severance might be increased by 25%; in really munificent cases, severance might even be doubled. The company might also extend medical benefits. How long will you have to decide? The window isn't overnight, but it's not an eternity. While you may have heard rumors about the impending early retirement offer for several months, usually you'll have about a month to decide, once the plan is unveiled.

A few years back, when corporate slenderizing first began in earnest, the suggested early retirement age might have been 62 or 60. Now, as restructuring becomes a way of life throughout the land, some companies are offering early retirement packages to those as young as 55 or even 50.

The implication of the offer is clear. "Here's a good package," the company tells you. They're not threatening you. But the message is clear. "You may want to leave now. Make up your mind. If you don't, there could be changes in your job status in the future."

On top of the extraordinary trauma of deciding whether or not to retire, you'll also have to determine whether to take lump sum distributions from various retirement plans, if they're offered. For a detailed analysis of whether or not you should take the lump sums, see the next chapter: "To Roll Over, or Not to Roll Over, That Is the Question."

Try to put the emotional part of this offer aside, as best you can. Do the math, and figure out whether the offer is, in fact, too good to be true.

As traumatic as retirement is, you're just retiring from a job. Not from life.

Your retirement date is one of those sea changes of life. A crucial factor is how your replacement income—pension, Social Security, IRAs, and other investments—is stacking up. In addition to replacing real income, you may want to replace psychic income.

CHAPTER 25

To Roll Over, or Not to Roll Over, That Is the Question

Hamlet had it easy. With "To be, or not to be," he was merely wrestling with the question of whether life was still worth living.

If you have just been offered the chance to receive the entire contents of your pension fund at work—because you've retired, changed jobs, or your plan has been terminated—you have a much tougher question: "To roll over or not to roll over." Do you take the money you've just received and put it in an IRA account, or do you give yourself the chance to ignore the slings and arrows of everyday living and take the money now?

We weren't kidding when we said this is an extremely difficult question. In fact, this could be one of the most important decisions—financial or otherwise—of your life. Why? Because odds are—if your retirement plan has been perking along nicely for a while—the lump sum your employer has just given you is the largest check you will ever receive.

And if that isn't daunting enough, consider this: that lump sum may well be—once you've retired—your primary source of financial security. For many people, the amount of their pension dwarfs their other retirement savings, and Social Security benefits, *combined.*

So what do you do? Do you roll the money over, or don't you?

It's hard to give you a short answer, but unless you have important reasons *not to,* it's usually best to roll the assets over.

Remember where that money is coming from. The check didn't come from heaven, it came from a retirement plan. Your retirement plan.

You *are* going to live longer than you think. There is a *chance* that you are going to outlive your retirement assets. You may want to continue to save the money—in a tax-deferred IRA rollover.

This large source of money that is causing you sleepless nights could have come from only one place: a qualified tax-deferred retirement plan, be it a pension, profit sharing, 401(k), Keogh, or other salary-deferral savings plan, such as a 403(b) plan. By "qualified," we simply mean that the plan is in compliance with the various federal laws and regulations that govern retirement plans.

The rules can be complex, say, for a large pension plan. Strict adherence is demanded before a plan is qualified, under the tax code, for tax-favored treatment. (If an employer isn't in tune with the assorted regulations, the government can get nasty, "disqualifying" the plan, which in effect means that the tax incentives are withdrawn and the roof has fallen in.)

But let's assume *your* plan is safely qualified. So the next question is, why are you getting this money now? Surprisingly, that may be very simple. Here are some possible answers:

1. **You are no longer employed by your company.**
   Maybe you've retired. (If so, congratulations.) But it is also

possible you have resigned, been forced to retire early, or been downsized, or, well, fired.

For people who have been recently "let go," there is a natural tendency to want to stick their retirement money in the checking account, to help pay the bills. While it is understandable, it is a very expensive source of money.

First, the normal income taxes on the money are due.

Second, if you are under 55 there probably will be a 10% penalty on top of that.

It is best to leave tapping into the retirement money as a last resort.

2. **Your plan has been terminated.** You're still gainfully employed, but, for whatever reason, your plan has ended. A good example would be the termination of a qualified stock purchase plan. Many stock purchase plans are thriving, and may well continue to do so for many years. But some plans (see Chapter 10) were established to take advantage of corporate tax breaks, and when those breaks ended, so did the plan.

3. **The distribution was made because the employee died.**

There are some important differences between pretax and after-tax contributions. You can only roll over money that was contributed *pretax* to your retirement fund. Money on which taxes have already been paid can't be rolled over. The law is very specific on that. But that, as we will see in just a moment, is actually a very good thing.

But before we get there, let's use an actual example to show how rollovers work in practice.

Suppose you'll be getting $100,000—of which $10,000 is your after-tax voluntary contribution, $40,000 is your employer's contribution, and $50,000 is the cumulative earnings or gains that have been produced by the $50,000 that you and your employer have put in. You're allowed to roll over *all* the money that's never been taxed, in this case that adds up to $90,000.

What about that other $10,000? That's the good news we talked about earlier. Since you've already paid taxes on it, it's now yours tax-free. This may be hard to believe—but the government *really* doesn't want you to pay taxes twice on the same amount.

Your Employer May Say No

Do all qualified plans qualify for lump sum payouts? No. Your retirement plan must specify that it will allow lump sum distributions. ERISA allows but doesn't demand it. Your employer has the final say.

In a defined contribution plan, you'll probably be allowed to take your vested amount as a lump sum. You may be running the investments; they're probably not pooled with other employee contributions; the money is yours.

But if your employer pension plan is a defined benefit plan, as many older pension plans are, the employer will probably say no. You will, as we said before when we were discussing defined benefit plans in Chapter 7, probably receive the money on an annuitized basis when you reach your former employer's normal retirement age. (However, if you are willing to settle for reduced benefits, you might be able to start receiving your money earlier. Check with your former employer for details.)

It's Not Really a Windfall—You've Earned It

You've lived quite nicely up until now, without having your retirement money burning a hole in your pocket, so think long and hard before you go and spend this windfall. Better yet, just put the money into another retirement account. (The government, by the way, is giving you the same advice, if you are retired, or have changed jobs, and are under 55. If you spend the money now, not only must you pay whatever taxes are due—more on that in a second—but the money may be subject to a 10% penalty for early withdrawal.)

Oh, all right. We'll make one little exception. If the amount of the distribution is small—and small is up to you, we've never met a dollar we didn't like—then take the money and go have a good time. (By the way, we could define "small" as less than, or equal to, your annual bonus from work. If you don't get a bonus, it's two weeks' gross pay, or less.)

If the amount is more than that, roll the money over. If it is less than that, go buy yourself a present, or go away for a nice, long weekend. Treat it as a one-time gift—taxable, of course—from your boss, and have a good time.

The Marvel of Compounding (Tax-Deferred)

If the government can't convince you with the enticements of an IRA, maybe the wonders of compounding will.

Quite often, in this book, we've talked about what a wonderful thing compound interest is. And nowhere is that more true, than when it comes to rollover accounts. Here's a quick example of how a $50,000 distribution could grow tax-deferred in an IRA rollover:

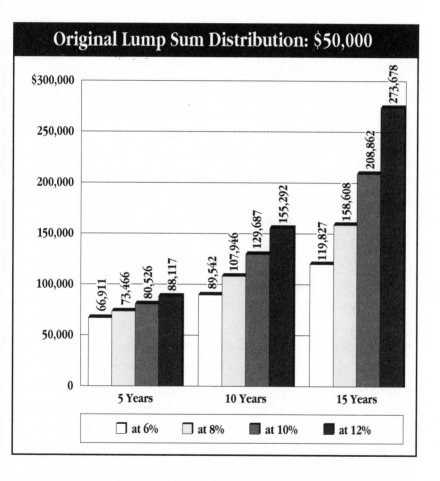

Original Lump Sum Distribution: $50,000

	5 Years	10 Years	15 Years
at 6%	66,911	89,542	119,827
at 8%	73,466	107,946	158,608
at 10%	80,526	129,687	208,862
at 12%	88,117	155,292	273,678

Not bad, huh?

This example underscores what we have been saying all along about saving tax advantaged, and saving smarter: the longer you can leave the money in an IRA, the bigger the benefits of tax-deferred compounding.

Taxes, Taxes, and More Taxes

If you do think about spending the money—and you'd be less than human if you didn't at least *think* about spending it—you'll find your decision in large part, like so many other financial decisions in your life, revolves around tax considerations. In its simplest form, the decision on what to do with your rollover money boils down to this: do you pay taxes now or pay them later?

Remember, the money in your retirement account has been growing tax-**deferred.** Your employer's contribution, plus the interest and dividends that money has earned, has never been taxed. Plus, there is a very good chance that your contribution was made with pretax dollars. Even if it wasn't, whatever money your contribution has earned has been growing tax-**deferred** as well.

We put the word "deferred" in boldface in the preceding paragraph to underscore something that you may have forgotten. The government has so far allowed this money to grow, without demanding its share, based on the understanding that one day the taxes will actually be paid. That day of reckoning? When you withdraw the money.

If you start spending your pension money today, the taxes are due today.

Suppose, as you cruise through your 60s in retirement, that your health is incredible, you don't presently need the money, and all you want to do is keep on smilin', and keep on deferrin'. (Although you really know you're defying the odds, you see no reason why *you* can't live forever.) The government's paternal smile on tax deferment is just that—very compliant as you age from 59½ to 70½, then the approving smile fades slightly, as it turns into a frown of tax collection. (At least we've never met a smiling tax collector.)

For when you reach 70½, the tax bell starts tolling in earnest. All good things come to an end.

You'll be reminded, not too gently, that all those lovely years of tax forbearance are over, and you'll be required to begin a systematic—that is, regular—takeout of those hefty retirement assets which have heretofore been sheltered.

We're tempted to say the party's over, but that's not really true.

For the takeout from an IRA can be based on your life expectancy, and what that really means is that you take money out for the rest of your life. The party's just begun!

But let's not worry about what happens when you reach 70½, in terms of taxes, till later. (In the first part of this book we told you how to *save* money for retirement; in this latter third of the book, we're telling you how to *spend* money from your assorted retirement nest eggs.)

To go back to the central question of this chapter, deciding to take the money now has consequences other than taxes. How you answer the question of "to roll over, or not to roll over" will go a long way toward determining your future financial flexibility. You'll have more options now, if you take the money, but conceivably less later.

If you use your retirement money today for a 180-day trip around the world, to pay for the elaborate wedding of the century for your daughter, or even to buy the dream retirement home that has just come on the market, you won't have the money sitting in an account somewhere, when you retire.

That could be okay.

The current opportunity may be too wonderful to pass up. That perfect home may be priced at 50% below the market, for example. As always, it's your call. It's your money. But remember, again, what your grandmother told you: You can't eat your cake and have it too.

However, you can eat half your cake, and have half of it left over. There is something known as a partial rollover, which, just as the name implies, allows you to spend some of your retirement money now, and roll over the rest. If you get a total distribution, you can roll over any portion you want.

The money you don't roll over will be taxed as ordinary income and forward averaging will not apply. (Consider forward averaging—explained on the next page—very carefully. If you're eligible, it might be to your advantage.)

But please note, if you actually receive your distribution after January 1, 1993, and then decide to roll over any part of it, an automatic 20% tax withholding will apply to the total distribution. And if you are under age 59½, you very likely will be hit with a 10% tax penalty for early withdrawal on the amount *not* rolled over.

It's Five Minutes to Midnight

Okay, that takes care of the background.

On to the big question, what do you do with the money if you receive a lump sum distribution? It's a decision that you will have to make relatively quickly. From the time you get the lump sum, you're allowed 60 days to roll it over. If you wait any longer than that, the government assumes that you plan to keep the money,

Spreading Taxes—with Forward Averaging

How does forward averaging work? Forward averaging simply utilizes the tax rate from a single return rate schedule that would apply to one-fifth or one-tenth of the taxable distribution amount.

Your age may limit which one you can use. According to the Tax Reform Act of 1986, people who were age 50 *before* January 1, 1986, can elect either 5-year or 10-year forward averaging for distributions from qualified plans.

Let's look first at 5-year averaging. Suppose you are eligible for 5-year averaging, and let's say you're getting a $100,000 lump sum. First you calculate that part of the distribution that is subject to ordinary income taxes. Then you subtract the minimum distribution allowance, if any, and you divide that amount by 5. You figure out what your taxes would be on that amount (as if you made no other money that year), then you multiply that amount by 5. (And 10-year averaging works the same way, since it may lower your taxes on the lump sum.)

Forward averaging is generally a wonderful thing, and like all wonderful things, it comes with qualifications and restrictions.

Even if you don't qualify for forward averaging you may have a shot at another tax break.

If you were age 50 before January 1, 1986, and participated in your employer's plan before 1974, you may elect to treat part of the distribution—the pre-1974 part—as a capital gain. That money will be subjected to a 20% tax. Post-1973 proceeds will be treated as ordinary income. Some restrictions on the use of forward averaging are listed below:

- You must have left the company—or, to put it in the IRS parlance, "you must have separated from service."

- You can use 5-year averaging only once in your lifetime. And it's only available to you if you're 59½ or older, unless you were over age 50 before January 1, 1986, in which case you are "grandfathered," according to the law, and can use 5-year averaging even if you're not yet 59½.

- You are not eligible for either 5 or 10 year averaging unless you have been in a plan at least 5 years.

If all this is slightly confusing—ask your tax adviser for help.

and all taxes—and the 10% penalty if applicable—will have to be paid.

Note that we say, "if applicable." Here are some exceptions:

1. You are 55 and "separated from service."

2. You are totally and permanently disabled as defined by the plan.

3. You use the money to meet a pressing financial need caused by medical expenses.

4. You've chosen to take the lump sum in annuitized payments.

5. You have received the money as a beneficiary.

Deep in a new law, the Unemployment Compensation Amendments Act of 1992 (which will become effective January 1, 1993), is an important change in the lump sum taxation scheme. The law pushes you more than ever toward a rollover decision.

Under the old law—prior to this law passed in 1992—you first could decide that you wanted to receive a lump sum, and then after you got it, you had up to 60 days to decide what to do with it. That still works—up to a point.

The old rules said that if you decided to move the assets before the 60-day expiration into your IRA, that's fine—the tax deferral continued. A major change in the new law says that unless you tell your employer (who in turn, tells the trustee of your retirement assets) *in advance* to transfer the assets *directly* to the new trustee of your choice (which could be an IRA custodian or trustee, or a trustee for another qualified plan or to an eligible annuity), your employer will be required to withhold 20% of the lump sum and turn it over to the IRS. You get the 80%.

Suppose that happens. You could still—within the parameters of the 60-day rule—elect to ship the 80% to an IRA. You could even make up the 20% difference—*somehow,* out of savings or other assets, or from a loan—in order to bring the full rollover up to 100%. Once you complete that rollover, within the 60-day rule, you eventually will be able to reclaim the 20% withholding when you file your income taxes. But in the meantime, you've lost the use (tax-deferred earnings) of the 20%, you've had to do a lot of scrambling, and it's downright cumbersome to go through the hassle of getting it back.

The way to avoid all this is simply to do advance planning. Since you will most likely know of your lump sum options some months before the D day—your final decision deadline back to your employer—you should not have to make a panic decision overnight.

Very early in this book we mentioned a service that is available at many financial service firms. It's usually free. You'll simply tell them the amount of your lump sum distribution, whether or not you're eligible for forward averaging (which is a way to get a special tax treatment), a few other facts on your tax bracket, and back will come a computer printout that compares your options. The options range from best possible taxation of your lump sum to rolling over and continuing the deferral.

Much of the decision process revolves around your immediate monetary needs, and your long-term retirement needs. Talk to your tax adviser or your financial consultant.

Our advice? If you are not going to spend the money, transfer or "roll over" it immediately—from one trustee to another. If you fail to do that, and receive the lump sum, minus the 20%, don't wait till day 59, make a frenzied deposit with an IRA custodian, and then struggle to get back the 20% from the government.

Let us give you the worst case we can think of. You've gotten your lump sum distribution (minus the 20%), but then decide to roll it over. Something always seems to get in the way. You wake up one fine Sunday morning to find that it's been exactly 60 days since you got the check. You are out of luck. Gloomy Sunday. Even if you deposit the money as soon as your financial services house—bank, whatever—opens Monday morning, you are too late. Backdating isn't allowed. The IRS tends to follow the book carefully on this one. They *know* how to watch a ticking clock.

Two other quick points to make on the 60-day rule.

First, you have 60 days from the time you receive the check, not from when the check is dated. However, to repeat, in case you failed to move trustee to trustee, our recommendation is to roll the money over well within 60 days of the check's date. It will make dealing with the IRS so much easier, should it come to that.

Second, suppose while you're pondering what to do with the money, you invest your funds short term, say, in a money market fund, and then, well within the 60 days, you roll it over. Fine. But you can only put into the rollover the exact property and amount of money you received from your retirement plan. (However, if you sell the property—say, the securities or bonds—before you

---

The Dreaded IRS Checklist

For the first few years after ERISA became law in 1974, and retirement plan rollovers were allowed, there were so few large lump sum distributions that auditing them was barely on the taxman's list.

Now that millions of rollovers happen annually, and now that reporting of distributions to the IRS is more automated, and now that the lump sum distributions can be well into six figures, and some are for a million plus, you can be sure that the audit priority for rollovers is much higher on the dreaded checklist.

roll the proceeds over, the cash amount you roll over cannot exceed the value of the initial distribution.)

Any earnings that your money has received since it has been out of the plan are taxed as ordinary income. Of course, since you are going to roll the money over quickly, there shouldn't be a whole lot of interest or dividends to worry about. After all, most people have some warning that they will be getting a lump sum distribution, so it shouldn't take them 60 days to make up their minds about what to do with it.

Why would you take the full 60 days? Well, if you haven't given the subject of rollovers any thought, it certainly can take some time to figure out what to do with the money. After all, you have to decide among three difficult choices:

1. **Do you even want to take the money?** Just because it has been offered doesn't mean you have to take it. You can leave the money in the company retirement plan. Why would you leave the money there? You might decide that your employer—or his trustee—can manage the money more efficiently than you could in an IRA rollover.

2. **You can take the money and roll it over.** (That raises the question of what you should invest it in. We'll deal with that in a minute.)

3. **You can treat the money as current income.**

Let's examine the tax consequences of each decision.

If you leave money in the present plan, the expectation is that you won't withdraw it until you really need it, which will probably be when you retire. If you take this route, nothing really changes. Your money continues to grow tax-deferred.

An important factor in this decision is not tax-related. It's very basic: How good has the return been? If you're pleased with the results—the total return per year—you may want to keep the same management. But if you think you—in partnership with your financial consultant—could do better in self-directing these assets, this may be the time to move.

You take the money in one lump sum, and roll it over into an IRA. There is no limit on how much money you can put into an IRA, if it's coming from a qualified pension plan. Once the assets are safely lodged in the IRA, future earnings—dividends, interest, and/or capital gains—are tax-deferred until you take them out. Normal rules on IRA withdrawals apply (see Chapters 11 and 31). So in essence, if you choose this option, you are basically substituting your own IRA for the company pension plan.

If You Can—Should You Leave It There?

When you leave a job where you have accumulated retirement benefits, you are faced with the question of whether the investment managers or investment opportunities at your old job are superior to those available to you through an IRA rollover.

If you desire to keep your money in the qualified plan at your old employer, you should be aware of some basic concerns:

- If your benefits are less than a certain amount—generally $3,500—your employer may be able to force you to take your money out of the plan.
- The investment management may change, thus you should check periodically that your investments are still meeting your objectives.

The rules under which you are allowed to leave your money in a qualified plan are complex. You should consult your accountant for guidance.

Take the money and have fun (or invest it otherwise).
You can do with the money as you wish, once you remember to put enough aside to pay the taxes—and penalty, if any—that are due. As we've said, your contributions were all previously growing tax-deferred. And if indeed the rollover is coming from money that you had in a salary-deferral plan such as a 401(k), your basic contributions weren't taxed either.

It is now time, alas, to pay the piper.

But that does not mean you should pay through the nose. If you decide to take the money now, and not roll it over tax-deferred, the best thing to do may be to use a forward averaging method (again, *if* you're eligible) to lessen the pain.

If You Decide to Roll It Over

Okay, you've opted to roll the money over and transfer it to an IRA.

Since an IRA is an IRA is an IRA, whatever IRA you put it in is perfectly fine, right?

*Wrong. Although all IRAs look alike, they're not identical. While the law allows you to take your qualified lump sum distribution and put it into an existing IRA—the one that you have been steadily funding to the tune of $2,000 a year—*our advice is not to do it. Open a second IRA, just for your rollover. Just in case . . .

In the financial planning biz, this second IRA, or rollover IRA, is called a "conduit IRA." This is an IRA whose holdings are restricted to money or securities that have come only from a qualified retirement plan. By setting up a second IRA, you can literally have your new retirement account serve as a conduit from one qualified retirement plan to another. It could work as a conduit a year from now, or 20 years from now.

Why would you want to do this? Here's an example. Let's say

that years from now you end up working for an employer who offers a qualified retirement plan, and his plan will accept rollover contributions. You like the new plan. If you had earlier set up a separate IRA account for your rollover money, you can move your old pension funds, plus all your tax deferred earnings and gains from this rollover account, into your new employer's retirement account, and take advantage of whatever investment options he has to offer. As a bonus, you may still eventually be able to take advantage of forward averaging if you choose later to take a lump sum distribution.

However, if your rollover IRA is tainted by even as little as $1 from a regular IRA—that is, the rollover is mixed with funds from a contributing account, such as your "traditional" IRA, the one you have been putting $2,000 a year in all this time—you won't be able to ever move that money to a qualified plan. Once the tainting is on the books, it's irreversible.

Let's give one more example, to make sure this is clear. Say you change jobs at age 40, and you leave your old employer having accumulated some $100,000 in retirement money. Following our advice, you'd put that $100,000 into a new, or conduit, IRA. Then after depositing the check, you trundle off to start work at another company, one that does *not* have a qualified retirement plan.

Ten years later, on your 50th birthday, you decide it's finally time to go into business for yourself. As a self-employed individual, you decide to set up a new qualified retirement plan for yourself. We'll also assume that over the decade you haven't tainted the IRA rollover account with any new IRA contributions.

You can now take that old IRA rollover (including the tax-deferred earnings and gains that had accumulated over the last 10 years) and plop all of it into a new plan which you have established. If you had been earning 10% a year on the $100,000 roll-over—which between dividends, interest, and gains would not be out of the question—you would be starting your new plan with $259,374. A pretty good start, we'd say.

When You're Absolutely, Positively Retiring

Now that we've given you solid reasons for separating a regular IRA from a rollover IRA, let's give you the one situation we can think of where you may not have to do it.

Let's say you are 65, and absolutely, positively are retiring. You have $30,000 in your regular IRA, and you are going to be receiving $300,000 in a lump sum distribution from a pension account. You're not interested in averaging—you want to take out your money on a slow-release program from the IRA.

Since you're never going to work again, and thus won't have a new qualified plan anytime in the future, there's no need to preserve the theoretical benefits attributed to a qualified plan. You won't have to manage one large account, and one small one. You can combine your two IRAs, for the sake of asset management efficiency. Your custodial fees, if any, will be less.

How Will You Get the Money?

That's not as silly a question as it may sound.

Most of the time you will receive the lump sum distribution by check—assuming you've not had the money or property sent directly to a new trustee. The distribution should always be accompanied by a detailed statement that breaks out the distribution into voluntary and employer contributions. (You'll need this for tax purposes—even if you move the distribution trustee to trustee. If you're going to continue tax deferral the IRS may well want proof that the sum came from a qualified plan.)

However, there are some employer plans that will allow you to transfer assets other than cash—stocks and bonds, for example, that are in your account—to your IRA rollover account. You'll have to check ahead of time to see if the custodian of your rollover account restricts you to cash.

Once the money is in your rollover, you can, of course, take it out, but the same rules governing IRA withdrawals still apply. If you withdraw the money before you're 59½, you may have to pay the taxes due, plus, you may be hit with a 10% tax penalty for making an early withdrawal. After age 59½, and up to age 70½, you can take out as much—or as little—money as you wish without a penalty. (You do, of course, still have to pay the taxes due on the amounts you withdraw. And, as we said before, once you reach age 70½, you do have to start withdrawing the money and you'll be taxed accordingly.)

Don't Be Surprised—First Thing in the Morning

"What do you mean my new custodian won't accept anything other than cash?" we hear you cry. Well, custodians of some rollover accounts can only accept cash. The bylaws of their institutions limit them to only cash, or cash equivalents. In an operational sense, they aren't built to hold stocks or bonds. If you transfer 1,000 shares of stock to them, they are likely to say, "Thanks, I'll sell the stock first thing in the morning."

That's why you have to check in advance. Don't be surprised.

What Do You Invest the Money In?

Given the complexity of all the rules governing rollovers, the answer to this is relatively simple. Once you roll the money over, your first thoughts will probably be to put it into exactly the same sorts of investments that you have previously determined will lead to a comfortable retirement. (See Chapter 15, "Allocating Your Assets.")

If you were fortunate, and your previous plan allowed you to self-direct the investments, you'll probably be able to continue the same asset allocation and replicate the previous choices. But your investment world now expands dramatically. Suppose the plan had been a defined contribution plan, such as a 401(k), which gave you a handful of alternatives—from a money market fund to a bond fund to an equity fund. Now—through an IRA rollover—you could continue that same allocation, if you wish, but the number of choices in each category will probably increase tenfold, or maybe even a hundredfold.

Instead of having two bond fund alternatives, say, you now could pick and choose from literally hundreds of funds, and thousands of individual bonds. On the equity side, the explosion is even greater. Where before you might have been restricted to mutual funds, now—if you wish—you can buy individual stocks and bonds. (In many self-directed IRAs, there are few restrictions on investments—see Chapter 11.)

If the lump sum money is coming from a defined benefit plan, you probably had no previous control over the investments, and so the myriad potential investment choices in an IRA rollover will seem even more dazzling.

Receiving a lump sum distribution can be a nice, but relatively minor, financial event.

Or, as pension plans mature, and 401(k) and other retirement plans build, the lump sum—in size—can be enormously important. So big or small, it's time for a reappraisal. If you had been running the investments in the account post-rollover it might have been years since you shifted allocations.

We don't quarrel with past investment choices, but now—particularly if it's a sea change for you—may be the time for a new strategy.

Your age, whether you're still working or retired, how your other assets are faring, what you want to do with your retirement assets—all these elements should be factored into your grand retirement planning strategy.

We end this chapter with an admonishment. Remember where this lump sum is coming from. It's coming from your retirement plan.

You are going to live longer than you think. You may very well outlive your retirement assets.

So think again (and again) before you're tempted to take that lump sum and spend it otherwise (no matter how laudable the purpose).

CHAPTER 26

Social Security—Part II: How It Works for You

Earlier—way back in Chapter 6—we talked about both the past and the future of Social Security. We know of no serious auditor of Social Security—in economic or social policy think tanks, in academia, in the Senate or House, and even in the Social Security Administration itself—who doesn't believe that as we move well into the twenty-first century, Social Security, as it's currently structured, could run out of money. As the nation turns to fewer young and more old, this may happen as early as 2040.

The "real conflict," as A. Haeworth Robertson, the former chief actuary of the Social Security Administration, puts it, " . . . will not be between today's elderly and the baby boomer. Rather, it will be between the baby boomers and their children."

But in this chapter we'll give you the good news. For just about everyone—from a boomer to a retiree of next year—can rest a bit easier.

We obviously won't make light of the worries that future generations may face, but this guide is primarily concerned with *your* concerns. So unless your 5-year-old is truly precocious, and between savage bouts with Nintendo is reading this book—a preposterous idea, we know—we're assuming all *present readers* are old enough to be assured that they will indeed get *some* Social Security benefits.

Your next question: How much? Our answer: It all depends.

The balance of this chapter is on the nuts and bolts of Social Security. We'll explain:

- How to build Social Security "credits."

- How to estimate your future Social Security benefits.

- Taking your Social Security benefits early.

- Taking your Social Security benefits later.

- How to keep working—and still receive Social Security benefits.

- What Social Security family benefits are.

- How to apply for benefits.

Let's start with Social Security "credits." The trick is to *make sure* you earn enough.

Except for people who are getting benefits as a dependent, or as a survivor of someone who paid into the Social Security system, the basic premise behind Social Security is simple: you must work and pay taxes into Social Security in order to get something out of it.

Checking on Your Credits

As you work, and pay your Social Security taxes, you earn Social Security "credits." You receive one credit for each $570 of earnings (in 1992) you have per quarter, with four being the maximum number of credits you can earn each year. (The amount of money you need to earn a credit—surprise, surprise—goes up each year.)

If you were born in 1929, or later, you need 40 credits (10 years of work) to qualify for retirement benefits.

We know. We know. You want to know about people born *before* 1929. They need fewer credits. If you were born in 1928, you need 39 credits; 38 if born in 1927; 37 if born in 1926; and so on back through time.

If you stop working before you have enough credits to qualify for benefits—that is, got married young and/or dropped out of the work force for a while—the credits you earned while you worked remain on your Social Security record. If you later return to work, you start picking up credits again exactly at the point where you left off.

No retirement benefits are paid until you have the requisite number of credits.

If you don't qualify for Social Security, because you lack the necessary credits, or you receive only a little in Social Security benefits, you may still be eligible for Supplemental Security Income. To learn more, call the Social Security Administration at 1-800-772-1213 and ask for the booklets called *SSI: Supplemental Security Income* and *When You Get SSI: What You Need to Know.*

During your working lifetime, you'll probably earn many more credits than you need to be eligible for Social Security. Those additional credits *do not* increase your eventual Social Security benefits. All is not lost, however, since your benefits are based, in part, on the amount of money you earned during your working lifetime. So, the longer you work, the larger the benefit—up to a point.

The exact formula is enough to send a rocket scientist back to school, but it works something like this. The Social Security Administration adds up all the years you have worked, and then takes the 35 years in which you earned the most money to determine your benefits. (If you worked fewer than 35 years, they count every year.) Next, all your contributions to Social Security are totaled, and then divided by 35 to determine your average adjusted earnings for Social Security benefits.

Note the wording: *Your contributions to Social Security.*

You may have made $5 million dollars in 1992, but you stopped paying Social Security taxes after you earned $55,500. (This maximum taxable amount is indexed, and therefore it will increase from year to year.) So as far as Social Security is concerned you've made

---

How to Qualify—Back to Work

Making sure you have enough credits is a key reason we suggest you periodically check with the Social Security Administration to make sure you have the necessary credits. If you find out today that you don't, you still can do something about it.

For example, say you worked for only a couple of years out of school, got married, and decided to stay home and raise your family. Good for you. But now you're in your 50s or 60s, thinking about retirement, and find you are short five credits. Our advice: get those credits! Get a part-time or full-time job; or if you're self-employed, be conscientious in filing self-employment taxes—whatever works. Make sure you qualify for Social Security, so that you can get back some of the money that you paid in all those years ago.

---

just $55,500 in 1992, for the purpose of helping to determine your average adjusted earnings for Social Security calculations.

Once the Social Security Administration has figured out how much you have made in an average year, it takes that average adjusted earnings and multiplies it by an adjustment factor.

The adjustment factor is designed to even things out. In theory, you will receive half your base-year income annually in Social Security benefits, if you don't qualify for the maximum.

However, the more money you make, the less proportionally you will receive relative to your earnings. So, someone with a low income may receive 60% of his base year, while someone with a higher income may just receive 40%, or even less. In any event, no matter how much you earned, you won't receive more than the maximum set by law, which in 1992 was $1,088 month for someone retiring at age 65.

Estimating Your Future Benefits

In the abstract, this gets a bit confusing, but for your particular case, it needn't be. The Social Security Administration will give you a free, *personalized* estimate of how much money you will be entitled to upon retirement. All you have to do is call the Social Security Administration (at 1-800-772-1213) and request an Earnings and Benefit Estimate Statement. Fill out the simple form they send you, and you'll receive by return mail your complete earnings history, along with estimates of your benefits at retirement.

Since the government has been keeping a record of your earnings, you won't be asked to list how much you have made in the past.

In fact, the government will list it for you, on the printout you receive. Take a long look at those numbers to make sure they are right. (The form contains information on how to correct the history if it's wrong.)

Because the history will determine exactly how much you will receive in Social Security benefits, we suggest that you request the Earnings and Benefit Estimate every three years—just to make sure they've got everything right. You've paid payroll taxes your entire working life; you don't want to be shortchanged.

When you request the benefits estimate, you'll be asked to project how much you think you will make each year between now and retirement. Be conservative. If you expect a sizable increase, by all means put it down. But if you're nearing retirement and are now at—or near—your peak earning years, don't let wishful thinking influence your prediction.

The government will take your figure and then assume both an inflation rate, and an average wage growth rate for the economy, adjust your payout by the things we talked about before, and give you an estimate of how much you will have coming to you once you retire. (Along with your projected Social Security benefits, they'll also send you estimates of disability or survivors' benefits that might be payable.)

But the most important part of the package, of course, is how much you are entitled to, once you reach full retirement age.

What's the "Full" Retirement Age?

"Full" retirement age?

It's a new phrase that has entered the retirement planning lexicon which governs how much you'll receive in retirement benefits and when.

When Social Security was created back in 1935, the average life expectancy was 61, and that may explain why 65 was chosen as the age at which people could start drawing "full" or normal Social Security benefits—that is, 100% of what they were entitled to. The odds back then said that not a whole of people were going to be receiving retirement checks.

Why Is 65 the Magic Number?

There is no definitive explanation of why age 65 was chosen back in 1935 by Congress, but we can speculate on why 65 became the magic number.

Here are a couple of explanations that have been offered through the years.

Several countries had already set precedent by adopting 65 as *the* age. It's believed that Congress might have borrowed the concept specifically from Germany's Chancellor Otto von Bismarck who declared back in the nineteenth century that 65 was to him the perfect mandatory retirement age. (Some historians believe that since some of his aging generals were becoming obstreperous he instituted the policy so he could gracefully get rid of them.)

Another reason for picking age 65 in this country was that it would serve as a prompting device. It would nudge 65-year-olds out the door.

Although Social Security was clearly designed to have long-term benefits, it may also have been the hope of President Roosevelt, and our legislators, that there would be short-term gains to the hordes of jobless as well.

True, there were not a whole lot of 65-year-olds alive and working during the Depression, but there were some, and if they left work, their place could be taken by younger people, many of whom were on bread lines.

Since the mid-1930s life expectancies for men and women—as we have pointed out—have steadily increased and 65 just isn't as old as it used to be. (Let us mention that the spiritual father of rock and roll—Charles Edward Anderson Berry, known to most of us as Chuck—is now on the far side of 65. He was born in 1926. You may be older than you thought!) As a result of Americans' longer life expectancy, and the government's need to keep the program on a solid base, the "full" retirement age is increasing gradually.

This increase, which will start in the year 2000, will occur in small steps and will continue until full retirement age becomes 67 for *everyone born after 1959.*

The increase in full retirement age affects *everyone* born in 1938 or later.

The following table tells the story:

Age to Receive Full Social Security Benefits:

Year of Birth	Full Retirement Age
1937 or earlier	65
1938	65 and 2 months
1939	65 and 4 months
1940	65 and 6 months
1941	65 and 8 months
1942	65 and 10 months
1943-1954	66
1955	66 and 2 months
1956	66 and 4 months
1957	66 and 6 months
1958	66 and 8 months
1959	66 and 10 months
1960 and later	67

Retiring Early

So, when can you start getting the money?

No matter when you were born, the answer is age 62 at the earliest, provided you have earned the 40 necessary Social Security credits. However, the longer you wait—up to age 70, anyway—the more money you get. (Deferred benefits, which we will talk about in a minute, reach their maximum at age 70. Even if you delay in applying for Social Security until you're 80, you won't get any more money than you would if you applied at age 70.)

The idea of paying less money to people who retire early, and more to those who choose to wait, makes sense. It is governed by life expectancy tables.

If you start taking your benefits early, you'll get smaller checks, but more of them. If you retire later, you'll get fewer checks but each one will be bigger.

A simple example will show how this works. Let's say you were born in 1937. According to the table on page 416 your full retirement age is 65. If you start receiving your Social Security benefits at 62, you will receive 20% less each month than you would have if you had waited until 65 to start receiving your Social Security benefits. If you took the money at 63, there would be a 13.33% reduction. If you wait one more year, to 64, you'd suffer a 6.66% cut.

If your full retirement age is older than 65—that is, you were born after 1937—you will still be able to start taking your retirement benefits at age 62, but the reduction in your monthly check is going to be greater than it would be for someone whose full retirement age is 65. Again, this makes sense. *They* are starting their retirement benefits three years before their full retirement age. *You* are starting even sooner, up to five years sooner for someone born in 1960 or later, so the reduction in benefits should be bigger. How much will your benefits be reduced? Well, if you were born in 1960 or later, and opt to retire at 62, your benefits will shrink by 30%.

Given all this, when should you start receiving your Social Security benefits? At 62? At full retirement age? Not before you turn 70?

Our answer—it depends.
It depends on:

- both spouses' life expectancies. (An expectancy, of course, is not just based on the cold actuarial assumptions, but also can be a calculated guess on your part, taking into consideration your family history, your present health, and life-style);

- whether or not you or your spouse may want to work part-time (if so, keep in mind the fact that you may face Social Security benefit reduction);

- your overall financial situation.

As we have said from the beginning, Social Security should not be your sole source of your retirement funds. We expect your pension and other investments to make up the bulk of your retirement income, and the longer you work, the greater those benefits could be. Not only will you probably be making more money in your later working years, but all that additional time on the job may also be increasing the value of your company pension, and it will certainly be adding to the value of your own supplemental retirement plans: 401(k), IRAs, and the like.

Also, remember how Social Security benefits are calculated. They are based, in part, on how much money you earned while you worked. The more you earn, up to a point, the greater the benefits you'll receive when you retire.

And finally, you simply may not want to retire. If you don't want to, don't. As we'll explain in a moment, the Social Security structure will reward your work ethic.

But let's say neither your pension nor your base earnings year will be affected if you retire tomorrow. (You, like most of the people who are serving as our examples, have already qualified to receive the maximum Social Security benefits you legally can.)

If this is the case, it makes sense to take the money at age 62, instead of waiting.

If you wait until full retirement age to start collecting benefits, you will receive more money in the long run—but the long run is exactly that: a marathon.

If you wait until your full retirement age, and for the sake of argument let's say it is 65, it will take you until age 76—11 years— just to catch up with someone who started receiving benefits at age 62.

If You Become Disabled

Sometimes poor health, and not financial planning, forces people to retire early. If you are unable to continue working because of medical reasons, consider applying for Social Security disability benefits.

The amount of disability benefits you receive is equal to what you would have received if you retired at full retirement age. For more information, call the Social Security Administration at 1-800-772-1213 and ask for the booklet called *Disability.*

It is relatively easy to understand why that is so. Someone who starts receiving benefits at age 62 has a three-year head start on someone who waits until age 65. While it is true they are only receiving 80% of the benefits they would have received if they waited to age 65, those three years of additional checks add up fairly quickly. So quickly, in fact, that it will take our 65-year-old a full 11 years to catch up. After that, of course, the 65-year-old would pull steadily ahead.

But given how long it takes to catch up, taking the money now seems like the best course of action.

But what about inflation? Sure, if you stop working before your full retirement age, you get the money earlier, but aren't you vulnerable to inflation? After all, you are getting less money that you would if you waited. Isn't inflation going to make those funds shrink further?

No. The law governing Social Security calls for automatic cost-of-living increases. Once you start receiving benefits, the amount will go up automatically if the cost of living rises. Yet another reason to take the money now.

By the way, if you do decide to take Social Security early, you'll be in good company. In 1956, only 2% of Social Security beneficiaries took their benefits before age 65. Today, that number is 68%.

Retiring Later

Suppose you don't want to retire. There is, of course, a world of difference between Social Security and private employer pension plans. Employer plans vary as to whether you will receive additional benefits if you stay beyond your company's normal retirement age. If your company plan is a defined contribution plan, your own benefits should continue to increase year by year. But if your employer plan is a defined benefit plan, you may not receive any *extra* benefits for your years of service after normal retirement age. (See Chapter 7 for more commentary on employer plans; the best way to find out is simply to ask your employer.)

You've decided you really do like your job. You have no great desire to quit the "rat race." You've always said you plan to work until they carry you out, and you mean what you say. Do you lose out by not taking your Social Security retirement benefits early or at full retirement age?

The answer: No. In fact, you benefit in two ways.

First, you'll be adding another year—or two or three or four—of high earnings to your Social Security record, the record that determines how much your retirement benefits will be.

But even if you have already qualified to receive the maximum benefits, your check will be increased for each year you delay receiving Social Security.

Depending on when you were born, *each year* you delay receiving Social Security can mean a 1% to 8% increase in your *annual* benefits, as the chart on page 422 shows.

A quick example will underscore the information in the chart. Let's say you were born in 1954. Your full retirement age, as the table on page 416 makes clear, is 66. But suppose you don't retire until you're 69. Your yearly benefits would be 24% more than they would have been if you retired at 66. Why? Because you receive an 8% yearly increase for each year you wait. You postponed retirement for three years beyond your full retirement age, so your retirement benefits are increased 3 (years) times 8%, or 24%.

Now, contrast that to someone who turned 60 in 1993, and has also decided to retire at age 69.

Her yearly benefits would increase 22%. Why? Well, because she

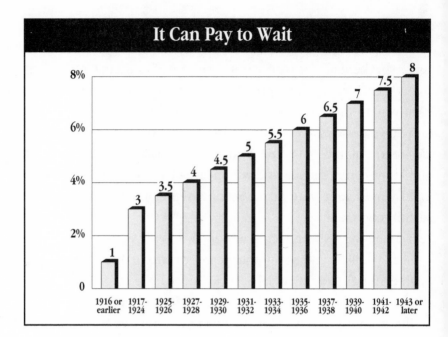

It Can Pay to Wait

Chart showing percentage by birth year:
- 1916 or earlier: 1
- 1917-1924: 3
- 1925-1926: 3.5
- 1927-1928: 4
- 1929-1930: 4.5
- 1931-1932: 5
- 1933-1934: 5.5
- 1935-1936: 6
- 1937-1938: 6.5
- 1939-1940: 7
- 1941-1942: 7.5
- 1943 or later: 8

was born in 1933, her full retirement age is 65, unlike our boomer's 66. That means she is postponing her traditional retirement age by four years. So, we will multiply four times the yearly increase she will receive because she has postponed retirement. As the chart above tells us, people born in 1933 receive an additional 5.5% for each year they wait. So, our 60-year-old would receive an additional 5.5% × 4, or an extra 22%, a year, by waiting.

It seems inequitable at first blush. But remember, given the steady increase in Social Security taxes over the years, the boomer has paid a lot more money into the system than his elders have.

There are two things to remember if you decide to delay retirement. First, be sure to sign up for Medicare at age 65.

Second, remember there is no benefit in postponing receipt of your Social Security benefits past the age of 70. Once you reach age 70, the annual yearly increase you receive for delaying receipt of your benefits stops. You've already maxed out, so you might as well take the money.

If You Work and Get Social Security at the Same Time . . .

Things get a little bit complicated, but not overly so. Here's what you need to remember to keep things straight: You can still receive retirement benefits if you continue to work, provided your earnings don't exceed certain age and income limits.

Those limits?

People aged 62, 63, or 64 could earn up to $7,440 in 1992, without reducing their Social Security benefits. For people 65 to 69 the limit was $10,200. (In addition to an annual increase in maximum earnings based on the average earnings of all employees in the country, Congress is considering raising the limit significantly.)

A Primer on Federal Health Programs

Here's a basic primer on Medicare. Medicare, the nation's federal health insurance program for those 65 and older, has two parts: hospital insurance and supplementary medical insurance. Most people have both parts.

Hospital insurance, called Part A, covers inpatient hospital care, and certain follow-up care. You've probably already paid for Part A; it's funded through a portion of your Social Security taxes.

The supplementary medical insurance, called Part B, pays for physicians' services, and some other services not covered by hospital insurance. Medical insurance is optional, and a premium is charged. In 1992 the premium was $31.81 a month. Be aware that this premium increases annually because of the inflation index. For much more on these federal health insurance programs, see Chapter 30.

People who are 70 or older do not have an earnings limit. They can earn as much as they can without reducing their Social Security benefits.

People under 70 can still earn up to the limit, without reducing their benefits. If they earn more than the limit, some or all of their benefits will be cut to offset what they earn.

Before we explain in detail how that reduction works, let us underscore an important point. Your Social Security benefits are only reduced if you *earn* too much money *through working.* The amount of money you receive from your investments, or from your pension, does not affect the Social Security benefits you receive. Well, there is one exception we should address. If you receive a pension from work which was not covered by Social Security—for example, you worked for the federal civil service, or in certain state or local government jobs—your Social Security benefits may be lowered, or offset, by the pension you receive.

However, if any of these exceptions do affect you, or someone you know, call the Social Security Administration and ask for the pamphlets *Government Pension Offset* and *A Pension from Work Not Covered by Social Security.* A reminder: Any benefits you receive might be taxed—we'll get more into this in a few paragraphs.

If you do work, here's how your age will govern your benefits (which means you will receive a smaller check from Social Security):

If you are under 65, then $1 in benefits will be withheld for each $2 you earn above the limit.

If you are 65 through 69, $1 in benefits will be withheld for each $3 you earn above the limit.

Let's take two examples to show how this plays itself out in practice.

Suppose you decide to retire at age 65, your full retirement age. That would give you about $800 a month in Social Security benefits, or $9,600 a year.

However, after about 73 seconds—give or take 60 seconds—of retirement, you start to go stir-crazy, and you soon pick up a part-time job that produces $20,000 a year in income.

We know that's more than you are allowed to earn, without reducing benefits. The only question is how much will the benefits be cut? To figure that out, we take the $20,000 in earnings and subtract the maximum you are allowed to earn without affecting benefits, $10,200 (in 1992).

That leaves a difference of $9,800. We divide the $9,800 by three—since for people aged 65 to 69 $1 in benefits will be deducted for each $3 that are earned above the limit—and get $3,267.

What this means is that you will receive annually *all but* $3,267 of your Social Security benefits.

In other words, you will receive $6,333 in Social Security (the $9,600 you would have been entitled to, less the $3,267 you are penalized by working.)

This would make your total income—from Social Security and your part-time job, anyway—$26,333.

Would you have been better off working less? It's a judgment call.

Let's say you had limited your part-time income to exactly $10,200. (A lot of people receiving Social Security benefits work only up to the point where their part-time job will affect benefits.)

In that case, you would receive your full $9,600 of Social Security benefits, in addition to your $10,200 in earnings. Total income (from Social Security, plus job): $19,800. True, that's only about three-quarters of what you would have received if you had kept on working until you had earned $20,000, but presumably you would have had only to work half as hard to generate $10,200 in income, as opposed to $20,000.

Let's take one more variation to make sure this is clear.

To keep things relatively simple, we'll keep everything the same, except your retirement age. In this example, we'll have you retiring at age 62.

Here, the calculation would look like this:

Earnings	$20,000	
Minus limit	7,400	(the limit is lower because he retired earlier)
Difference	$12,600	

We then take the difference and divide *by two,* since $1 in benefits is deducted for each $2 in income that someone under full retirement age earns. That means your benefits would be reduced by $6,300.

But remember, you retired at 62, and not at your full retirement age of 65, so you will only receive $7,680 in benefits (80% of the $9,600 a year you would have received) to begin with.

So when we subtract the $6,300 "penalty" from your already reduced Social Security benefits, we find that you will receive just $1,380 in Social Security annually, or $115 a month.

This second example was designed to underscore what should be an obvious point: if you're going to be making a few bucks after you are officially retired (that is, after you've started receiving Social

Security) you are probably better off not taking Social Security to begin with. It's better to wait a year or two until you really have stopped working so hard. (It really isn't a hardship. Remember, for every year past age 62 that you delay receiving Social Security benefits, up until age 70, the benefits increase.)

If there were ever any doubts that working—to any appreciable degree—and collecting Social Security don't mix, the IRS has abolished them once and for all. If your adjusted gross income is greater than a relatively small amount, you'll probably have to pay taxes on a portion of your Social Security benefits, whether or not you work.

It's sad but true. Here are the details.

If you filed a federal tax return as an "individual" you will have to pay taxes on your Social Security benefits if your "combined income" exceeds $25,000.

What is "combined income?" The IRS defines it as your adjusted gross income, as reported on your federal tax form, *plus* nontaxable interest you've received, *plus* one-half of your Social Security benefits.

If you file a joint federal tax return, you will pay taxes on your Social Security benefits if your combined income—that is, your adjusted gross income, *plus* nontaxable interest, *plus* one-half of your Social Security benefits—is greater than $32,000.

Exact details are spelled out in IRS publication 554, *Tax Benefits for Older Americans,* and publication 915, *Tax Information on Social Security.* But here's one thing you know for sure, before you pick up either booklet: if you are planning to work after you are "retired," taking your Social Security benefits is not a good idea, if you expect to make any *significant* money at your "post-retirement" job before you turn 70.

Family Benefits

Just because you are receiving Social Security benefits doesn't mean no one else in your family can.

Obviously, if your spouse worked, he (and for this example we'll assume the nonworking spouse is male) is entitled to receive the full benefits he qualified for while working.

But even if your spouse did not work—or did not work enough to qualify for Social Security—he can still receive benefits, as can your children, under certain conditions.

Here's how:

The maximum benefit for a spouse who does not qualify for his own retirement benefits is one-half of the retired worker's full benefits.

Can your nonworking spouse opt to start receiving retirement benefits before his or her full retirement age? Yes. However, just like a retired worker who takes retirement benefits early, the benefits for him will also decrease by a fixed amount for each year the benefits are taken early. For example, a nonworking spouse who decides to take benefits at age 62, when his full retirement age is 65, would receive only 37.5% of the retired worker's full benefits.

What about a divorced spouse? Can he still get benefits, even if he never worked? Yes, under the following conditions:

1. The marriage lasted at least 10 years.

2. The divorced spouse is at least 62 and unmarried.

3. The worker is at least 62.

If they have been divorced for at least two years, the husband, in this case, would be entitled to receive benefits, even if his former wife were still working. He would receive the same amount of benefits as he would have had the marriage lasted. *And note:* His benefits have no effect on the amount of benefits that either the worker, or the worker's current husband, if there is one, can receive. (By the way, in many states the divorced spouse may be entitled to a portion of their ex's retirement plans.)

Children, too, can qualify for Social Security, and indeed some 3.5 million of them are currently receiving benefits.

There are three ways a child, defined as someone under age 18, can get benefits from Social Security or SSI.

1. **They are dependents of a father or mother who is collecting retirement or disability benefits from Social Security.** They also can receive survivor benefits should that parent die.

2. **They have been disabled since childhood.** Survivor benefits normally stop when a child becomes 18 (19 in the case of a full-time student). However, those benefits can continue to be paid into adulthood, if the child is disabled. To qualify, the child must be the son or daughter of someone who is getting Social Security retirement, or disability benefits, or of someone who has died, *and* the child must have a disability that began prior to age 22.

3. **They also may qualify to receive SSI benefits.** (For further information on the guidelines covering children, call the Social Security Administration [1-800-772-1213], and ask for the following three booklets: *Survivors; When*

*You Get Social Security Retirement or Survivors Benefits
. . . What You Need to Know;* and *Social Security and SSI
Benefits for Children with Disabilities.)*

How Do You Sign Up?

You can apply for benefits by going to your local Social Security
office, of course, but you can also sign up by telephone. And you
don't have to wait until your birthday. You can apply up to three
months before the date you want your benefits to start.

What will you need to apply?

- Social Security number.

- Birth certificate.

- W-2 forms, or self-employment tax return for the year
  before.

- Spouse's birth certificate and Social Security number, if he or
  she is applying for benefits.

- Children's birth certificates and Social Security numbers, if
  applying for children's benefits.

- Central assets or checking or savings account information,
  if you want your benefits directly deposited.

Special note: The Social Security Administration requires that
you submit original documents, or copies certified by the issuing
office. You can mail the documents to Social Security, which will
make photocopies and return the originals. Or you can bring them
with you in person. When it comes time to submit documents, we

prefer the hand-carried approach (especially if you're a believer in Murphy's law).

A final thought about Social Security brings the chapter full circle to what we cautioned you about very early in this book.

There is no doubt that if no substantial changes are made in the twenty-first century there will be a problem funding Social Security, as the number of working people continues to decline. When Social Security was enacted, there were 49.1 people working, for every person who had retired. Today that number has shrunk to 3.4 people working to 1 retiree, and in the year 2020—when the oldest boomer is 74—it's estimated that it will be 2.4 workers to 1 retiree. Some demographers have predicted that the ratio will be 1:1 in the year 2042.

One of the perennial proposals offered as a way of helping solve the Social Security problem— which comes up as regularly on the

---

A Wonderful Idea: Direct Deposit

Allow us some more pure editorializing: We think direct deposit is a wonderful idea.

You don't have to worry about your check being lost, stolen, or misplaced.

You won't have to make a special trip to the bank, so you won't have to worry about bad weather, feeling poorly, or that you are going to be away from home on the day the check arrives.

You'll have your money available at the opening of the business on the day your payments are scheduled to arrive in the mail. (Social Security benefits are paid on the third day of the month. If the third falls on a weekend, or on a Monday holiday, benefits are paid the previous Friday.) If the check is deposited into an interest-bearing account, such as a money market fund, you begin earning interest on your money immediately.

---

floors of Congress as do the cherry blossoms each spring nearby in the tidal basin—is to require Social Security recipients to undergo a "fairness test," one that would be based on income.

Currently the rich and poor are equally entitled to draw benefits upon retirement. A future test might reduce benefits going to retirees with higher net worth. There is always an inherent problem in defining "fairness." This is a contentious issue. On the one hand, people who have put money into Social Security say they want their benefits, regardless of how large their net assets may be; the other side says, "if you don't need it, you shouldn't get it."

It's been suggested that the baby boomers upon their retirement will either have to accept less money from Social Security, or else their children will have to pay more in increased Social Security taxes. Neither is a particularly pleasant option.

Another possible solution, suggested by A. H. Robertson, the former chief actuary of the Social Security Administration, may be to raise the "normal" retirement age even higher—perhaps to age 70 or later—for those who will be retiring in the twenty-first century.

Since our experience tells us that baby boomers hope to retire earlier, and not later, extending the "normal" retirement age doesn't necessarily mean they will work longer. They may still choose to take early retirement. If so, their Social Security benefits will be proportionally less.

Will this major change in retirement age ever become law? We don't know. But as we pointed out on page 416, Congress already has raised the age once, from the traditional age 65 to age 67 for people born in 1960 and later.

What we do know is this: Individuals should not rely on Social Security to be their major source of retirement income. At some point the nation will have to come to grips with the funding gap that will be facing Social Security sometime in the next century.

If you are reading this book, the odds are you won't be totally beholden to Social Security in order to have a comfortable retirement. At the very least, you now know that there are Social Security benefits waiting for you. Just consider all the options, and then determine what's best for you.

CHAPTER 27

Insurance—Protecting Against the Unexpected

If you want a pleasant retirement, it isn't enough to accumulate assets. You also have to protect them. That's where insurance comes in. In simplest terms, insurance provides a way to protect against the unexpected. Life insurance protects your family, if you die prematurely; annuities (the subject of Chapter 18) protect you if you live longer than your money lasts; and disability insurance protects you if a long-term injury, or illness, prevents you from earning a living. Insurance may help cover long-term needs—personal, social service, and medical care—in your later life.

The amount and type of insurance you need depends on your personal situation. For instance, one of the primary reasons why people buy life insurance is to provide financial security for their dependents. But you can also use insurance to provide funds for specific future goals, such as paying for a child's education, providing additional funds for your own retirement, and protecting the estate you've spent a lifetime building—since insurance proceeds can be used to pay estate taxes. (Insurance proceeds are generally paid to heirs free of all income taxes, and without the costs and delay of probate. It's important to have sufficient cash ready, since estate taxes are generally due within nine months of death.)

In this chapter we will briefly go through the types of insurance available, pointing out the specific places where each policy can be helpful as you go about planning your retirement.

Let's begin with life insurance.

There are, in essence, two types of life insurance: term and whole life. Term is temporary insurance, while whole life is a permanent form of insurance that combines pure insurance protection with asset accumulation.

There are numerous variations on each type of insurance, but let's start with the basics.

Term Insurance

Term insurance provides pure insurance protection for a specific time period, be it a year, or five years, or even longer. It is pure death-protection insurance, with no cash value or investment component.

Term life insurance works just like fire or car insurance. Term insurance only pays a benefit if the insured event (that is, death) occurs. Your beneficiary collects only if you die within the term covered by your insurance.

Term insurance offers the most protection for the lowest cost when you are young—because you are, statistically speaking, unlikely to die anytime soon. However, under traditional term policies—called "annually renewable term"—the premiums will generally increase each time you renew the policy and could become prohibitively expensive as you grow older.

To get around the problem of having your premiums increase as your age does, a second type of term policy, "decreasing term," is available. Under this policy, the premium remains the same each time you renew your coverage, but the amount of coverage that same premium buys decreases over time, as you grow older. This kind of policy can be used where the risk of loss will decrease over time, such as in a mortgage protection insurance policy. Since your outstanding loan balance steadily shrinks over the life of the mortgage (after all, your monthly mortgage check goes to repay principal as well as interest), there is no problem in having a decreasing term policy that is earmarked for paying off your mortgage, should you die.

Because term insurance provides short-term, rather than lifelong coverage, it is best suited for temporary needs. Term is a good choice for younger couples (such as the Schmidts) with growing families who generally require a large amount of insurance at a minimum cost.

The Schmidts—they're the couple from St. Louis we profiled in Chapters 1 and 2—have two children to raise and put through school. They have mortgage payments to make. And they, as we have seen, haven't accumulated a lot of assets to fall back on, should anything happen to Carl, or Connie for that matter. Remember that other young couple—the Harrisons from Texas? They recently married; they're both in their mid-20s, are both working, and presently are childless. They won't need as much term insurance as the Schmidts. But if their family situation changes, they'll need to reexamine their family needs and add some term insurance.

Term insurance can create an instant estate, at the time when it is needed most, and the proceeds from the policy may be quickly available on an income-tax-free basis.

There are four other brief points to make about term insurance:

1. While most people who work have some life insurance coverage through their employer, it is usually not enough to support a young family for any extended period of time. And only in the rarest of cases would it be sufficient to pay off a mortgage and put the children through school.

2. Term insurance can be an excellent choice for women who are raising a family and not working outside the home. Traditionally, couples don't carry insurance on the spouse who isn't employed, yet the cost of replacing the child care, housekeeping and other services they provide—to be very blunt—could create a real financial hardship for their families should they die.

3. The flexibility that term insurance offers is something you might want to consider if you have a large expense—such as college tuition—coming up.

   Suppose you have decided you're going to send your newborn twins to some Ivy League schools. That cost will total somewhere near $400,000 by the time they're ready to go to college. Your children's Ivy League future could be in big trouble if either parent died prior to paying the tuition bills. One solution? You could take out enough term insurance to cover the cost of both educations. The insurance would only be in place until the children are through college. This is one way to make sure the bursar will get paid. Many people who buy term insurance for a specific temporary need—such as making sure that money is available to put their children through college, or to pay off the mortgage in case they die—also buy whole life insurance policies to provide for permanent insurance needs.

4. Some policies are convertible into permanent (that is, whole life) coverage. Yes, you will have to pay a higher premium, but under this conversion feature you may not have to take a new medical exam.

Whole Life Insurance

As the name implies, whole life (which is also known as ordinary life) policies cover you for your entire life, and not for a set term.

Another difference from term insurance is that your scheduled annual premiums never change and your amount of coverage will not decrease as you age.

A third difference is that the policy earns a value against which you may generally borrow funds, if you wish. Term policies, on the other hand, have no cash value.

In the early years, the premium charged is higher than the true cost of protection, and in the later years, it is substantially less than what term insurance would cost. This is why whole life policies

---

Benefit of Term Insurance—at Retirement

This type of policy is not normally used for this purpose. There is no cash value that can be used to supplement retirement income. However, death proceeds can be used to provide retirement income for the surviving spouse.

cost much more than comparable term insurance when you're younger, but they eventually become less expensive than term as you grow older. The additional money you pay in during the early years of whole life coverage (the amount of premium above the cost of pure protection) goes toward: *(a)* off-setting the true cost of the insurance coverage as you age and *(b)* creating the policy's cash value.

That is the key to understanding how whole life works. Whole life insurance is an integration of term insurance and a savings program.

While the policy is in force, your cash value builds up on a tax-deferred basis. If you need the money, you can generally borrow against the policy (but under certain policies the loan may be taxable). If you die, the outstanding loan balance is subtracted from the proceeds. Should you cancel the policy, you receive the "savings" component of your insurance premiums, less whatever "surrender charge" the policy may have.

Participating whole life policies pay dividends that you can use to reduce the premium due on the policy, or to buy additional insurance, or you can take the dividends in cash.

Those dividends are not the same as dividends you receive on a stock. Instead, they represent a return of the portion of insurance premiums you have paid that were not needed to cover the cost of the policy's death protection, guaranteed cash value, and administrative expenses. As a result, they are treated as a tax-free return of capital, until the total amount of dividends you receive, when added to all other amounts withdrawn from the contract, exceeds what you have paid in premiums.

Even after your children have grown, you might need a whole life policy to provide a nonworking spouse with the income required to maintain a comfortable life, should you die first. Similarly, if you pay for the care of an elderly parent, or an incapacitated relative, you might buy a whole life policy to make sure that care can be continued regardless of what happens to you.

Another important reason for buying whole life—especially when you are older—is to preserve the estate you have spent a lifetime building. Whole life insurance can provide the liquidity needed to pay "transfer costs" incurred at your death, thereby keeping your estate intact for your heirs. Those transfer costs can include: federal estate taxes, state inheritance taxes, funeral costs, medical expenses, probate and legal fees.

Variations on the Whole Life Theme

Survivorship whole life, aka joint and last survivor or "second to die policies." This is a whole life policy that insures two people, traditionally husband and wife. The death benefit is paid at the time of the second death, when it is generally needed to pay estate taxes.

Because of the timing of the death benefit payment, the cost of this policy is less than comparable single life plans. That's the good news. The flip side is that the surviving spouse does not get the proceeds since they pass on to the *couple's* heirs or estate.

Benefit of Whole Life Policies—at Retirement

The policy's cash value can be used to generate monthly income at retirement. The policy can be structured to provide substantial retirement income. You pay the premiums, earn tax-deferred income on the "savings component" of the policy, and the death benefit proceeds can help preserve the value of your estate.

Survivorship plans are available in both fixed-rate and variable life versions, and can be funded on either a single premium, or annual premium basis. (More details on what these things are in a few pages.)

Universal life, which combines insurance and tax-favored asset accumulation, has become one of the most popular insurance programs over the past several years, and it is easy to see why. The main reason is flexibility.

With a universal life policy you can vary the amount you pay in premiums. You can raise the amount, lower it, or even skip a payment. (Obviously, the road you choose affects the eventual payout.)

The rate of return that the cash portion earns is flexible as well. With universal life the rate paid is often based on some specified financial index. However, you will receive a guaranteed minimum return, regardless of what happens to market interest rates.

Universal life also provides much greater flexiblity in choosing the amount of death benefit protection so that you can better meet your changing financial needs. As a result, it is particularly attractive for individuals with a long-term orientation who are seeking to create an estate for their heirs.

If you need funds for a child's college education, your own retirement, or some other purpose, you can usually borrow against

---

Benefit of Second to Die Policies—at Retirement

The policy provides excellent cash accumulation because of the low mortality costs. The money is paid out only after the second death, when estate taxes are due. Also, it's possible to borrow against the cash value in these policies—just as you can with the traditional whole life policies.

your policy's cash value at favorable interest rates, without incurring any tax liability in most cases.

Universal life typically costs less than traditional whole life policies, but more than term insurance.

Scheduled premium variable life. This policy combines permanent insurance protection with a flexible investment plan that allows you to invest the cash value in a broad spectrum of investment choices.

As with traditional whole life policies, you may pay premiums as frequently as monthly, and the policy, again like typical whole life coverage, also provides a minimum guaranteed death benefit. Another difference here is that the death benefit may increase, should your investments do well. Of course, what that means is that the policy's cash value fluctuates with investment performance. You're in charge of the portfolio mix, and naturally the investment performance isn't guaranteed. You'll have a wide variety of investments to choose from. For instance, you could put the money in stock, bonds, and money market portfolios. You pick the alternative, or alternatives, that best suit your objectives. And you can generally shift your investments to meet changing economic conditions or your own personal needs.

You can invest your portfolio to fit that asset allocation planning that you have done for your other investments.

Variable life offers the potential to earn higher tax-advantaged returns than you could with either whole life or universal life policies. It may be a good choice, if you are interested in beginning a long-term asset accumulation program, but of course a variable portfolio by its nature *does* carry more risk.

Single premium whole life. As the name says, with this type of whole life policy, you pay a lump sum up front and receive permanent insurance protection. In addition, you have the potential for growth in the cash portion of the policy.

Different policies offer different accumulation features. The policy may pay a competitive fixed rate of return, with the first two, three, or five years being guaranteed. It's also possible to buy a variable life policy on a single-premium basis. This would give you a variable return through a wide choice of investment options that can include stocks and bonds, and other securities.

Most of the insurance plans we've discussed so far are primary vehicles to cover you and your spouse. Beyond mandatory insurance—covering your car and your home—don't ignore excess liability insurance (often known as an umbrella policy), just in case someone has an accident while visiting your castle.

Disability Insurance

Statistics show that a third of all people will be disabled for three months or longer between the ages of 30 and 65. That's why you should be thinking about disability insurance. Any accident, or illness, that keeps you out of work for an extended period of time can quickly eat up your retirement savings.

You may have some disability protection available through an employer plan, government workers compensation program, and Social Security (see Chapter 26—for Social Security benefits for the disabled), but these coverages can be limited in scope. Besides, the higher your income, the less adequate these benefits may be in maintaining your life-style. And so you may want to take out an individual long-term disability policy.

How large should that policy be? Large enough to maintain your current standard of living, minus the other income and benefits you would have coming in while you're disabled. There's one other thing to keep in mind about disability policies. Most insurers will not pay you 100% of your gross income. (They want you to have an incentive to go back to work.) Typical policies pay 60% of what you are earning when you become disabled. If the disability policy premiums have been paid by you, any benefits you receive will be tax-free. Even with the discounted payout, you might receive in tax-free payout just about as much as your former after-tax income.

Examine this component of the coverage carefully. Some policies say if you can do *some* kind of work, they will not pay benefits, or the benefits they will pay will be reduced. The better policies pay benefits if you can't perform *your own occupation.*

Long-Term Care Protection

As a rule, our crystal ball is pretty cloudy. But here is a prediction we make with a fair amount of certainty: Long-term care insurance is fast becoming one of the most popular insurance products available.

People *are* living longer, and it is likely that a portion of that extended life span will be spent in a nursing home, or under some form of medical care or supervision. Current estimates are that people who are 65 or older face a 40% chance of spending some time in a nursing home during their lives.

Long-term care is so important (and is so relatively new) that we want to separate it as a subject from these more well known insurance categories in this review. So for our discussion of long-term care, see Chapter 30.

What's the Risk?

Some insurance companies—in the late eighties and early nineties—faced severe problems because of the quality of their real estate holdings and the quality of their junk bond holdings.

How can you analyze an insurance company? Here are some facts to consider:

If the company's invested assets are diversified, that tends to limit the downside risk of poor performance in any one product line.

Total mortgage concentration should be weighed. What's the ratio of mortgages in default to total mortgages? What's the company exposure to the commercial market (which has tended to be much more troublesome than the residential field)?

Liquidity these days is more important than ever.

In short, any thorough evaluation of an insurance company should include a close scrutiny of the company's general financial stability. As we suggested earlier, check the various insurance rating services for their appraisals.

Insurance Needs—They Change

Elsewhere in this guide we ask you not to let cobwebs grow on your assets. We advise constant review of your investments—at the least on an annual basis, but for many of you who prefer to be more active in your overseeing duties, investment reviews will be a quarterly task.

Your insurance coverage, too, should be reviewed periodically. You certainly don't need to tackle it quarterly, but an annual inspection of your life insurance needs is a good idea.

It may make sense for you to decrease (or, as the case may be, increase) the amount of insurance you carry. Your personal profile—your spouse, your dependents no longer being dependent—may change. If so, your insurance needs may change. Another milestone: when you hit the big 50, or your children finally leave home, that may be the time for you to reduce some life coverage.

At age 50—when you're probably somewhere between 10 and 20 years away from retirement—that's also the time to dig into estate planning (our next two chapters). Before you drop any insurance, see how it might fit into estate planning. Once you've dropped a given policy—you may not *easily* be able to replace the coverage.

At these various reviews, you may want to decrease or even eliminate your contributory coverage if you no longer have dependents (because of death or divorce, for example; less traumatically, changes may be warranted because your children are grown up, thank you, are doing well, and to your great relief, you're no longer thinking of them as dependents).

But then—as we mentioned earlier—you may also want to increase your coverage if you've faced other major changes: if you have recently married, if you had a child, if you purchased a home, or if you now anticipate even larger education expenses—perhaps for graduate education—for your children.

Of all the milestones which call for insurance review the most important is when you retire. That's the time—if you had been slightly derelict in terms of insurance review in the immediately preceding years—when you *must* get down to business. Sit down—both you and your spouse—with your financial adviser, and put all your plans to the test.

How much insurance do you need? It depends on your age—and what you're trying to protect.

Insurance, in its many guises, protects you against the unexpected. Insurance can protect your assets. As you move through the stages of life, periodically review your insurance needs—decreasing, increasing, or adding different protections.

CHAPTER 28

Reducing Estate Taxes

The sole purpose of estate planning is to make sure your assets are handled after your death in a way you would have approved of had you lived. Solid estate planning means taxes are avoided.

If you just keep this point in mind, estate planning—a generally macabre and difficult subject—becomes a lot easier to deal with.

For example, people like Milton Quincy, our 75-year-old video packager, have worked an entire lifetime to accumulate assets that are now worth millions of dollars. In the process of accumulating that wealth, Milton tried to keep the amount of money he had to pay in taxes to an absolute minimum, and he also tried to keep people from prying into his financial affairs.

His estate planning—which revolves around minimizing federal estate taxes and avoiding probate—is designed to make sure that those two goals are fulfilled even after he dies.

Leave More for Your Heirs and Less for the IRS

Up until this point, our focus has been on helping you develop a diversified asset strategy. Saving more, saving systematically, saving smarter, saving tax-advantaged, and diversifying those savings is the best way we know to get rich—albeit slowly.

However, we have to admit we have been leaving out a lot—in some cases as much as 55%—of the picture. *All the saving you have done will be worth a lot less, if you don't do careful estate planning.*

With estate taxes as high as 60% (for estates valued between $10 million and $21 million), an estate you worked a lifetime to build can be wiped out after your death. Careful estate planning is a vital part of your overall retirement strategy because it can assure that your wealth is transferred to the people and charities you choose—in a way that best cares for their needs. Proper planning lets your beneficiaries—and not the IRS—keep as much as possible.

And the odds are we are talking about a lot of money. You *are* undoubtedly worth more than you think you are. And just about all those assets are going to go into your estate.

Now consider this. A $2 million estate, growing at just 5% a year, will double in approximately 14.5 years, and the estate tax liability will grow right along with it. In fact, it could grow even faster.

Consider a 65-year-old couple. Their life expectancy is about 20 years, that would make their current $2 million estate, assuming 5% growth, worth $5.3 million at their death.

However, based on current federal estate tax rates, their tax liability would increase from $780,000 to approximately $2.5 million over that time, as the following chart shows.

449

What this chart clearly explains is that while their estate is expected to grow by 165% over those 20 years, their estate tax will increase by 220%.

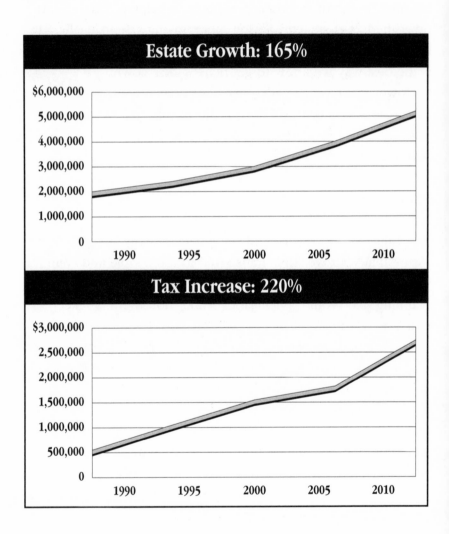

The reason for that is simple. Estate taxes are progressive. The larger the estate, the higher the tax rate, as the following chart shows.

Federal Income Tax Rates

Taxable Income up to		Amount of Tax (15%)		Rate on Excess
$35,800	$3,600	$5,370	$540	28%
86,500	10,900	19,566	2,584	31%

☐ Married Filing Jointly   ☐ Estates and Trusts

Federal Estate Tax Rates

Taxable Amount	Amount of Tax +	Rate on Excess
$500,000	$155,800	37%
750,000	248,300	39%
1,000,000	345,800	41%
1,250,000	448,800	43%
1,500,000	555,800	45%
2,000,000	780,800	49%
2,500,000	1,025,800	53%
3,000,000	1,290,800	55%
10,000,000	5,140,800	60%
21,040,000	11,764,800	55%

Most states impose some form of state inheritance or death tax. These tax rates vary from state to state. In addition to those local taxes there may be probate costs, legal fees, and other expenses associated with settling the estate. The entire tab could erode more than 70% of the estate's value.

That's the bad news. The (limited) good news is that there is a federal estate tax credit available (subject to certain limitations) for the death or inheritance taxes paid to the state.

What's in Your Estate?

Stocks, bonds, real estate, and other investments you own; cars, art, jewelry, and other personal property, all are part of your estate. Your estate may also include half the value of property you hold jointly.

Offsetting these assets are your outstanding debts, such as mortgages, income and property taxes, personal loans, and charitable contributions.

Also deducted are funeral expenses, attorney's fees, and other costs associated with settling your estate. These expenses alone could average 5% of the estate.

Your retirement benefits, such as pension, profit-sharing, and qualified stock purchase plans (and your IRA and Keogh plans), plus the proceeds from your life insurance policies, will probably go direct to named beneficiaries, and so will bypass the estate and probate costs, but taxes will still be due.

A key point in summary: If the spouse is the beneficiary, pension assets and life insurance may pass outside probate, but may *still* be part of your taxable estate.

Federal Estate Taxes 101

Federal estate taxes are determined by the fair market value of all the assets an individual owns at death and are due on estates in excess of $600,000.

Why are there no federal estate taxes due on the first $600,000 of your assets? There are, but the Federal Unified Estate and Gift Tax law gives each person a tax credit (called the Unified Credit) of $192,800.

Because of the Unified Credit, you can leave at your death, *or* give away during your life, up to $600,000, free of federal gift and estate taxes.

When you start talking about estate tax credits and gifts in the same breath, things can get confusing. Let's make sure this is clear.

Anyone can give away up to $10,000 a year to as many people as she likes, without suffering federal gift tax consequences, *and without affecting the Unified Credit* at the time of the giver's death.

However, if you exceed the $10,000 annual limit, your Unified Credit is reduced dollar for dollar.

There is a second way you can leave assets free of estate taxes. If you are married, you can leave any amount of property to your spouse (if a U.S. citizen) free of federal estate taxes, thanks to an unlimited marital deduction.

The deduction doesn't eliminate estate taxes. It just postpones them until the surviving spouse dies. At that time, both estates will be taxed.

If you think about it for a minute, you'll understand how the marital deduction can create a good news, bad news situation.

The good news, of course, is that all the assets from one spouse can go to the other *free of estate taxes.*

The bad news is that you can lose the Unified Credit in the process, since $600,000 of those assets would have been free of estate taxes anyway.

Providing Your Spouse with a Lifetime Income

To get around that problem, many couples create a "credit shelter trust," which usually goes by the less awkward name of an "A-B," or "bypass trust."

At the time of death of the first spouse, property equal to the Unified Credit remaining for that spouse is placed into a trust. (Remember, you can give away part of the Unified Credit during your lifetime, so you may not be entitled to shelter the full $600,000 upon your death.) The trust is usually set up to provide lifetime income to the surviving spouse, and gives him or her access to the principal if necessary. (This access, however, may be limited to a certain annual percentage of the assets.) More about trusts in the next chapter.

Checking Up on Beneficiaries

Most retirement plans—such as your employer pension plan, your IRA, Keogh, or SEP—require you to name a beneficiary. (Pension proceeds to a beneficiary are generally not probated but are included in your estate.) When you're reviewing terms of your will is also the appropriate time to review your various beneficiary designations—ranging from your retirement plans to your life insurance policies. *Remember:* Your will does not alter what your beneficiary forms state.

Here Are Some Estate Planning Basics

By taking certain relatively simple steps, you can significantly reduce your estate taxes and allow your estate to pass to your heirs with a minimum of cost and delay.

At the very least, you should prepare a will, and *review it every three years* to make sure it corresponds with changes in the tax law, and changes in your own personal circumstances. (You had another child; Aunt Sonya and you had a major falling out and there's no way on God's green earth that you are ever going to leave her the good china; you've decided to give more money to your church and less money to your alma mater.)

If you die *intestate,* that is, without a will, the laws of the state in which you live will determine who inherits your property, and the distribution may not be what you would have chosen. (The wide variance of state laws is yet another reason why—if you move from one state to another on retirement—it's imperative to review your will with a local attorney.)

For example, in many states your spouse will receive only one-third to one-half of your estate if you die intestate. The remainder would be distributed to your children or parents. You also forfeit some opportunities to reduce estate taxes (details in a minute), and you often expose your heirs to lengthy legal proceedings and added expense, if you die without a will. And, of course, state law makes no provisions for favorite charities or other groups you would like to support.

First Things First—Writing (and Updating) Your Will

You should have a will.

And so should your spouse. And that's true even for a nonworking spouse.

Let's say the husband worked and the wife stayed home during the marriage, and when he died, he left everything to her.

Fine, you say. No problem. But in real life there can be a big problem. What happens to all those assets if she dies intestate? The state will distribute the assets. *Both husbands and wives should have wills.*

And as those wills are being drawn up you should think about how the property in your estate is owned.

If you are married, realigning the ownership of assets may save a substantial amount of estate taxes. For example, a married couple with joint assets valued at $1.2 million or greater might want to consider dividing their assets between them, that is, switching to single-name ownership. That way each spouse can take maximum advantage of the Unified Credit, which shelters estates worth $600,000 or less. In an estate valued at exactly $1.2 million, you can save your heirs $192,800 in estate taxes by preserving each spouse's Unified Credit.

In addition, you should think about giving away some of your assets now. That will reduce your taxable estate.

You can give up to $10,000 a year ($20,000 per couple; $10,000 comes from him, $10,000 from her) to each of as many people as you like, without any federal gift tax consequences. Gifts that exceed the $10,000 limit, as we said, reduce the Unified Credit available to your estate.

Making Sure You Can Pay the Estate Tax Bill

Odds are that no matter how much care you take in planning your estate, there will be a tax bill to pay. A well-defined estate plan should not only minimize estate taxes but also provide sufficient liquidity to take care of the taxes due. Liquidity is important because estate taxes must be paid within nine months of the date of death.

Finding the money can be a problem, particularly when the tax bill is big. If there isn't enough cash in the estate, you have three choices:

- **Borrow the money.** You can borrow against the assets in the estate, but a loan is only a short-term solution. It will have to be paid back.

- **Sell investments.** This can be an unattractive choice, particularly if nonliquid assets—such as real estate—must be sold at distressed prices.

Generosity Has Some Limits

You are capable of giving a lot of your estate away each year with no tax consequences. For example, by gifting $10,000 per parent to each of their four children, a couple can give away a total of $80,000 each year without incurring any federal gift tax.

Similarly, if this couple has eight grandchildren between their four children, each grandchild can also receive $10,000 from each grandparent.

If these very wealthy (and very generous) grandparents were gifting all this to their children and grandchildren, they would be reducing their taxable estate by $240,000 a year.

- **Use life insurance.** This is an option we mentioned, in
passing, in Chapter 27, on insurance, but it is worth repeat-
ing here. Life insurance is a highly efficient method of meeting estate taxes. The insurance proceeds may be received
income-tax-free, and they also may be free of estate taxes.

An intriguing way of using the insurance proceeds is through
a life insurance trust. Although trusts will be the subject of the
next chapter, let us discuss insurance trusts here, since they are applicable.

As we said, life insurance proceeds are generally not subject to
income taxes, but if you are considered to be the owner or control-
ler of the policy, the proceeds are treated as part of your taxable
estate, and could actually increase the estate taxes due.

To get around this problem, you can remove the proceeds from
your estate by setting up a life insurance trust to own the insurance
policy.

You make annual gifts to the trust, and the trustee uses the
money to purchase the insurance policy.

You could assign ownership of an existing policy to the trust,
but if you die within three years of transferring the policy, the
proceeds may be considered part of your estate.

Estate Planning Checklist

- Do you have a will?

- Does your spouse have a will?

- How are your assets owned? Jointly? Individually?

- Do you plan to make gifts to colleges or charities, as part of settling your estate?

- Have you decided who should inherit the property after both you and your spouse are dead?

- Have you set up a custodianship for yourself—if you become disabled?

- Have you chosen guardians for any minor children?

- Should all your children or grandchildren be treated equally, or are there any special medical or educational requirements?

- Have you chosen an executor for your estate?

- Is your spouse comfortable managing money, or should funds be left in trust?

- Have you planned for your children/grandchildren's education?

- Have you arranged for your parents' long-term health care needs?

- Have you taken care of your own or your spouse's long-term care needs? (Some possible ways of meeting long-term care costs will be shown in Chapter 30.)

If there's ever a time, in your life-long financial planning efforts, when you *must* go to the experts—it's now, as you work on reducing taxes. Use them. Make them—lawyers, accountants, estate planning specialists—your partners.

You've worked too hard to build an estate to see it eroded by unnecessary taxes. Proper estate planning lets you minimize taxes and direct where your assets are going after your death.

CHAPTER 29

Trusts: A Crucial Part of Estate Planning

A trust, like estate planning, is often thought of as an esoteric and difficult subject. But it isn't. At its most basic, a trust is nothing more than a legal arrangement that transfers ownership of assets from a grantor—the person who establishes the trust—to a trustee. The trustee administers the trust, and manages the assets for the beneficiaries, according to the terms established in the trust document.

The trustee can be any individual—friend, family member, anyone you want—or a corporation, such as a bank trust department.

Trusts can play an important role in your overall financial and estate planning. They combine tax-saving opportunities with the ability to manage your assets in such a way that they provide for your family the way you want now—and after your death.

That's a point worth underlining; many people think trusts can go into effect only after someone's death. That is not so. The transfer of ownership of assets from your control to a trust can occur at any time and for any reason.

And as long as we are talking about misconceptions, there are two others we would like to get rid of at the start.

A trust does not have to be run by someone else. You can manage a trust you set up until you become too ill to run it, or die. (And at that time, your spouse or children—or any other person you have designated—can take it over.)

Finally, people think that just because you establish a trust you somehow have lowered—or eliminated—estate taxes.

Not true. Establishing a trust, in and of itself, may not automatically lower your taxes. But there are various ways you can use trusts to transfer assets to beneficiaries and *reduce current income, gift taxes, and/or estate taxes.* (Gift and estate taxes are now usually referred to as "transfer taxes.")

Trusts 101

In the broadest sense, there are two kinds of trusts.

A trust created while the grantor is alive is called a *living,* or *inter vivos,* trust. A trust established by will is referred to as a testamentary trust.

Living trusts come in two forms. They can be either *revocable,* or *irrevocable.*

With a revocable living trust, you retain full control over the assets you place in trust while you are alive. You can put money in, take money out, change the terms or even revoke the trust as you please.

One advantage of a revocable living trust is that it can eliminate the need for a court-appointed conservator to manage your financial affairs should you become incapacitated.

If you name a successor trustee in your trust, that trustee can continue to manage the assets in your trust—according to your instructions in the trust provisions—if you are no longer mentally or physically able to continue to act as your own trustee.

The second advantage of a revocable living trust is that it *allows you to avoid probate.*

An irrevocable trust is just that: a trust that cannot be changed or terminated. You would establish an irrevocable living trust if your objective is to obtain income and/or estate tax savings *and you are willing to relinquish control over the assets while you are alive.* That is key. If you transfer property to an irrevocable living trust, it will be excluded from your estate because you have relinquished all ownership rights and control of that property. (This would not be true if you established a revocable living trust, since you still would have control of the assets. Assets placed in a revocable trust become part of your estate.)

Why would you establish a trust? There are nine good reasons, in addition to the potential savings in estate taxes:

1. You believe the beneficiary is unwilling, or unable, to invest, manage, or handle the responsibility of an outright gift. (For example, he lacks the legal, emotional, or intellectual ability to handle a large amount of assets.)

2. You want to postpone full ownership, or prevent ownership, to a specific group of individuals.

3. You fear an outright transfer of assets would lessen the beneficiary's dependence on you.

4. To spread the proposed gift among many beneficiaries.

5. To hedge the appreciation/depreciation of the gift.

6. Trusts may be able to provide protection from both the donor's and beneficiary's creditors.

7. Privacy. Trusts do not pass through probate, the legal process of administrating a will.

8. Trusts can be used if you are concerned that an outright gift to a minor child may end up with the wrong person or relative.

9. You might want to be able to assist the charity of your choice.

Income Tax Treatment of Trusts

Who pays the tax on trust income depends on who is receiving the income.

- If you have established a revocable living trust and are its sole beneficiary, you and the trust are considered to be the same taxable entity. You report the income on your 1040, and your Social Security number serves as the trust's taxpayer identification number. The trust itself is not required to file a separate tax return.

- If other beneficiaries receive income from a trust—either revocable or irrevocable—then the trustee must file, on behalf of the trust, an income tax return and he also must report the distributions made to beneficiaries on Schedule K-1 of Form 1041. (The beneficiaries must report the income they receive on their personal income tax returns.)

- If an irrevocable living trust, or testamentary trust, retains any income or capital gains (instead of distributing them to the beneficiaries), the trustee must again file an income tax return on behalf of the trust, using the trust's own taxpayer identification number.

This raises an interesting point about how trust and individual tax rates compare.

Dividend and interest income earned on investments held in trust is taxed at exactly the same 15%, 28%, and 31% tax rates as investments held outside of a trust.

However, as the chart on page 451 showed, higher income tax rates apply at significantly lower levels of trust income.

For example, a trust is taxed at the 31% rate on taxable income above $10,900, while a married couple filing jointly could have taxable income of $86,500 before the 31% rate bracket applies.

Note: Both trusts and trust beneficiaries are also liable for state taxes on the taxable income they receive.

Because of this difference, it makes sense to distribute income annually to beneficiaries—since they are taxed at a lower rate— rather than hold it in an irrevocable living, or testamentary trust.

Your Family Gets the Income, Your Charity Gets the Assets

Suppose you want to make a tax-advantaged gift to charity, yet keep income from the assets you are donating to pay for a child's education, or supplement your own retirement income? A **charitable remainder trust** may be the solution.

When you place assets in a charitable remainder trust, you, or other family members, receive income under the terms of the trust for life, or for a specified period of time. Then the assets pass to the charity of your choice.

The nice thing about this arrangement is that you receive a charitable deduction on your *current* income tax return that is equal to the present value of the charity's interest in your property. The deduction is based on your age, the percentage to be paid to the income beneficiary, and the value of the assets placed into trust. Any appreciation in trust assets remains outside your estate for tax purposes.

A charitable remainder trust can be particularly useful if you want to increase the annual income you are receiving from a highly appreciated asset—such as a piece of undeveloped land in a rapidly growing area—that is yielding you little or nothing. The trust can sell the asset, avoiding the substantial capital gains that would result if you disposed of it, and reinvest 100% of the money in assets that may produce a higher yield.

But be careful with this strategy. The unrealized capital gain will be considered a tax preference item and could subject you to the alternative minimum tax (AMT).

The AMT is a concern if the total of preference items, plus adjustments, increases your tax base to the point where, when taxed at a flat 24%, the resulting number is larger than the regular income tax you'd otherwise have to pay.

It takes a fair amount to trigger the alternative minimum tax. For example, if you had taxable income totaling $200,000 in 1991, you would need preference items, and adjustments, that exceed $45,700 before being subject to the AMT.

To make these strategies particularly effective, you can combine them with a life insurance trust.

Here's how it works.

At the same time you are establishing the charitable remainder trust, you establish another trust that names children, or other family members, as beneficiaries. That trust buys a life insurance policy on your life in a face amount that is equal to the value of the property being transferred to the charitable trust. Alternatively, the trust buys a policy that is at least equal to the after-estate-tax value of the assets that you plan to place in the charitable remainder trust.

You contribute a portion of the income resulting from the charitable trust's investments, and the tax savings from your charitable deduction to the insurance trust so that it can pay the premiums on the life insurance.

When you die, the insurance proceeds pass to your heirs free of federal estate tax.

The diagram on page 467 shows how it works.

Another type of charitable trust, known as a *charitable lead trust,* allows you to preserve and pass assets on to your children or grandchildren, while still helping the charity of your choice. The charitable lead trust is the exact opposite of the charitable remainder trust, as the chart on page 468 shows.

The income from assets placed in a lead trust goes to the charity for a specified number of years and the principal is returned to your beneficiary when the trust terminates. The higher the annual payment to the charity and the longer the term of the gift, the smaller the gift to your heirs. It is anticipated that your heirs will receive at least the value of the original corpus. Any appreciation above that will escape taxation.

Trusts should be a crucial part of your financial and estate planning. They combine tax saving opportunities with the ability to manage your assets in the way you want—both now and after your death.

466

Charitable Remainder Trust

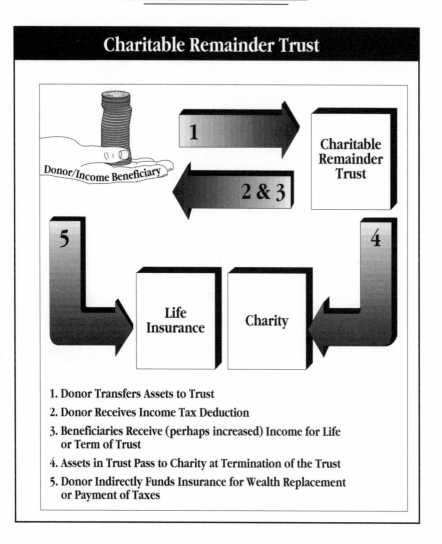

Donor/Income Beneficiary

1 → **Charitable Remainder Trust**

2 & 3 ←

5 **4**

Life Insurance **Charity**

1. Donor Transfers Assets to Trust

2. Donor Receives Income Tax Deduction

3. Beneficiaries Receive (perhaps increased) Income for Life or Term of Trust

4. Assets in Trust Pass to Charity at Termination of the Trust

5. Donor Indirectly Funds Insurance for Wealth Replacement or Payment of Taxes

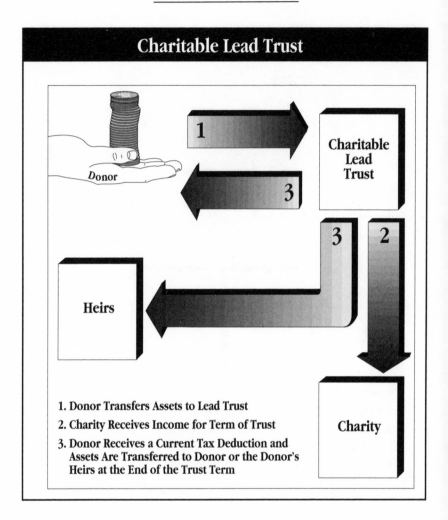

Charitable Lead Trust

Donor

1

Charitable
Lead
Trust

3

3   2

Heirs

Charity

1. Donor Transfers Assets to Lead Trust
2. Charity Receives Income for Term of Trust
3. Donor Receives a Current Tax Deduction and
   Assets Are Transferred to Donor or the Donor's
   Heirs at the End of the Trust Term

CHAPTER 30

Meeting Medical Costs

You travel a lot, and you are sophisticated. You would never, ever, be seen browsing in those tacky souvenir shops that seem to overrun every tourist area. You know the kind. They offer T-shirts with such sayings as:

> My parents went to
> SAN FRANCISCO
> and all I got was
> this lousy T-shirt

For San Francisco you can substitute New Orleans, Orlando, or Yellowstone, or any other destination. (And for "parents" you can substitute grandparents, if you like.)

Admit it. You've seen these shirts. Always from a distance, of course. You may have even seen, in the back of the store, the shirt that read:

> GET EVEN
> Live long enough
> to be a burden
> to your kids

That T-shirt is a laugh; but it is also a prophecy, one that we tried to back into discussing, since it is the most serious—even the *most* somber—part of retirement planning: who will take care of you, if you are no longer able to take care of yourself?

We *are* an aging nation. We can expect an extended life for many reasons; the biggest one being that traumatic events, those that in the past were life threatening, are so much more treatable these days thanks to extraordinary advances in medical technology.

That's great, of course, but this extended lifespan has to be paid for somehow and that can get quite expensive.

We have to caution you about the rest of this chapter. It is much more fun to plan active retirement activities, such as figuring out which of the 10,000 Indonesian islands you really want to visit, than it is to face up to the somewhat pleasureless job of figuring out how you will take care of yourself some 20, 30, or more years hence.

Assuming you really don't want to be parented by your children—or at least, not excessively—you'll have to plan for the time when you may well need long-term care.

LTC—from Day Care to Nursing Homes

Before we give you the odds of you requiring it, let's define long-term care (LTC). It covers a broad range of personal and social services and medical care—from nursing homes to home health care to adult day care—for people who are unable to care for themselves for an extended period of time.

Major illnesses can often be beaten. It's the debilitating ones, that can, to put it mildly, wear you down, physically, emotionally, and financially.

Or you may be in fine mental health but you've run out of steam.

You may suffer a chronic illness: severe arthritis, diabetes, or you've had a stroke or a heart attack, or you suffer from Alzheimer's disease. Because of illnesses, you may need help with the necessities of each day: dressing, eating, and simply moving around. You're far from dead—you just need help.

Face it. The time may come in the twilight of your life when you may need long-term care.

Most long-term care is provided at home—through visiting nurses, therapists, or homemakers, or by your family—but you may require institutional care. This could range from basic custodial care in a nursing home, which is mostly nonmedical, to more intensive care involving daily nursing care or rehabilitative help. You may need around-the-clock care.

None of this means that on the day you retire, you'll suddenly need a walker, and require LTC. In fact, of those 65 to 69 only some 13% need *any* form of long-term care.

Add some 20 years to that, however, and the need—not surprisingly—becomes much greater. Of those aged 85 and older, more than 50% will require long-term care, at least once in their lives.

Is your glass half full or half empty? The fact that almost half of those 85 and older *don't* need LTC is an extraordinary testimony to (take your choice): good living, good blood lines, good medicine, or good thoughts.

However:

- About two in five Americans 65 and older end up in nursing homes at some point in their lives. Of those, some 26% stay more than a year, and 11% stay 36 months or longer.

- It's projected that 55% of Americans will have, over their lifetime, cumulative nursing home stays that add up to more than a year.

- Costs for long-term nursing care currently average between $30,000 and $60,000 per year. (Costs are highest in the large, metropolitan areas. Costs also vary because of the type of facility you require.)

- When the baby boomers retire, according to a recent report from the government's General Accounting Office, the projected number of disabled elderly will range anywhere from 14 million to 27 million.

Suppose you don't need a nursing home, and can exist with home care. This is fine for your morale. It's certainly more comforting to be at *home* with your familiar things.

The most loving home care—but not necessarily the best care—might come from your spouse. Amidst all these statistics, it's difficult to quantify how much long-term care is tender, loving care.

A Call for Help

But there inevitably will come a time when outside help is needed. You may be alone now; or your spouse simply may be incapable of tending to you. Perhaps meals will be delivered to you, or you'll be getting transportation help. Home-care costs can range from $20 to $100 per visit. On a daily basis (and your needs don't take the weekends off), home-care costs currently can range from $7,300 to $36,000 annually. That's in today's dollars. Using current cost estimates, and assuming a 5.8% annual increase for the next two decades, when today's 50-year-old reaches 70, nursing home care could *average* $90,000 a year, and home-care costs could be $67,540 annually.

What Do You Mean—I'm Not Covered!

Those are scary numbers, you concede, but you aren't worried. "I've got insurance," you say. "Between my current medical plan and assorted government plans, I'll do just fine. Right?"

We wouldn't bet a pleasant retirement on it.

It's possible that once you retire your employer will continue to pick up all your health care costs, but this largess is increasingly rare.

Maybe your employer will pay part of your benefits, with you picking up the difference. That is more common, but still not guaranteed.

For many employees, once you retire your health insurance stops. You may be able to continue under the company's health plan, if you are willing to pick up the premium. That's better than nothing. You may not get the employer rate, but your costs might still be 15% to 25% less than what it would cost if you were to walk in off the street. Still, it is not the world's best deal.

While a basic medical plan is a necessity—no matter who is

paying the premium—because it probably covers hospitalization and physicians' care, it is not enough. *Basic insurance plans seldom include long-term health care coverage.*

And things are bound to get worse, from a former employee's perspective. Many employers, quite within their legal rights, are reducing their medical benefits to retirees. It is a trend that is picking up speed.

Corporate management is blunt about this. Companies are fighting desperately to hold down, or even reduce, their medical benefit costs for the working, and they—the corporation and its shareowners—tell you they can no longer afford to shoulder the soaring medical costs of retirees. This harsh, but realistic, look at medical costs is particularly onerous to the boomers. They may have seen their parents well covered by employer plans once they retired. All that past benevolence is going the way of the dodo.

If you are a baby boomer, only one person in this world of shrinking entitlements is going to take care of you in retirement, and you know who that is. *You.*

Medicare—Medigap—Medicaid

Let's look at the government programs: what they cover and what they don't.

Medicare is the federal program, for people 65 or older, which will help with hospital and doctors' bills and other medical expenses for those relatively short-term acute illnesses, such as a heart attack or an accident, and those vexing ailments to which the elderly are prone, such as a broken hip or pneumonia.

Most of the high medical costs of short-term disability could be well covered with Medicare. Think of Medicare as help in the short term.

But Medicare *does not* pay for ongoing custodial care—the kind of care that most elderly people will require in one form or another as they age. Medicare usually is limited to 100 days of skilled nursing care, and that care must follow a hospitalization. Even then, you'll be responsible for some copayments, and the skilled nursing facility must be Medicare-certified. Since many nursing homes are not skilled nursing facilities—and of those that are so categorized, not all are Medicare-certified—there can be a shortfall. In short, Medicare pays for only a small fraction of long-term health care expenses.

As for home health care, Medicare coverage is even more sparse.

Since it's estimated that no more than 65% to 70% of your health care cost will be covered by Medicare, the difference will either have to come out of your pocket, from any medical benefit plans you might have assumed from your employer, from new plans that you might have bought, or from **Medigap,** a supplemental policy that helps to fill the Medicare shortfall.

There are different levels of Medigap coverage, depending on which policy you pick, but the most comprehensive policies—and obviously, the most expensive ones—will pick up your deductible (the out-of-pocket slice of your doctors' bills), as well as diagnostic tests, and prescription drugs, preventive care, and possibly even treatment abroad. (Remember, you do want to go island hopping in exotic corners of the world. In addition to all those Indonesian islands there are those hundreds of Norwegian fjords that may deserve checking out.)

But as full as some Medigap coverage can be, it, too, will not cover long-term care costs.

Finally, as a last resort, there's **Medicaid,** which provides long-term care for those with little or no financial resources.

In order to qualify for Medicaid, you must literally spend your life savings down to a minimum level. The rules are complicated, and since this program is a joint federal-state operation, rules will even vary state by state. But Medicaid is essentially a welfare program, and you would have to be at the near-poverty level for it to kick in. We hope you'll never have to resort to it.

However, there are no guarantees. The Senate Select Committee on Aging has reported that about two-thirds of single elderly persons and one-third of married elderly persons who enter nursing homes will be impoverished within six months.

Frightening to Look At, More Frightening to Ignore

If all this seems frightening, it's because it *is* frightening. Those who are either retired or facing retirement over the next several years are obviously more acutely aware of future medical costs, but the boomers are increasingly becoming more fearful of the future. In the most recent Merrill Lynch Retirement Planning Survey, 57% of pre-retirees, those aged 45 to 64, and 47% of the boomers aged 25 to 44 said that the issue of long-term care is "extremely important." Some 60% of the pre-retirees and a surprising 57% of the boomers worry that long-term health care costs "could ruin me financially."

They have reason to worry. A couple who are both 45 years old in 1992, according to current projections and assumptions, can expect to need $240,000 to cover general health care and long-term care costs *alone* when they turn 65 in 2012.

How, as part of your retirement planning, can you provide for long-term care? An even better question to ask is, "Can I afford *not* to buy long-term care insurance?"

If you have few substantial assets, rely on the government. There's little incentive for you to somehow scrape up enough to buy LTC coverage. But if you, as an individual or as a couple, do have substantial assets, then you must be concerned that long-term care could significantly diminish your standard of living. One way to protect your assets is to buy long-term health care insurance.

How to Pay for LTC

When you were young, you needed whole life insurance. While working, you needed disability protection. Now that you're older, your insurance needs have shifted. Buying long-term care insurance can help to keep a couple's assets out of the nursing home's till.

Comprehensive long-term health care insurance, a rarity a decade ago, is much more readily available today. These policies are designed to protect your assets by giving you coverage for nursing-home care, and in many cases, coverage for home-care costs. The increasing graying of America has led, over the last 10 years, to a much wider array of insurance plans that offer LTC.

As always, premiums will vary depending on your age and the options you select. The younger and the healthier you are, the lower the premiums will be. For example, a fairly basic policy that provides for up to five years of nursing-home care, and five years of home health care, could cost a 50-year-old about $600 a year. For a 70-year-old, in good health, the policy might cost about $2,800 annually.

Read the fine print: premiums will vary, state by state, and there may be a waiting period before you are covered, and there may also be a maximum benefit that will be paid.

You often can tailor the LTC insurance program to fit your needs, but it is important that you make sure that degenerative diseases, such as Alzheimer's, are covered. You may even be given the option—at extra cost, of course—to increase your daily benefit amount periodically in order to offset inflation. If permitted, you would want your policy—once you've passed the physical and are covered—to be renewable for life. This means you would be guaranteed that your policy could never be canceled as long as you pay your premiums.

Some of America's larger corporations now offer group long-term health care policies to active employees, although it's still a rarity for the majority of companies. Although the cost must be borne by participants, the group premiums tend to be from 20% to 30% lower than an individual would pay.

You also may be in luck—when it comes to finding LTC coverage—if you look at your own existing life policy. For in recent years more life insurance companies have been adding what is called a "living benefit rider" to their whole life or universal life policies. This lets you draw on a portion of the policy's death benefit if you come down with what is diagnosed as a terminal illness. Because this addition of a special rider is expected to become more readily available in the future, this might be more available to the boomer then it would be to the pre-retiree.

Another type of rider is even specifically designed to cover some long-term care costs.

The cost of your life insurance policy will undoubtedly be increased if you want an LTC rider, but still, adding the rider, if offered, may be less expensive than buying an individual LTC policy. If you exercise this rider there may be other trade-offs (such as reducing the death benefits), so ask your insurance expert to give you a full explanation of benefits and costs.

In retirement, you'll happily discover that many of your living expenses will go down. But one expense that can only go up is your health care expenses. The simple fact is that those costs climb with age.

One recent study found that out-of-pocket health care expenses have more than doubled (in constant dollars) between 1961 and 1991. Part of the reason for that, of course, is the rising cost of health care. But another big reason is that employers—and the government—are now requiring people to pay a larger percentage of their health care costs.

What are other options in paying for LTC? In Chapter 23, we reviewed the increasing importance of a reverse mortgage as a way of generating a cash flow when you're retired. This can be particularly important in financing long-term care in *your own home*. Or you may want to use a sale leaseback. A third option: Tap your home equity as a way of meeting these costs. (This is somewhat like a reverse mortgage.)

If you're hit with long-term care expenses, and you have no coverage, consider drawing down the cash value of your whole life policy. There may be a substantial value lurking there, and a loan against your policy may even be tax-free.

No Sugarcoating—Sorry

This chapter—probably more so than any other in this guide—may have been a somber reading experience. Sorry. There's no way to sugarcoat it.

In focus groups around the country, with both pre-retirees and folks who have already retired, we've discovered that few people really fear death, and they don't really fear the process of dying.

They are, however, overwhelmingly scared of one thing: that they'll outlive their money and die in poverty.

In the next chapter, which is also our last, we'll give you pointers on spending down with grace and verve, and we'll show you a relatively painless way of doing annual financial checkups.

If you can figure out how to pay for long-term health care should the need arise, the rest of your life will be far easier.

You can even go ahead and buy that tacky "Get Even . . . " T-shirt if you want to. Your children will laugh.

But in real life don't give that gag T-shirt life. Don't be a burden to your children (or your spouse).

In retirement, you will need not just basic medical care but also long-term care. LTC is a critical part of retirement planning. Planning now—whether you're 40 or 70—for long-term care will reduce one of the greatest worries that the elderly face: the fear that they will outlive their resources.

CHAPTER 31

Spending Down

Once you've retired, the ride isn't over. It's only begun. We'll concede it's a cliché to say that "today is the first day of the rest of your life." But a slight twist on that cliché does produce a truism: "Now that I'm retired, today *is* the first day of completely managing *my* financial future for the rest of my life."

Here's why that's true.

When you worked, your employer managed your salary. Sure, you earned it, and yes, because of your extra efforts or adrenaline at the right time you might even have had some control over the size of the bonus you'd receive. But still, your employer—and not you—decided exactly how much you'd make each year.

Your employer may also have managed your pension.

Well, now that you've retired, the old days are gone. You have just become manager of just about all of your financial fate.

Why *almost* all? There are a couple of reasons.

First, you can't do much about the size of the Social Security check you'll receive. It's set (although you'll be pleased to see that it changes periodically to keep up with inflation). And your pension payout, if it's from a defined benefit plan, is fixed as well (although it's probably *not indexed* for inflation).

But all the rest of your retirement assets—and that "rest" will account for *at least 60%* of your retirement income if you're typical—is yours to manage and spend.

What retirement assets are we talking about? Your 401(k) or 403(b) plans; your profit-sharing or employee stock ownership plans, your SEP, Keogh, or regular IRAs, and what may be most crucial to your retirement, your rollover IRA.

Obviously, those are not all the resources you will be drawing on. You also have your nonretirement assets: your savings, banking, and brokerage accounts, insurance and annuity assets, and, of course, your real estate.

Real Estate—Important, but Not Always Liquid

For many people, real estate is the biggest asset they have, and what to do with it poses the biggest question they face in retirement. Retirement is the time that you have to decide whether you want to convert your real estate into money. You may have some income-producing rental properties, or non-producing land. You would categorize them as nonliquid, for it's not always easy to convert real estate into cash. Land rich; cash poor.

Most likely your biggest investment in real estate is your home. Do you sell the house (and/or the vacation home as well) and move to a smaller condo or co-op? Or maybe you sell the big house and move permanently to the vacation home.

As this list of assets shows, you have a lot to manage, and, if you planned right, a lot to spend.

Converting Assets into Fun and Comfort

We like to think of retirement as the time when you are "spending down," figuring out how you are going to use the assets you worked a lifetime to accumulate so that they produce the most fun and comfort for you.

It may be possible just to live off your investment income and Social Security, and leave the rest to your beneficiaries.

If that's what you want to do, fine. But please accept the fact that hearses don't have luggage racks. You may be tempted to say, "if I can't take it with me, I'm not going." But the fact is you *are* going sometime. Night is coming.

Why not enjoy the time—the daylight—you have? Isn't that why you saved for retirement in the first place? Milton Quincy—our 75-year-old video packager from Pasadena—is not going to cut back on traveling to Europe and enjoying the good life once he stops work. He's spending down with grace and verve. Why shouldn't you?

We are not talking about going through 100% of your savings in the first 30 seconds of retirement. But if spending 5%, or even 10%, of your principal each year will make retirement enjoyable, why not do it? After all, with any luck (and/or careful money management) your remaining assets will be performing well enough to offset the reduction.

Your Education Continues

We hope you are prepared for retirement. Indeed, helping you to prepare is why we wrote this book. But how much pre-retirement planning did you absorb? You may have been lucky. Your employer may have sent you to seminars. And if you were really lucky, your employer welcomed your spouse at those meetings as well.

Great, but don't stop learning now. Go to financial planning seminars whether they are sponsored by an employer, financial consultants, your local community college, or public library. Learn as much as you can.

And one of the things you may have to learn is how to share your financial planning with your spouse—if you haven't already.

We are going to take an educated guess and say that only one of you has been running (worrying?) about the investment side of the household. In years past, the man took the lead. That changed considerably with the rise of dual-income families. That's certainly to the good. But odds are what didn't change was the fact that only one person handled the money.

So if it has been a one-person show—now is the time to change.

Suppose the most knowledgeable of you dies first? What happens to the surviving spouse?

To avoid this worry, it's important that you *both* become knowledgeable about your financial affairs.

How do you do it?

In addition to both of you attending financial seminars, make sure you both meet periodically with your financial adviser. Make it a three-party partnership.

Sharing Decisions—Big and Small

We know that any major financial moves (such as, "Should we sell the mansion and move 3,000 miles to Big Boulder?"; or "Should we roll over the $500,000 pension plan, or pay taxes now?"; or "Should we change our wills?"; or "Should we set up new trusts?") result from family discussions. And they're probably extensive. At least they should be.

What we're asking—now that you're retired—is that even the most minor investment decisions be joint ones from now on. This is the easiest way for the spouse who was not closely involved with the family finances to find out *(a)* what's going on, and *(b)* to gain the information she (or he) will need to make decisions on her (or his) own, should the day come.

As a kid, you learned how to ride a bicycle by using training wheels at first. Then you made the big move. The wheels came off and your father, mother, or big sister or brother ran alongside the

---

Widows and Widowers

The actuarial facts prove the conventional wisdom that women outlive men. Women outlive men on average by about four years (the male at 65 has a life expectancy of 18 years; the female's expectancy is 22).

In 1990 the U.S. Census Bureau estimated that there were five times as many widows in the United States as there were widowers. Of widows under the age of 45, some 54% remarry, so says the Census Bureau. Of widows over 45, only 9.5% remarry.

---

bike for a time or two to give you support. And suddenly you knew how to ride.

It's almost the same with managing money.

Learn how. Fall off once or twice. (We know of *no one* who hasn't bought, and survived, at least one turkey in his financial lifetime.) But unlike the lifetime mastery of a bicycle once you no longer need help, when you're managing money and trying to decipher the maze of taxation and investments, call on big brother or big sister. It's perfectly acceptable to get advice.

Get help—not just from your financial consultant, but also from your spouse.

You don't need to go it alone.

A Checklist for the Retired

To help you get ready to solo, we've prepared a checklist:

Review your will once you've retired, and thereafter at least every three years. In tandem with that, review the beneficiaries of your life insurance policies and retirement accounts.

It is possible after you pass age 70½, to make the mandatory withdrawals that the law demands based on the combined life expectancy of you and your designated beneficiaries.

For example, if your spouse is your beneficiary, the combined expectancy is based on the actual age of you and your spouse—regardless of whether the difference is one year or thirty. But if the beneficiary is not your spouse—say it's your child or a grand-child—then there is a limit of ten years that can be counted as the age differential in the combined expectancy.

And, of course, a change of beneficiaries cannot always be done automatically. A spousal consent may be necessary. This particularly would be necessary in community property states. As always, when in doubt, check with your lawyer.

This will give you a chance to adjust your will, to reflect the changes in your life. There may have been a death in your family, or you might have gotten divorced. A child, or grandchild, might have been born. Once the trauma—good or bad—is over, adjust accordingly.

If you've been sloppy, and have forgotten to designate a beneficiary, it will *all* go to your estate. Do you want that? It can be very costly.

Also, as part of this review, make sure the executor named in your will is still the appropriate choice. Things (and people) change.

Calculate IRA withdrawals. Annually, you must determine exactly how much you will be required to withdraw from your IRA in the coming year. The regulations *require* you to do this once you've reached 70½. Here's the general rule on minimum distributions from retirement accounts: They must begin by April 1 of the calendar year following the calendar year in which you reached age 70½. This minimum distribution is based on life expectancy tables from the IRS. If you were "grandfathered" by a special "election" provision under a 1984 law, you *might be receiving* an exception to the minimum distribution rule. (See your tax adviser.) As to that minimum distribution, some IRA custodians will do the calculating automatically for you.

Review your disability insurance. Having disability insurance while you're employed is a good idea, since it will replace lost earnings if you are unable to work for an extended period. However, now that you are not working, it's not needed.

Review your whole life policy as well. Your children have long left home, your spouse will be provided for in all sorts of other ways, so do you need whole life insurance? Other than to pay your estate taxes, probably not.

If you don't need the insurance, it makes sense to cash it in, assuming there's some cash value. That's especially true since life insurance policies—with cash value provisions—often have a low yield. You are probably better off investing the money elsewhere. Or you may want to convert the cash value into an annuity.

Consider charitable contributions. In retirement, paying taxes seems somehow even more onerous than it did while you were working. If you are thinking about increasing your charitable giving to increase your tax deduction—and decrease the value of your estate—remember that contributions are limited to 50% of your adjusted gross income for the year.

Think about selling your home, to free up some of the equity there. Don't forget the one-time $125,000 exclusion in capital gains that you are entitled to.

Review cash reserves. You may have maintained a sizable (as much as six months of your former salary) cash horde as an emergency fund while you were working. That money—which you kept liquid and so is low yield—was there to make sure you could pay your bills if you were suddenly laid off.

Well, you *are* happily "laid off" now. You're officially retired. Now that you're retired, it probably makes sense to take that money—or at least most of it—and invest it in something that will produce a higher return.

Adjust cash flow. From your assorted sources of income, you'll need to create a steady cash flow to cover your retirement expenses. After you account for the set monthly income (Social Security, and a regular pension or annuity), what other assets—including your IRA or your other retirement plans—will you need to tap?

In order to produce a steady (that is, predictable) stream of income, you may need to shift some assets—in both retirement accounts and nonretirement accounts—into short-term investments. This would be done so that you would receive both income and a return of principal. Ladder your maturities—spread the investments over a three- to five-year period so that some come due each year. This will be particularly important to retirement accounts such as IRAs—when you'll eventually be forced to take out some of the principal each year.

Review trusts. You may have, years ago, set up a combined trust, say, for your kids. Now might be the time to look anew at those trusts. Needs may have changed.

For example, since you set up the trusts your daughter may have married Boca Raton's richest polo player, while her twin brother decided to give up his promising medical career to become a (struggling) conceptual artist living in Bisbee, Arizona. Maybe, just maybe, you'll want to change the trusts. He may need a bigger slice of your loot than she does. (Be prepared to spend *lots* of time explaining your reasoning to your daughter. Despite her new-found wealth, she's bound to be unhappy.)

We've already conceded how difficult it is for parents to talk to their children about what they will be leaving them. But just as you had the responsibility—as your children were growing up—to have other painful talks about serious things, this is the time for one more serious talk. Sit down with them; write a letter. Just do it.

If you find all this is just too difficult to talk about, your ultimate cop-out is letting your will do the talking for you (something we do not advise).

Sign up for Medicare. When you're 65, you're eligible to sign up for Medicare.

Limit your part-time income. Not everyone who retires from the big one is totally, absolutely, 100% retired. You may be eager to do some consulting, to work part-time. You want to work, not solely for the dollars, but also for the psychic income. It's nice for a gray-hair to be wanted.

Work if you wish—but remember that Social Security benefits are not taxed *unless* your adjusted gross income (including tax-free income and half your Social Security and, of course, earned income) exceeds $25,000. The taxable amount would be half the excess over $25,000—but no more than half of your Social Security benefits. (Back in Chapter 26, page 423, we go much more into detail on the Social Security rules.) Once you're 70, there is no earnings limit, as far as Social Security is concerned.

Offset inflation. Annually you should check to see that the *after-tax* return on your investments is staying ahead of inflation.

If you make 4% on your money, while inflation is running at 5%, you will be steadily losing ground each year. In retirement, you should be pleasantly thinking about how many "frequent flyer" miles you can rack up, and not worrying about the purchasing power of your investments. Being too conservative can be the most unconservative course of all.

Review risk tolerance. This almost goes without saying, but we'll say it anyway. When you do your annual review of how well your assets are doing, also review how—if at all—your risk tolerance level has changed now that you are retired.

Your principal goal now might be preservation of capital, so you may want to shift more of your assets into things that produce income today. (But *never, ever* put everything into investments with a fixed return. You always need some of your assets—even if it is as little as 20%—in stocks, in order to counter inflation.)

Thin down. Eventually after people retire they get around to "thinning down" their possessions. You'll finally get around to cleaning out the attic, going through the kids' accumulated stuff. They may not have lived in your home for decades, but somewhere you will have tons of mementos from their school days. Listen to your wise uncle: send *your* kids (who may well be old enough to have *their* kids starting to hoard stuff—the chain is never-ending) the stuff you don't want.

Let them have the ruthless job of throwing it away. Of your other unwanted possessions, some will go to charity, some to a tag sale, and most to the trash heap.

While you are thinning down, don't forget your financial accounts. They can probably use a little thinning down. See if it makes sense to:

- consolidate your savings accounts

- consolidate your brokerage accounts

- consolidate your IRAs

If you do, it will be easier to tell at a glance how your investments are doing, and you might even save some money on management fees and commissions. Weed and feed your accounts.

I know it's here somewhere. In the next five minutes could you find your:

- Will

- Birth certificate

- Income tax returns for the last three years

- Property deeds

- Automobile titles and registration

- IRA statements for the past year

- Other retirement account documents

- Bank and savings accounts

- Insurance policies

- Brokerage account statements for the last three years

Where do you keep all this? A copy of your will (or wills) will obviously be kept by your attorney. But we would suggest that in your home office, or your den, you keep one "master" locked fireproof file cabinet (which are available, these days, in either designer colors or veneered finishes) for these prime documents.

Shift income. Shifting income? How is that possible? Your Social Security, annuity, and/or pension checks will be coming to you as regularly as clockwork. What's there to shift?

You do have some flexibility. As you know, if you are between the ages of 59½ and 70½ you can take out as little or as much as you want (need) from your IRA each year. You can be systematic, or be erratic.

Since that's the case, do some planning. If you're getting extra income this year (perhaps you've disposed of some assets), you may not want to take anything out of your IRA.

Once you're 70½, you have to—by law—start a systematic withdrawal from most retirement accounts (including IRA, SEP, Keogh, pension, and qualified savings accounts), but you can still shift some money around to fit your financial needs.

Suppose in one year you get a windfall, or you simply reap the profits from some other investments. If that's the case, you can opt to take out no more than the mandated minimum from your retirement accounts.

Let's say that in the following year you'll be getting no extra money from your other accounts or assets. You can always decide to withdraw *more* than the minimum. This is perfectly legal. You can *always take out more* than the minimum, but *never less.* So even if you're beyond 70½, you can still have some leeway in shifting income. Never say never. Or never say always. It may be that from some of your accounts you are taking money out on an annuity basis. That is, it's a fixed amount you're withdrawing. If that's so, then you may not have any leeway to vary the withdrawal.

You also might be able to defer income (and thus taxes) one year to the next by buying short-term discount obligations, such as zero coupon CDs, or Treasury bills with maturities of a year or less. You won't be taxed on any of the interest, until the security or obligation matures. So you can buy the zero coupon this year and have it mature the next.

Budgeting Expenses—Some Up, Most Down

Budgeting. In the decade or so preceding your retirement, you were probably adjusting your budget, trying to figure out how you could put every possible dollar away for retirement. You certainly were going through this juggling act if your financial planning efforts had rung an early warning—that you were facing a shortfall in building retirement assets.

But once you're really retired, new budgeting is an absolute must. Much has gone down in the expense ledger, but some has gone up. For example, on the expense side:

1. Your **commuting expenses** have vanished.

2. **Clothing expenses** are probably less as well. You're no longer dressing for success. You're dressing for fun and comfort, and probably will be spending less.

3. **Food.** The total cost is probably a wash. While working, some of your meals might have been subsidized, or even expensed, and you'll be eating at home more now. You'll have freedom to eat now when you want. We know of bona fide millionaires who can't resist eating dinner early, occasionally, to take advantage of the seniors' early bird discounts at many restaurants.

4. **Car expenses.** Should probably decrease slightly. While some financial advisers recommend having just one car once you're retired, we don't. The preservation of your marriage is more important than any potential savings. However, there will be no commuting, and the odds are that you won't need a new car as often.

5. **Utilities.** This may surprise you—but heating or cooling may go up. You're home more—so the off time for your climate system is less now.

6. **Hobbies, recreation.** Didn't cost you anything while you were working. You didn't have time (or much time). Now—as you'll soon discover—some hobbies can be great diversions, but some can be mighty costly.

7. **Travel.** This expense might take a big jump. At long last, you have time to travel. In some years the airlines give

seniors a break, in others they throw the discounts out the window. Either way, the odds say you will be traveling more.

Even if you get your wanderlust out of your system within the first couple of years of retirement, there still will be the children and grandchildren to visit. Or maybe you'll pop for them visiting you.

Your Annual Fiscal Checkup

Maintenance—good maintenance at the prescribed intervals—makes the world go 'round.

If you want your car to perform efficiently to a proper age, then you follow the manual when it tells you to check something at 5,000 miles, or maybe 15,000 or perhaps 25,000 miles. Thanks to the quality control of American (or substitute the country of your choice) manufacturers, you may even wait till 50,000 miles or five years for some maintenance checks.

And now that you're retired, and you've reached a certain age of wisdom, you go to your kindly doctor at least once a year. Or more often if needed. Even a minor creak might call for a checkup (or at least a phone call). These checkups are good for the peace of mind and body.

We end this guide with a plea for regular financial checkups in retirement. Just as your life may be shortened if you pass up the needed medical checkups, your financial life might not be quite as satisfying if your fiscal checkups are few and far between.

Do for your financial affairs what you do faithfully for your car and your body.

———

A few pages ago we talked about changes in expenses in retirement. Well, what about income? It, too, certainly will change.

On the income side, you're no longer getting a salary, but you are receiving Social Security, pension, annuity payments, and there may be IRA or 401(k) withdrawals. Plus, you'll have your non-retirement assets as well.

If you have prepared well, they all should add up to—or exceed—what you used to receive in salary.

If that is the case, spend down.

You have indeed **grown rich s-l-o-w-l-y.**

Congratulations.

AUTHORS' NOTE

Many of the figures we have cited—tax rates, retirement plans contribution levels, various contribution deadlines—change from time to time because of new laws, new regulations, and mandated cost-of-living adjustments. Obviously you must check to see what's current as you are reading this guide.

You also may have noticed that quite frequently in this book we compare cumulative investment returns, in various guises, ranging from 6% to 8% to 10% to 12%. In some years past a 12% total return has been reasonably achievable; in other years it may have been difficult to achieve. We can't pretend to know what the economic environment will be as you read this in future years, but we do argue that if you try to invest smarter in the managment of your assets—whether that means striving for 8% or 10% or 12%—that extra effort should be to your advantage over the long term.

What will the various rates of return be on your assorted investments when you're reading the book? We can't possibly hazard a guess, and if you need an authority for that unassailable nonprediction, we will cite J. P. Morgan. This is another apocryphal Wall Street story, but it is said that after the financeer testified on some weighty matter in Washington, the lawmakers had one final question for him: "What will the markets do tomorrow?" His parting shot, as he left the chambers: "Gentlemen, they will fluctuate."

His words can also stand as our parting shot. Rates of return *will* fluctuate.

Finally, you also have seen that quite frequently in these chapters we have advised you to seek professional guidance in managing your investments. Whether this comes from a financial consultant, your accountant, your attorney, or portfolio manager, you should not go it alone.

The world of investments is too complex these days for single handing.

ACKNOWLEDGMENTS

From all of Merrill Lynch the backing for this book has been very complete, but in particular, William A. Schreyer, chairman, Daniel P. Tully, president and chief executive officer, and Steven L. Hammerman, vice chairman and general counsel, have been steadfast in support of helping Americans find a better retirement.

For some years now John L. Steffens, an executive vice president of Merrill Lynch and also chairman of the Alliance for Aging Research, has been a missionary to not just Washington but to the nation as a whole on problems of the aging, and the need for America to rejuvenate its savings. His preface to this guide is the rightful starting point for this book's thesis.

Under the firm leadership of Paul Critchlow, William E. Sullivan, and Gerald E. Cremins, this project was kept on course; special thanks to these key executives: Harry P. Allex, Herbert M. Allison, Chuck Clough, Gail Farkas, Robert J. Farrell, John Fitzgerald, Barry Friedberg, Terry K. Glenn, Edward L. Goldberg, William Henkel, Alan Jones, Jerome Kenney, David H. Komansky, Debbie Mandelker, Nassos Michas, Thomas O. Muller, Thomas H. Patrick, Michael Perini, Robert Sherman, James F. Shoaf, Winthrop H. Smith, Donald Straszheim, Arthur Urciuoli, Patrick J. Walsh, William F. Waters, Madeline Weinstein, and Arthur Zeikel.

Acknowledgments

A former Merrill Lynch partner, the late Louis H. Engel, successfully brought Wall Street to Main Street some years ago in his book *How to Buy Stocks*. His pioneering educational efforts indirectly made this book possible.

Long before a major law change in 1974 created new ways of saving for retirement, a former Merrill Lynch executive, Thomas B. Sherman, foresaw that one day millions of Americans would be self-directing their own retirement accounts. His vision was the genesis of Merrill Lynch's retirement-planning services today. This project was also aided outside the firm by Steven Galef, Harold Kahn, David Nevin, John Orb, Charles Rotkin, Roy Rowan, Linda Ruby, and George Shinn.

Michael Jacobs, president of Viking, saw the value in what we were trying to say and for that we will be eternally grateful. Lori Lipsky is nominated for editor of the year. (First prize is six months' worth of sleep, so she can catch up.) Jonathon Lazear, who labored long and hard, deserves a special mention, as does Debbie Orenstein. At *Financial World,* Mark J. Meagher, Douglas A. McIntyre, Dexter Hutchins, and most especially, Geoffrey N. Smith, need to be singled out for their understanding of how long it takes to put a book together.

For their considerable help, our thanks to Merrill Lynch financial professionals from across the country: Sidney Art, Eugene Banks, Bruce Barth, Bernie Benson, Jack Benson, James Billington, Phil Blevins, Sr., Nicholas M. Brandjes, John Brannigan, Joseph Browne, Thomas Buck, Mary Burak, Donald Buske, Betty Cinq-Mars, Robert Costos, William DeReuter, Donna Ellenberg, Paul Fehrenbach, Joe Frierson, Linda Gibson, Red Goldstein, Thomas F. Grantham, Jack Gunter, Bert Halliday, James Heggie, Stanley Heilbron, Juliet Herman, Mary Kay Higgins, Robert Knapp, James Lusk, James McTiernan, Martin Manning, Linda Marcelli, Carrol Meredith,

Tony Provenzano, John Queen, David Rodkin, Rick Shrader, Irv Silver, Paul Simons, A. J. Staples, Brad Waddoups, Michael D. Williams, and David Witrovich.

From the home offices of Merrill Lynch, both in Princeton, New Jersey, and in New York City, we were given significant aid by: Mary Amberg, Susan Baker, Robert Barnett, Annmarie Cahill, Rene Campis, Millicent Citron, Bobbie Collins, Michael P. Cogswell, David Conine, Kay Cox, Stanley Craig, William Dennison, Deborah D'Errico, Greg Durrett, Angelo Esposito, Michael Feigeles, Dave Ferrier, Edward Gallagher, Janet Galvin, Mark Goldfus, Thea Grudzina, John Hele, David E. Hogan, Joseph Hollander, Chuck Humm, Rachel Kaplowitz, William J. Kehoe, Denise Kleis, Shawn Lapean, Linda L. Lowry, Doyle Lyons, Charles Mangano, Ann Michell, Steve Narker, David Nathans, Shelley K. Parker, Walter Power, Marilyn Reed, Kenneth J. Reifert, Claire Richardson, William Rittling, Lee Roselle, Edward Scharff, Alan Sislen, Barry G. Skolnick, Steve Smallwood, Peter Stingi, J. William Strott, Donald J. Tabone, G. Steven Thoma, Robert G. Volpe, Richard Walsh, James R. Wiggins, William A. Wilde, Andrew Wilmot, Donna Winn, Fred Yager, and Kevin Zuccala.

It would have been impossible to negotiate the legal mazes of this project without the sure guidance of Kenneth S. Spirer and Frank M. Macioce. They, as the authors' guardian angels, were aided by the resolute professionalism of Eileen Carley, David L. Dick, Lalit Jain, James McCarthy, and Dauna R. Williams.

The Employee Benefit Research Institute, a public policy research organization in Washington, D.C., has provided a wide array of publications and newsletters—many of which have helped us better understand private and public employee benefits programs in this country today. We also want to thank the College Board, Eric Cantor of the Investment Company Institute, A. Haeworth Robinson of the Retirement Policy Institute, and Anna Leider of Octameron Associates for their invaluable help.

Offering authoritative advice and constant encouragement were Mitchell S. Farkas and Kathy Hecht, and these financial planners and tax advisers: Robert Alderman, Roseanne Bassin, Donald B. Dulmage, Vern Martens, George May, and Eileen Russo.

John Galvin and John Michel, managers of Merrill Lynch's Retirement Plans and Services Department, have been persevering in their support of this book. From that department these professionals made meaningful contributions to this project: Maureen Introcaso, Ken Likely, Jill Nerz, Ray Shehata, Karen Walsh, Frank Waltzer, and Diane Yourcheck. For their wise counsel and friendship through the years and for their specific help with many facets of this book, special thanks to the Retirement Plans Department's John Coscia and William E. Starkey.

The authors were particularly blessed by the dedication of Bette Bloom, who coordinated the support of her associates Leigh Ann Mayer, Diane Baskin, Marilyn McHugh, and Bernadette Turi in the production of this manuscript. She was the mainstay; she synchronized the collective efforts of the many.

Collaborators, in the truest sense, were Amanda Sherwin and Roberta Cashwell, Rita Bock, Judith Gilpin, Jorge Rudko, and Margaret Zolotoy-Jones. A special thanks to Dick Rustin. His diagnosis of the needs of pre-retirees has been enormously helpful to the authors. A major voice in our reflections on the aging of America was that of Jane Halloran, Merrill Lynch's resident gerontologist.

Finally, with deepest gratitude, we thank William Clark. He is a giant tree in the forest. Each of the authors had separately considered writing on this subject. Clark caught the glint in their eyes, and turned their dreams into this book.

INDEX